ADVANCED spreadsheet projects in EXCEL

third edition

Julian Mott & Ian Rendell

DYNAMIC LEARNING

HODDER EDUCATION
AN HACHETTE UK COMPANY

The Publishers would like to thank the following for permission to reproduce copyright material:
Photo credits: **p.145** © Corbis Super RF/Alamy; **p.147** Photodisc; **p.148** © JLP/Deimos/Corbis; **p.149** Photodisc; **p.150** Stockbyte/Photolibrary.com; **p.151** © Motoring Picture Library/Alamy; **p.153** © Mark Bolton Photography/Alamy; **p.154** Photodisc; **p.156** © Image Source Black/Alamy; **p.157** © Formcourt (Form Advertising)/Alamy; **p.159** © Martin Harvey/Alamy.
Every effort has been made to trace all copyright holders, but if any have been inadvertently overlooked the Publishers will be pleased to make the necessary arrangements at the first opportunity.

t = top, *b* = bottom, *l* = left, *r* = right, *c* = centre

Orders: please contact Bookpoint Ltd, 130 Milton Park, Abingdon, Oxon OX14 4SB. Telephone: (44) 01235 827720. Fax: (44) 01235 400454. Lines are open 9.00 – 5.00, Monday to Saturday, with a 24-hour message answering service. Visit our website at www.hoddereducation.co.uk

First published in 2008 by
Hodder Education
an Hachette UK Company
338 Euston Road
London NW1 3BH

Impression number 5 4 3
Year 2012 2011 2010

Cover photo Jupiter Images
Illustrations by Tony Jones/Art Construction
Typeset in Goudy 10/12pt by DC Graphic Design Limited, Swanley Village, Kent
Printed in Spain

A catalogue record for this title is available from the British Library
ISBN-13: 978 0340 929 247

Contents

Introduction

Aims

This book is aimed at a number of Advanced courses of study within the National Qualifications Framework currently available in schools and colleges.

The book covers all the key software skills required in practical components of ICT and Computing specifications where a study of spreadsheets using Microsoft Excel is required.

The materials and approach used in the book are also applicable to students on many Computing and ICT related courses in further and higher education where a study of Microsoft Excel spreadsheets is necessary.

As well as covering many features of Microsoft Excel, the book offers advice and support materials for Excel projects including:

- designing the spreadsheet solution
- implementing the solution using Excel
- testing the implemented solution
- evaluating the solution
- user documentation
- choice of project.

Features of Microsoft Excel covered in this book

At this level, students are expected to make use of features beyond the simple arithmetic of +, -, *, / and straightforward formulas. The features of Microsoft Excel covered in this book are likely to be useful to many students.

Some of the features introduced are:

- linked worksheets
- named sheets, cells and cell ranges
- functions such as IF, COUNTIF, RAND and LOOKUP
- absolute references
- conditional formatting
- combo boxes, option buttons, spinners, scroll bars and check boxes
- macros to automate commonly used tasks
- message boxes
- UserForms for aiding and automating input
- pivot tables
- multiple scenarios

At the start of each unit, there is a list of the new features in that unit.

Students should be reminded that use of these features alone does not guarantee high marks, as many marks will be for how well they document the solution.

The book is intended only for guidance. Teachers and students should use the book in conjunction with the specification and examiners' reports.

How to use this book

The book assumes students have a working knowledge of Windows and Windows-based software.

The book can be used as a formal teaching aid by lecturers or students can work independently through the self-study units in class or away from the classroom.

Part 1 – Spreadsheet starters takes the student through a series of bridging units. These units are short, don't take long to complete and are designed to remind the student of the straightforward features of Excel. It is not necessary for students to do every bridging unit.

We have found this section useful in:

- reinforcing student knowledge
- helping to get to know students' abilities at the start of the course
- setting as homework
- giving practice in setting up a complete solution
- allowing students to work at their own pace

Part 2 – Building a solution in Microsoft Excel takes the student through a series of 22 self-study units which demonstrate further useful features of Excel, through the scenario of calculating the cost of an advertisement in a weekly newspaper, the *Denton Gazette*.

The scenario is fictitious and has been designed to incorporate as many features as is possible for demonstration purposes only.

These units should be worked through in sequence as they set up a spreadsheet solution.

In case of any problems, the files that should have been created by the end of each unit are stored on the website that supports this book.
Also on the website are some exercises to practise skills learned in this section.

Part 3 – Further Excel features looks at some more Excel features which students may wish to use in their projects through standalone self-study units (Units 23 to 26).

Part 4 – UserForm exercises looks at two Excel solutions that are UserForm driven. These can be used as extension material and a source of ideas for projects.

In *Part* 5 there are two practice assignments, one of which students should tackle to put the skills they have learned into practice. This is followed by 12 ideas for students' projects. Students could adapt a problem or undertake a similar problem to meet the demands of a real user.

Further ideas for projects are on the website that supports the book.

Part 6 – Documenting your project gives advice on how to document an Excel project. It covers the design, the implementation report, the testing, the user guide and the evaluation. It includes pointers, hints and examples of good practice.

Part 7 – Tips and tricks offers a range of useful tips to support the units and should provide interesting reading. These could be used as further activities for students. It is hoped that they can be the starting point for finding out even more about Excel.

Programming in Visual Basic

Generally specifications at this level do not require the use of programming. However some features in Excel such as UserForms and Message Boxes can only be implemented using a line or two of Visual Basic for Applications (VBA).

Students may enhance their solution in such cases by inserting a few lines of code or by tinkering with existing code. Details of how to insert a little VBA code are included in Part 2 and Part 4.

Compatibility issues

All software manufacturers bring out new versions every few years, tweaking the features a little and adding new ones. Microsoft Excel is no exception.

It is not necessary to have the latest software version. Although toolbars and dialogue boxes look slightly different in different software versions, all the materials in this book work in all versions of Excel.

Excel is also backwards compatible so that each version can open files set up in another version. This is exceptionally useful if students have a different version of the software at home from the version in school or college.

A note to students and lecturers

It is important to note that the solution used in the text is not being put forward for a particular grade at any level. The solution is fictitious and is aimed at showing the student the potential of Microsoft Excel and how software features can be incorporated to produce a working ICT solution.

All boards provide exemplar materials, support and training. It is vital that students and tutors follow the specification.

The documentation of ICT solutions at this level follows the system's life-cycle approach of specification, design, implementation, testing and evaluation. Again, though, different specifications and different solutions will have a different emphasis.

A word of real caution. Students must on no account copy materials in text books and submit them for examination. Moderators, examiners and the exam boards are very aware of published exemplar materials. You will be penalised severely.

Spreadsheet Projects in Excel Support Website

The website provided offers a number of support files.

Units 1 to 26 are supported with a unit file except Unit 21 which deals with the Visual Basic Editor and does not develop the system. This will enable students to pick up the solution at any point in the development.

A file for a tip and trick is included where appropriate. This should save development time particularly for teachers/lecturers wanting to demonstrate a particular feature in Excel.

A range of PowerPoint files offering advice and support will assist students in documenting the solutions they have developed and also allow teachers/lecturers to explain the key issues.

Further files are available offering ideas for project work.

Julian Mott and Ian Rendell have written two coursework books:

- *Advanced Spreadsheet Projects in Excel*
- *Advanced Database Projects in Access*

1 Spreadsheet starters

Spreadsheet starter 1: Comparing mobile phone costs

Features used:

- Column widths
- Copy and Paste
- Formulas
- AutoSum
- Absolute and relative references
- Colours, backgrounds and fonts
- Merge and Center
- Borders
- Removing gridlines

Selina is about to buy a 'pay as you go' mobile phone from T-Mobile but they have three different tariffs to choose from. You are going to set up a spreadsheet model which will work out the cheapest tariff for her.

You will then use the same spreadsheet to work out the best tariff for her friend Bryony.

Typical rates for calls and texts are shown below. Call charges are per minute.

T-Mobile	**Everyone**	**Mates Rates**	**Text Appeal**
Cross network calls	£0.12	£0.40	£0.40
Same network calls	£0.12	£0.05	£0.20
Landline calls	£0.12	£0.20	£0.20
Cross network texts	£0.10	£0.10	£0.03
Same network texts	£0.10	£0.05	£0.03

Entering the data

1. Open a new worksheet. Make sure that the Standard and Formatting toolbars are turned on. If not click on **View > Toolbars > Standard** and **View > Toolbars > Formatting**.
2. Click on cell **A2**. Click on **Format > Column > Width** and set the width to **18**.
3. Highlight columns B to D and set their width to **12**.
4. Highlight cells **B2** to **D6** and click on **Format > Cells**, click on the **Number** tab and choose **Currency**.
5. Enter the data as shown in Figure 1.1. (You do not need to enter the £ signs.)
6. Set the column headings in cells **B1** to **D1** to bold by clicking on the **Bold** icon.

7 Centre these column headings with the **Center** icon.
8 Save your file as **Phone.xls**.

Figure 1.1 ▶

Phone

	A	B	C	D
1		**Everyone**	**Mates Rates**	**Text Appeal**
2	Cross network calls	£0.12	£0.40	£0.40
3	Same network calls	£0.12	£0.05	£0.20
4	Landline calls	£0.12	£0.20	£0.20
5	Cross network texts	£0.10	£0.10	£0.03
6	Same network texts	£0.10	£0.05	£0.03

Sheet1 / Sheet2 / Sheet3

Selina thinks that in a month her use might be

- 10 minutes – Cross network calls
- 80 minutes – Same network calls
- 60 minutes – Landline calls
- 30 Cross network texts
- 80 Same network texts

Bryony thinks that in a month her use might be

- 100 minutes – Cross network calls
- 20 minutes – Same network calls
- 100 minutes – Landline calls
- 100 Cross network texts
- 100 Same network texts

9 Put the name Selina in cell **A8**.
10 Enter the tariff names in cells **A9** to **A13**. The best way to do this is to highlight cells A2 to A6, click on **Edit > Copy**. Click on cell A9 and click on **Edit > Paste**.
11 Enter the data for Selina in cells **B9** to **B13** as in Figure 1.2.

Figure 1.2 ▶

Phone

	A	B	C	D
1		**Everyone**	**Mates Rates**	**Text Appeal**
2	Cross network calls	£0.12	£0.40	£0.40
3	Same network calls	£0.12	£0.05	£0.20
4	Landline calls	£0.12	£0.20	£0.20
5	Cross network texts	£0.10	£0.10	£0.03
6	Same network texts	£0.10	£0.05	£0.03
7				
8	Selina			
9	Cross network calls	10		
10	Same network calls	80		
11	Landline calls	60		
12	Cross network texts	30		
13	Same network texts	80		

Sheet1 / Sheet2 / Sheet3

12 Enter the tariff names again in cells **A16** to **A20** and the column headings in cells **B15** to **D15** as shown in Figure 1.3.

Figure 1. 3 ▶

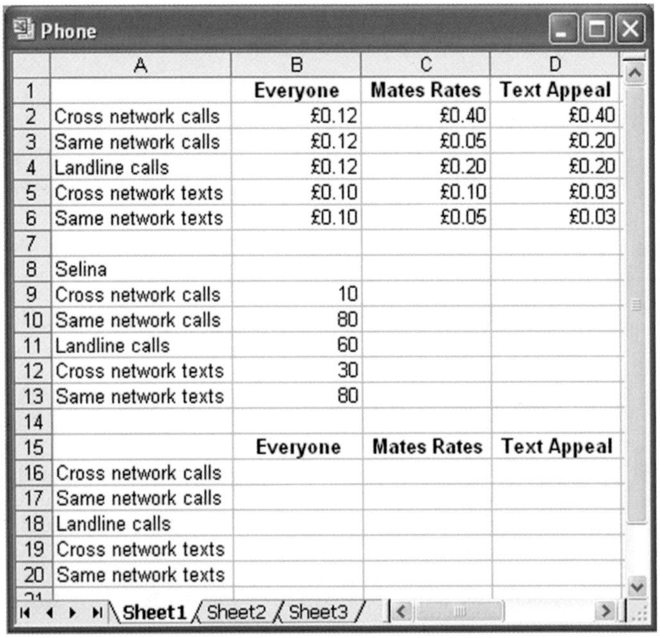

Phone

	A	B	C	D
1		**Everyone**	**Mates Rates**	**Text Appeal**
2	Cross network calls	£0.12	£0.40	£0.40
3	Same network calls	£0.12	£0.05	£0.20
4	Landline calls	£0.12	£0.20	£0.20
5	Cross network texts	£0.10	£0.10	£0.03
6	Same network texts	£0.10	£0.05	£0.03
7				
8	Selina			
9	Cross network calls	10		
10	Same network calls	80		
11	Landline calls	60		
12	Cross network texts	30		
13	Same network texts	80		
14				
15		**Everyone**	**Mates Rates**	**Text Appeal**
16	Cross network calls			
17	Same network calls			
18	Landline calls			
19	Cross network texts			
20	Same network texts			

Sheet1 / Sheet2 / Sheet3

We now need to enter the formulas that will calculate the cost for each tariff. To work out the cost of the cross network calls in the Everyone tariff, we will need to multiply B2 by B9 and store the answer in B16.

13 Click on cell **B16** and enter **=B2*B9**. Don't forget the equals sign at the start of the formula.

You should get the answer £1.20 as shown in Figure 1.4.

Figure 1. 4 ▶

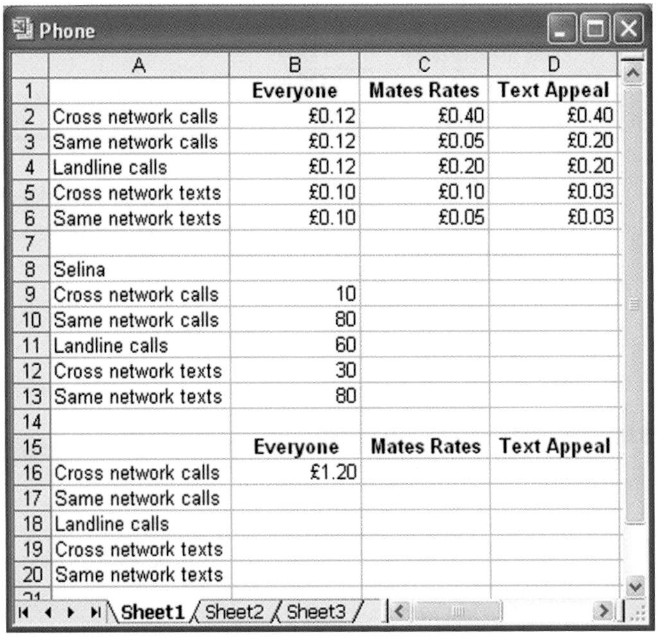

Phone

	A	B	C	D
1		**Everyone**	**Mates Rates**	**Text Appeal**
2	Cross network calls	£0.12	£0.40	£0.40
3	Same network calls	£0.12	£0.05	£0.20
4	Landline calls	£0.12	£0.20	£0.20
5	Cross network texts	£0.10	£0.10	£0.03
6	Same network texts	£0.10	£0.05	£0.03
7				
8	Selina			
9	Cross network calls	10		
10	Same network calls	80		
11	Landline calls	60		
12	Cross network texts	30		
13	Same network texts	80		
14				
15		**Everyone**	**Mates Rates**	**Text Appeal**
16	Cross network calls	£1.20		
17	Same network calls			
18	Landline calls			
19	Cross network texts			
20	Same network texts			

Sheet1 / Sheet2 / Sheet3

14 Click on cell **B17** and enter **=B3*B10.**
15 Enter formulas in cells **B18, B19** and **B20**.

As the formulas are similar, there is an easier way. We can replicate (copy) the formula in cell B16 as follows:

16 First delete the contents of **B17** to **B20**. (Select the range and press Delete.)
17 Highlight cells **B16** to **B20** and click on **Edit > Fill > Down.**
18 Click in cell **B21** and click on the **AutoSum** icon. Press ENTER. It will add the contents of cells B16 to B20.

Your total should be as in Figure 1.5.

19 Use the **Borders** icon and choose **Top and Bottom Border** and the **Bold** icon to format cell **B21** as in Figure 1.5.

Figure 1. 5 ▶

Phone

	A	B	C	D
1		**Everyone**	**Mates Rates**	**Text Appeal**
2	Cross network calls	£0.12	£0.40	£0.40
3	Same network calls	£0.12	£0.05	£0.20
4	Landline calls	£0.12	£0.20	£0.20
5	Cross network texts	£0.10	£0.10	£0.03
6	Same network texts	£0.10	£0.05	£0.03
7				
8	Selina			
9	Cross network calls	10		
10	Same network calls	80		
11	Landline calls	60		
12	Cross network texts	30		
13	Same network texts	80		
14				
15		**Everyone**	**Mates Rates**	**Text Appeal**
16	Cross network calls	£1.20		
17	Same network calls	£9.60		
18	Landline calls	£7.20		
19	Cross network texts	£3.00		
20	Same network texts	£8.00		
21		**£29.00**		

Sheet1 / Sheet2 / Sheet3

20 Enter a formula into **C16** to work out the cost of Mates Rates cross-network calls. Use **Edit > Fill >Down** and **AutoSum** again to fill in the rest of the column.
21 Repeat this for column D.

Your spreadsheet should look like Figure 1.6.

We can see that the Mates Rates would be the cheapest.

Figure 1. 6 ▶

Phone

	A	B	C	D
1		**Everyone**	**Mates Rates**	**Text Appeal**
2	Cross network calls	£0.12	£0.40	£0.40
3	Same network calls	£0.12	£0.05	£0.20
4	Landline calls	£0.12	£0.20	£0.20
5	Cross network texts	£0.10	£0.10	£0.03
6	Same network texts	£0.10	£0.05	£0.03
7				
8	Selina			
9	Cross network calls	10		
10	Same network calls	80		
11	Landline calls	60		
12	Cross network texts	30		
13	Same network texts	80		
14				
15		**Everyone**	**Mates Rates**	**Text Appeal**
16	Cross network calls	£1.20	£4.00	£4.00
17	Same network calls	£9.60	£4.00	£16.00
18	Landline calls	£7.20	£12.00	£12.00
19	Cross network texts	£3.00	£3.00	£0.90
20	Same network texts	£8.00	£4.00	£2.40
21		**£29.00**	**£27.00**	**£35.30**

Sheet1 / Sheet2 / Sheet3

22 Edit the data in cells **A8** and **B9** to **B13** for Bryony.

We can see that the figures adjust automatically and that the Everyone rate is much cheaper for Bryony.

23 Save your file.

Figure 1. 7 ▶

Phone

	A	B	C	D
1		**Everyone**	**Mates Rates**	**Text Appeal**
2	Cross network calls	£0.12	£0.40	£0.40
3	Same network calls	£0.12	£0.05	£0.20
4	Landline calls	£0.12	£0.20	£0.20
5	Cross network texts	£0.10	£0.10	£0.03
6	Same network texts	£0.10	£0.05	£0.03
7				
8	Bryony			
9	Cross network calls	100		
10	Same network calls	20		
11	Landline calls	100		
12	Cross network texts	100		
13	Same network texts	100		
14				
15		**Everyone**	**Mates Rates**	**Text Appeal**
16	Cross network calls	£12.00	£40.00	£40.00
17	Same network calls	£2.40	£1.00	£4.00
18	Landline calls	£12.00	£20.00	£20.00
19	Cross network texts	£10.00	£10.00	£3.00
20	Same network texts	£10.00	£5.00	£3.00
21		**£46.40**	**£76.00**	**£70.00**

Sheet1 / Sheet2 / Sheet3

24 Adjust the figures in cells B9 to B13 again. Choose your own figures. Which tariff is cheapest now?

You can also adjust the prices in cells B2 to D6.

Absolute referencing – copying the formula from B16 to C16 and D16

The formulas in columns C and D are similar to the formulas in column B. Couldn't we just copy them across? Let's try it.

25 Delete the data in cells **C16** to **D21** by highlighting the cells and choosing **Edit > Clear > Contents**.
26 Highlight cells **B16** to **D16**.
27 Click on **Edit > Fill > Right**.

We get £0.00 in cells C16 and D16. Clearly this is wrong.

Figure 1. 8 ▶

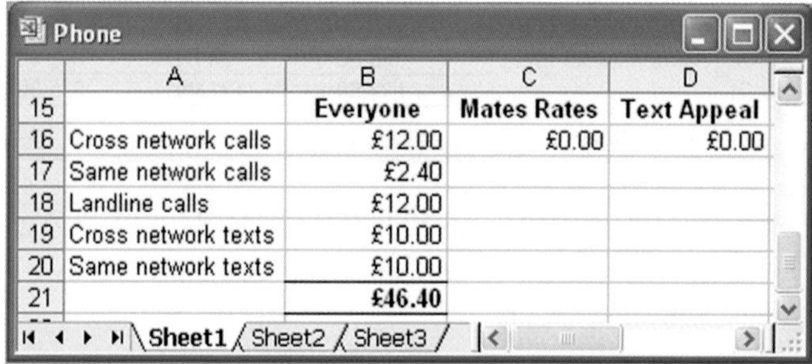

Phone

	A	B	C	D
15		**Everyone**	**Mates Rates**	**Text Appeal**
16	Cross network calls	£12.00	£0.00	£0.00
17	Same network calls	£2.40		
18	Landline calls	£12.00		
19	Cross network texts	£10.00		
20	Same network texts	£10.00		
21		**£46.40**		

Sheet1 / Sheet2 / Sheet3

This is because the formula in cell C16 is = C2*C9. Cell C9 is blank. The data required is in B9. This should not change as you replicate along the row. So we need an **absolute cell reference** – one that stays the same when copied. We indicate an absolute reference with dollar signs i.e. $B$9.

28 Click on cell **B16** and change the formula to **=B2*$B$9**.

It should still read £12.00.

29 Highlight cells **B16** to **D16** and click on **Edit > Fill > Right**.
30 Click on cell **B17** and change the formula to **=B3*$B$10**
31 Highlight cells **B17** to **D17** and click on **Edit > Fill > Right**.
32 Do the same for the other three rows.

The spreadsheet should now be working again.

The formulas should be as in Figure 1.9.

Figure 1. 9 ▶

Phone

	A	B	C	D
15		**Everyone**	**Mates Rates**	**Text Appeal**
16	Cross network calls	=B2*$B$9	=C2*$B$9	=D2*$B$9
17	Same network calls	=B3*$B$10	=C3*$B$10	=D3*$B$10
18	Landline calls	=B4*$B$11	=C4*$B$11	=D4*$B$11
19	Cross network texts	=B5*$B$12	=C5*$B$12	=D5*$B$12
20	Same network texts	=B6*$B$13	=C6*$B$13	=D6*$B$13
21		=SUM(B16:B20)	=SUM(C16:C20)	=SUM(D16:D20)

Sheet1 / Sheet2 / Sheet3

Hint: Switching to formula view

If you wish to see the formulas, hold down the CTRL key on the keyboard and press the back tick key (next to 1 on the keyboard). Press the same two keys again to switch back to normal view.

Alternative method using cell naming

Another way of setting up this table is to give a name to cells B9 to B13. Follow the instructions 1 to 8 as above.

1. Clear the data in cells **B16** to **D20**.
2. Select cell **B9**.
3. Click on **Insert** > **Name** > **Define**.
4. Enter the name **CC** (short for cross network calls) and click on **OK**.
5. Give names to cells **B10** to **B13**.
6. In cell **B16** enter the formula **=B2*CC.**
7. Enter similar formulas into cells **B17** to **B20**.
8. Use AutoSum in cell **B21** to add these figures.
9. Highlight cells **B16** to **D21** and click on **Edit** > **Fill** > **Right**.

Figure 1. 10 ▼ The formulas are shown in Figure 1.10.

Phone

	A	B	C	D
14				
15		**Everyone**	**Mates Rates**	**Text Appeal**
16	Cross network calls	=B2*CC	=C2*CC	=D2*CC
17	Same network calls	=B3*SC	=C3*SC	=D3*SC
18	Landline calls	=B4*LC	=C4*LC	=D4*LC
19	Cross network texts	=B5*CT	=C5*CT	=D5*CT
20	Same network texts	=B6*ST	=C6*ST	=D6*ST
21		**=SUM(B16:B20)**	**=SUM(C16:C20)**	**=SUM(D16:D20)**
22				

Sheet1 / Sheet2 / Sheet3

Improving the look of your spreadsheet

It is important to present your spreadsheet professionally, paying full attention to its appearance and general layout.

In Excel you can:

- change fonts
- change text size
- change colour
- change backgrounds
- add borders
- align data (left, right or centre) and many others.

We will use the options on the **Formatting** toolbar to improve the look of our spreadsheet.

1 Load the file **Phone.xls.**

We will start by positioning the sheet centrally on the screen by inserting rows and columns.

2 Drag across row headers 1 to 4 to highlight the first four rows and select **Insert > Rows**.

This will insert four rows.

3 Drag across column headers A and B and select **Insert > Columns** to insert two columns.

In the same way rows and columns can be deleted by highlighting the rows/columns that you wish to delete and selecting **Edit > Delete** from the menus. A number of formatting options are also available by highlighting the cell or cell ranges and right clicking the mouse button.

4 Highlight cell ranges **C5** to **F5** and **C19** to **F19** (hold down the CTRL key while selecting the second range) and select **Teal** from the **Fill Color** drop down on the Formatting toolbar.
5 With the cells still selected, select **White** from the **Font Color** drop-down.
6 In cell **C2** enter the text **Mobile Phone Cost Comparison Table**. Don't worry about column widths.
7 Drag across cells **C2** to **F2** to select them and click on the **Merge and Center** icon from the Formatting toolbar. Select again and alter the font size to 14 point. Again set the background colour to teal, the text to white and bold.
8 The next step is to highlight key areas with colour. Select cells **C6** to **F10** and **C20** to **F24**. Set the Fill Color to **Light Green**.
9 Highlight cells **C25** to **F25** and change the Fill Color to **Gray- 25%**.
10 Drag across cells **C12** to **D17** and click on the **Borders** icon, and choose **All Borders.**
11 Add the heading to cell **D12** and align the data as shown in Figure 1.11.
12 Click on **Tools > Options** and click on the **View** tab if not already selected. Uncheck the **Gridlines** to remove the gridlines from your spreadsheet.
13 Save your file.

Your spreadsheet should appear as shown in Figure 1.11.

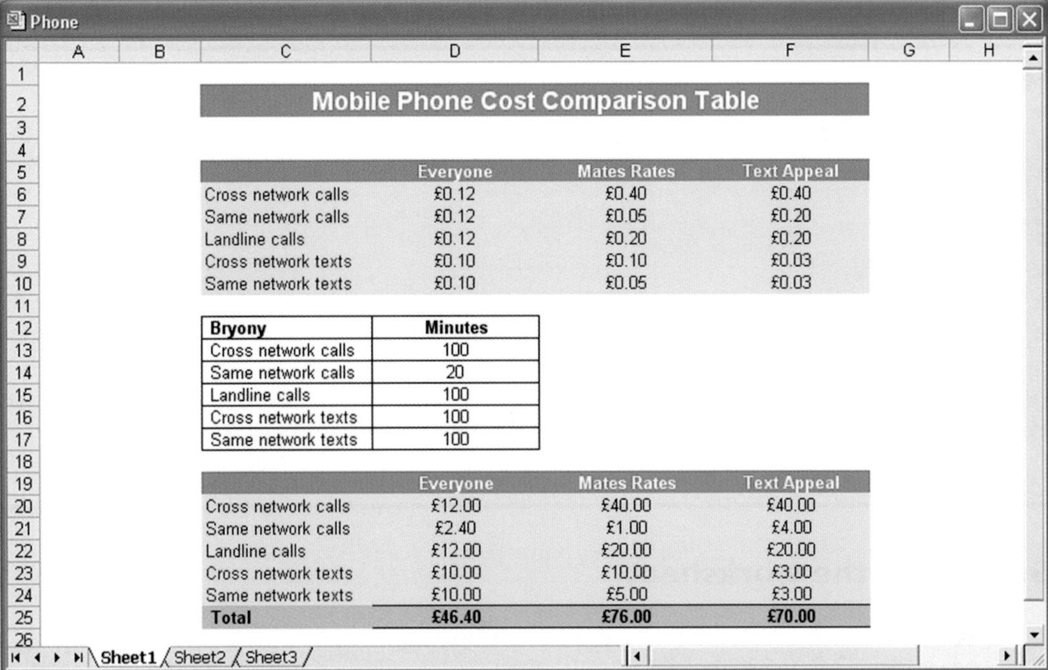

Mobile Phone Cost Comparison Table

	Everyone	Mates Rates	Text Appeal
Cross network calls	£0.12	£0.40	£0.40
Same network calls	£0.12	£0.05	£0.20
Landline calls	£0.12	£0.20	£0.20
Cross network texts	£0.10	£0.10	£0.03
Same network texts	£0.10	£0.05	£0.03

Bryony	Minutes
Cross network calls	100
Same network calls	20
Landline calls	100
Cross network texts	100
Same network texts	100

	Everyone	Mates Rates	Text Appeal
Cross network calls	£12.00	£40.00	£40.00
Same network calls	£2.40	£1.00	£4.00
Landline calls	£12.00	£20.00	£20.00
Cross network texts	£10.00	£10.00	£3.00
Same network texts	£10.00	£5.00	£3.00
Total	**£46.40**	**£76.00**	**£70.00**

Figure 1.11 ▲

Printing your spreadsheet is covered later in Spreadsheet starter 5. When printing it is important to consider the way your work will fit on the page, the paper orientation (portrait or landscape) and the addition of headers and footers.

You may wish to refer to the printing section now. Print your work with the page set to Landscape.

Spreadsheet starter 2: An invoice

Features used:

- Column widths
- Formatting borders
- Formulas
- =TODAY()
- Merging cells
- Print area
- Protecting and unprotecting sheets
- Data Validation

Excel is ideal for creating invoices (bills). It is important that your invoice looks professional. It is a good idea to find an invoice such as a gas bill at home and use this as the basis of your design.

You could also use a credit card bill, an electricity bill, a phone bill or a council tax bill for example.

Setting up the worksheet

1 Click on **File > New** to start a new spreadsheet.
2 Click on cell **C1**.
3 Click on **Format > Column > Width** and set the width of this column to **40.**
4 Format the width of columns B and D to **15** in the same way.

Figure 1. 12 ▼ Your spreadsheet will look like Figure 1.12:

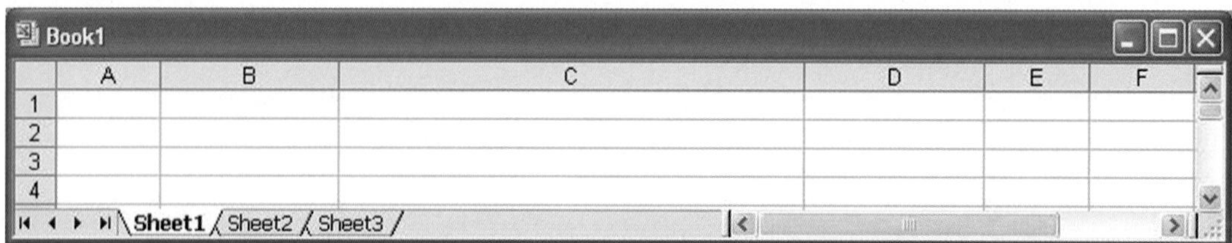

5 Now copy the headings from the screenshot below into your worksheet. Make sure that you format **Invoice, Quantity, Description, Unit Price** and **Total** to **Bold**. Save the file as '**Invoice.xls**'.

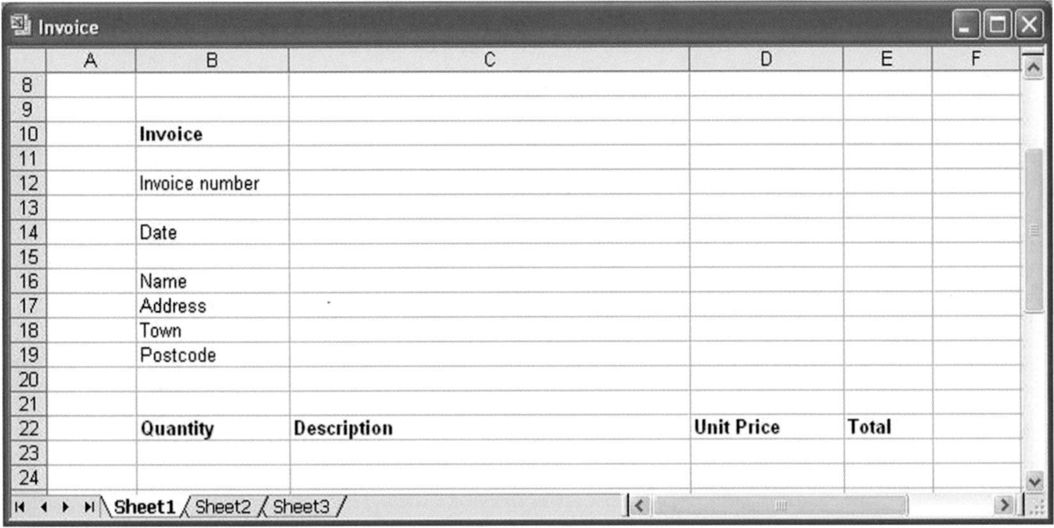

Figure 1. 13 ▲

Formatting borders

6 Highlight cells **B23** to **B36**. Click on the Borders drop-down on the Formatting toolbar and select **Outside Borders**.

Figure 1. 14 ▼

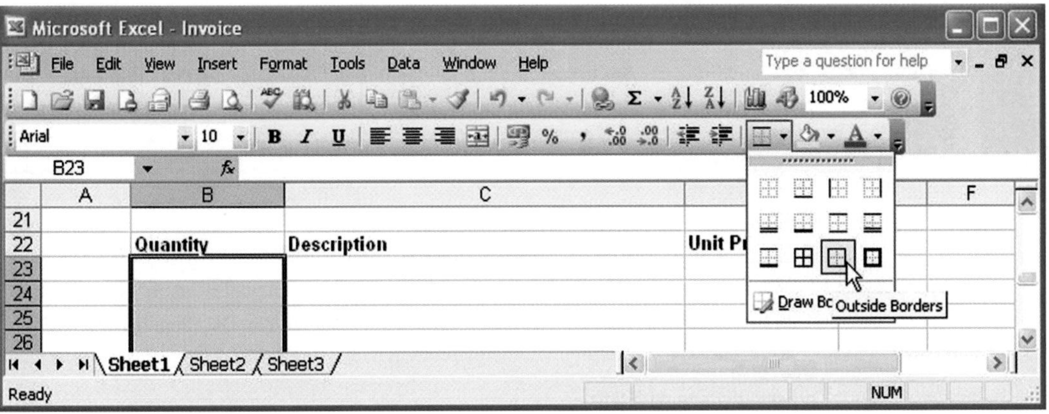

7 Repeat this for:

- Cells **C23** to **C36**
- Cells **D23** to **D36**
- Cells **E23** to **E36**
- Cells **C16** to **C19**
- Cell **C14**
- Cell **C12**

8 Highlight cells **B22** to **E22**. Click on the Borders drop–down on the Formatting toolbar and select **All Borders**.

Your spreadsheet will look like this:

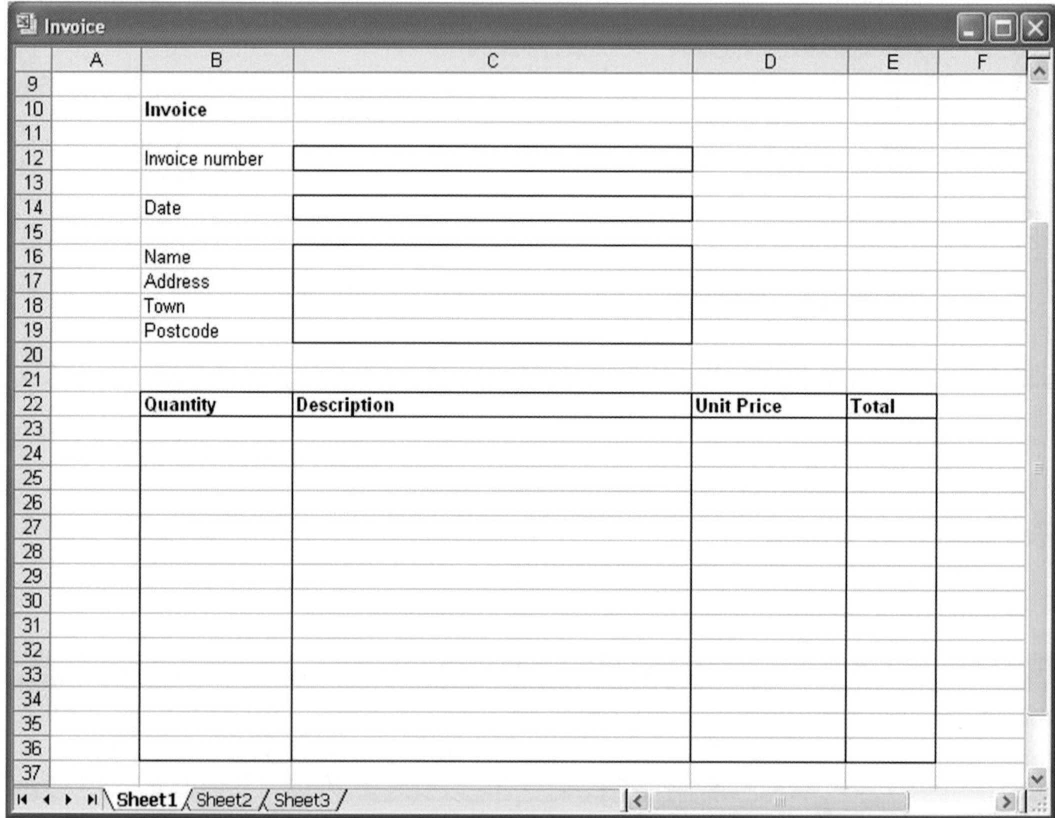

Figure 1. 15 ▲

9 Save your file as **Invoice.xls**.

10 Enter **4** into cell **B23**, **Dining Chairs** into cell **C23**, **79** into cell **D23**.

11 We need to work out the price of four dining chairs. The number of chairs is in cell B23. The price of each chair is in cell D23. So in cell **E23** enter **=B23*D23.**

You should see 316 in this cell.

Note: It is better to select the cells with your mouse than to type in the reference as you are less likely to make a mistake.

12 Highlight cells **D23** and **E23**. Click on the **Currency** icon on the Formatting toolbar.

13 In the line below, enter **1 Dining table** costing **255**.

14 In the line below that, enter **2 Easy chairs** at **143**.

15 Enter the formula into **E24** and **E25**. You can copy and paste from **E23** or replicate using **Edit > Fill > Down** or the Fill Handles. (See Tips and tricks number 5.)

16 Format cells **D24** to **E25** to currency.

17 Click in cell **E37** and click on the **AutoSum** icon and press ENTER.

Check that the amount in cell E37 is £857.00. The formula should be =SUM(E23:E36)

Figure 1. 16 ▼

Invoice

	A	B	C	D	E	F
21						
22		Quantity	Description	Unit Price	Total	
23		4	Dining chairs	£79.00	£316.00	
24		1	Dining table	£255.00	£255.00	
25		2	Easy chairs	£143.00	£286.00	
26						
27						
28						
29						
30						
31						
32						
33						
34						
35						
36						
37				Subtotal	£857.00	
38				VAT	£ 149.98	
39						
40				Total	£1,006.98	

Sheet1 / Sheet2 / Sheet3

18 In **D37** enter **Subtotal.**
19 In **D38** enter **VAT**.
20 In **D40** enter **Total**.
21 The VAT rate is 17.5%. In cell **E38** enter the formula **=17.5%*E37**.
22 In cell **E40** enter the formula **=E37+E38**. The total in cell **E40** should be £1006.98.
23 Highlight cells **D37** to **E40** and select **All Borders** from the Borders drop-down.

Entering the date

1 Click in cell **C14**. Enter the formula **=TODAY()**.

Remember: You must start with the equals sign and finish with the two brackets, but it does not matter if the word today is in upper or lower case.

When you press enter, you should see today's date in cell **C14**.

2 This is the first invoice so enter **1** into cell **C12**.
3 Select **C12** and **C14** and click on the **Align Left** icon.
4 Highlight cells **B1** to **D5.**
5 Click on the **Merge and Center** icon.
6 Put the company name in the merged cells. Format the size of the font to a suitable size, say 36 or 48 point. Add a logo near cells **E1** to **F5**.
7 Merge the cells **B6** to **D6** in the same way and enter the company's address. Similarly enter the phone/fax numbers and the email address.

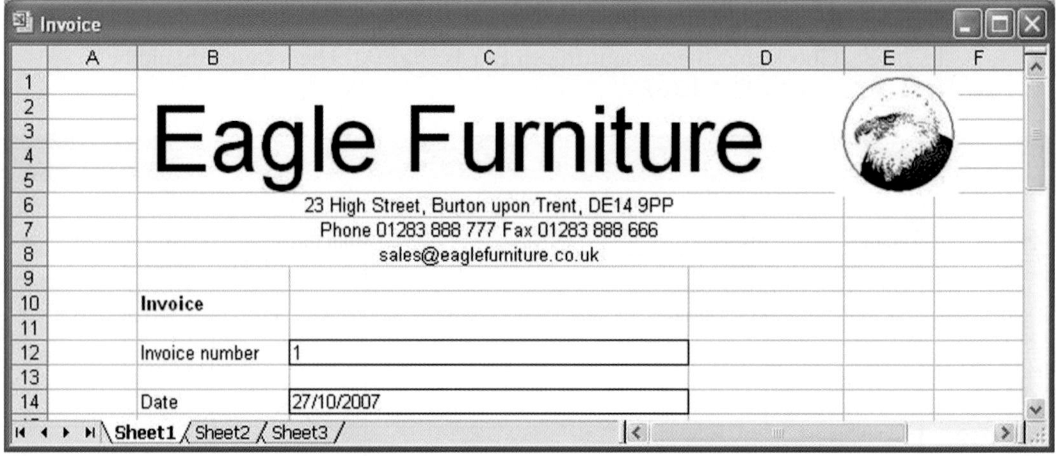

Figure 1. 17 ▲

8 Click on the **Print Preview** icon on the Standard toolbar to see what the invoice will look like when it is printed. We don't need to print column A, so close the print preview.

9 Highlight cells **B1** to **F42**. Click on **File > Print Area > Set Print Area**. Now only these cells will be printed.

10 You can change the font, font colour and background colours now if you wish.

Protecting the worksheet

How can we prevent the accidental deletion of data? We don't want to lose the logo, the company name, the column headings or the formulas in cells E37, E38 and E40, for example.

We do this by protecting the worksheet. First we have to decide which cells we want to be able to change. They are:

- **B23** to **E36**
- **C16** to **C19**
- **C12**

11 Highlight cells **B23** to **E36**.

12 Click on **Format > Cells**.

13 Click on the **Protection** tab.

14 Make sure that the **Locked** check box is unchecked.

Figure 1. 18 ▶

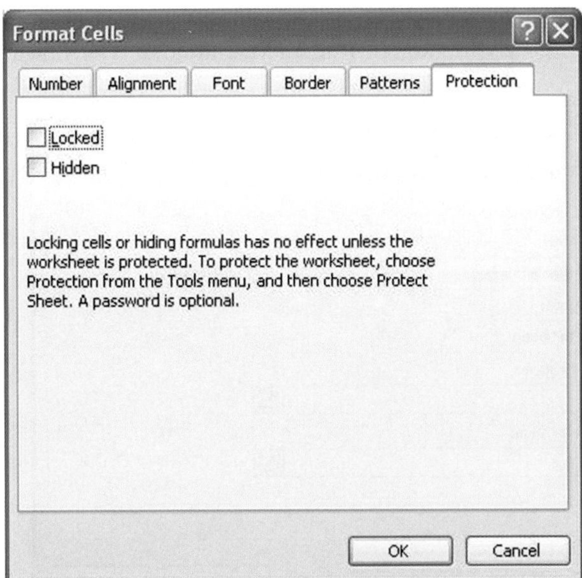

15 Do the same for cells **C16** to **C19** and then cell **C12**.

16 Click on **Tools > Protection > Protect sheet**. Click on **OK**.

17 Test that you can change the invoice number or the furniture purchased but you cannot edit the company address or the date.

Data Validation

We've all made clumsy typing errors such as typing 44 instead of 4. It could be a disaster if you sent an invoice to a customer for 44 chairs when you meant 4. How can we prevent such mistakes in Excel?

We can use the Data Validation feature.

1 Load the file **Invoice.xls**.

2 Select cell **B23**.

Normally customers do not buy more than eight chairs.

3 Click on **Data > Validation**.

A dialogue box appears.

Figure 1. 19 ▶

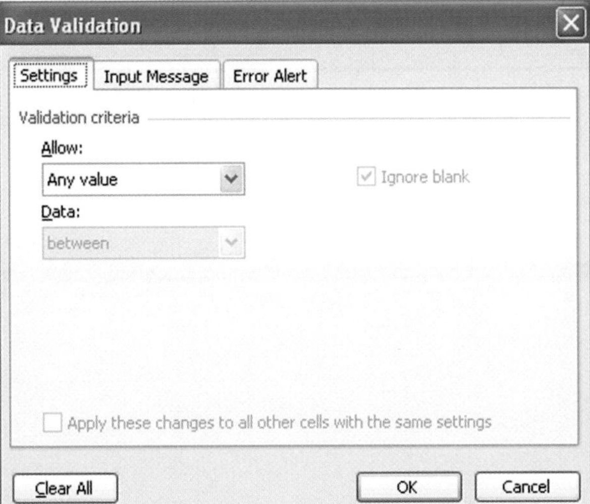

4 Click the **Allow** drop-down box and select **Whole number**.

5 Enter a **Minimum** of **1** and a **Maximum** of **8** as shown in Figure 1.20.

Figure 1. 20 ▶

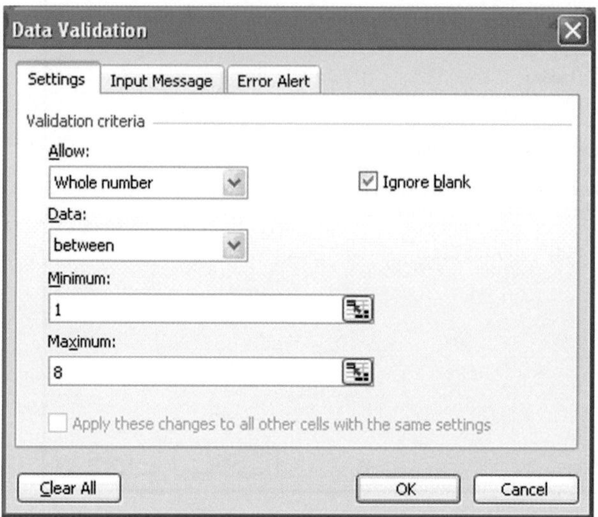

6 Click on the **Input Message** tab and enter the details as shown in Figure 1.21.

Figure 1. 21 ▶

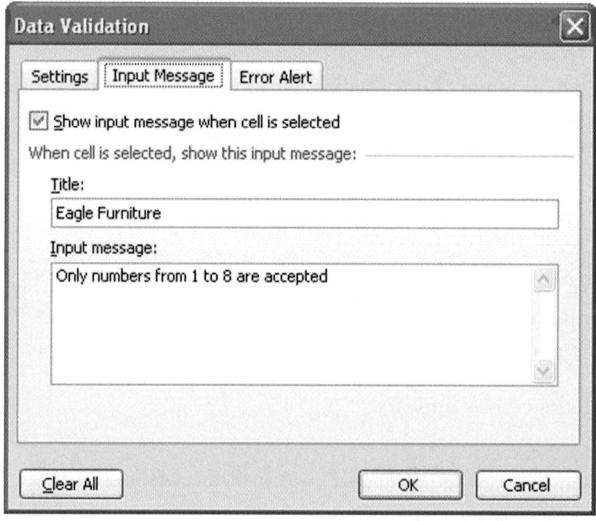

7 Click the **Error Alert** tab and enter the details as shown in Figure 1.22.

Figure 1. 22 ▶

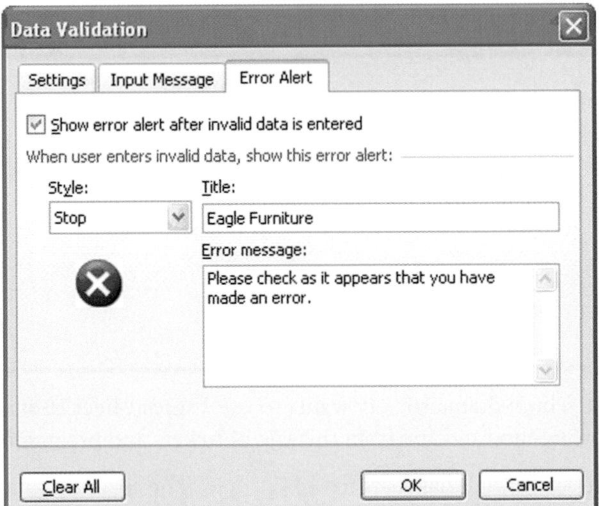

8 Test the validation check by entering the test data below in cell **B23**.

Test data	
0	rejected
1	accepted
3.4	rejected
8	accepted
9	rejected

Figure 1. 23 ▶

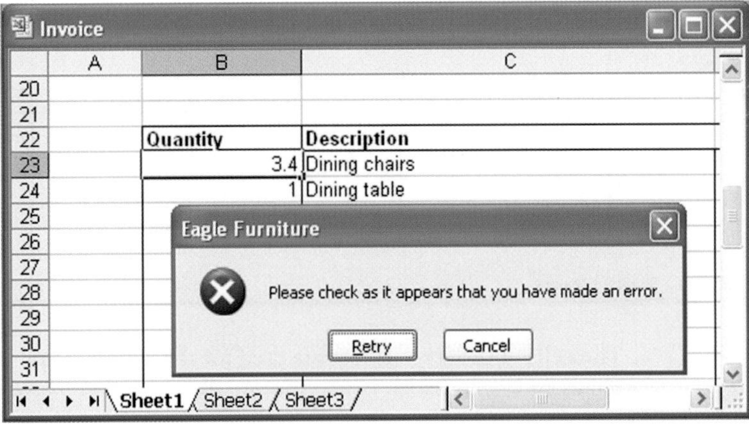

The Data Validation feature allows you to:

- set up maximum and minimum values for whole numbers (as seen)
- set up maximum and minimum values for decimals
- restrict the length of data in a cell
- let the user pick from a list
- select a date between a start date and an end date
- select a time between a start time and an end time
- allow the user to customise their own validation

If you want to practise setting up data validation, look at Dynamic Learning Exercise 9.

Spreadsheet starter 3: The school play

Features used:

- Formulas
- AutoSum
- Merge and Center
- Column widths
- Borders
- Colours, backgrounds and fonts
- Conditional formatting
- Multiple sheets

The school drama society wants to use a spreadsheet to store details of seat bookings and income from the sale of tickets and programmes.

The school hall has seats for 144 people. The seats are arranged in four blocks of six rows with six seats in each row.

Figure 1.24 ▼ The layout is shown in Figure 1.24.

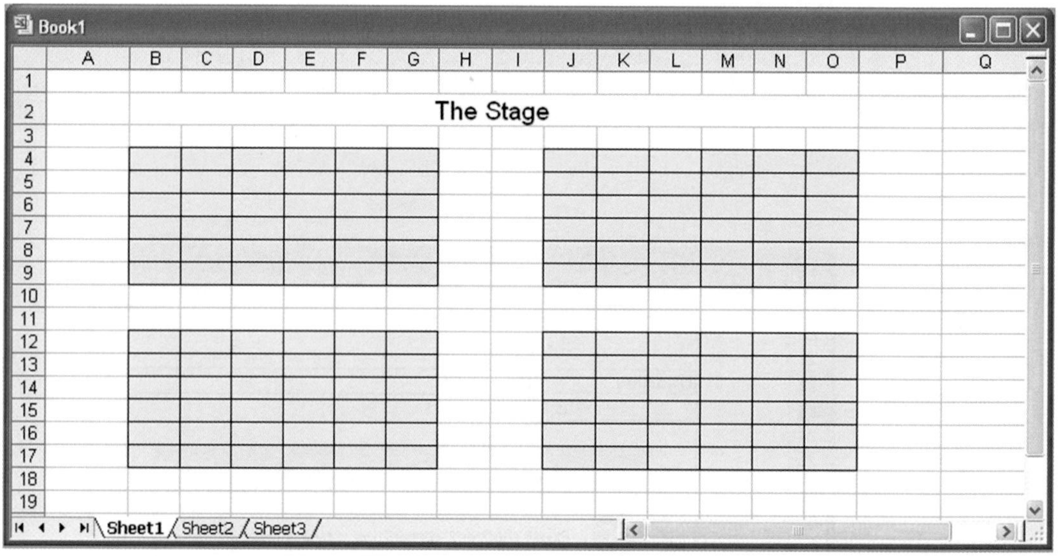

The cells of the spreadsheet are used for the rows of seats. Each cell will represent one seat.

When a seat is booked a number 1 is entered in the cell. Seats that are vacant are left blank.

The seats in the front two blocks are priced at £5.00 and the seats in the rear blocks at £3.00.

We will start by setting up the spreadsheet as shown. You will need to work in Landscape mode. Click on **File > Page Setup** and select **Landscape**.

1 Highlight columns B to O, and click on **Format > Column > Width** and set the column width to **5**.

2. Enter **The Stage** into cell **B2**. Highlight cells **B2** to **O2** and click on the **Merge and Center** icon to merge the cells for the stage.
3. Change the title to font size **16** point.
4. Highlight each of the four blocks of seats in turn and click on **Format > Cells** and click on the **Borders** tab. Click on **Outline** and **Inside** to format the borders of each cell.
5. Similarly for each block click on **Format > Cells** and click on the **Patterns** tab. Select a suitable fill colour.
6. Enter a **1** in some of the seats to show that they are sold.

You are going to design a spreadsheet model to store the number of seats sold in each row, the total number of seats sold and the total income from the sale of seats.

You may need to adjust the width of columns A, H, I and P to make your spreadsheet fit the screen.

7. In **Q3** and **R3** enter the headings **Seats sold** and **Income**.
8. In **Q4** you will need to put a formula that adds up cells **B4** to **O4**. Replicate this formula down to **Q9** using **Copy** and **Paste, Fill Down** or the **Fill Handle**.
9. In **R4** you will need to put a formula that multiplies the contents of **Q4** by 5. Replicate this formula down to **R9** in the same way. This formula multiplies the number of seats sold by £5.00 which is the cost of each seat in these rows.
10. You will need to repeat steps 8 and 9 for cells **Q12** to **R17** but remember the price in these rows is £3.00.
11. In cell **R19** set up a formula to add the contents of cells **R4** to **R17**. In cell **Q19** set up a formula to add the contents of cells **Q4** to **Q17**.
12. Extend your spreadsheet to store details of income from programmes sold. Programmes sell at £1.00. Assume that you sell one programme for every two people in the audience.
13. In cell **R23** set up a formula to add the contents of cells **R19** to **R21**.
14. Test your model so that as a seat is sold, the total number of seats sold increases by 1 and the income increases accordingly. Use your formatting skills to try and present your spreadsheet professionally (see Figure 1.25).
15. Save your file as **play.xls**.

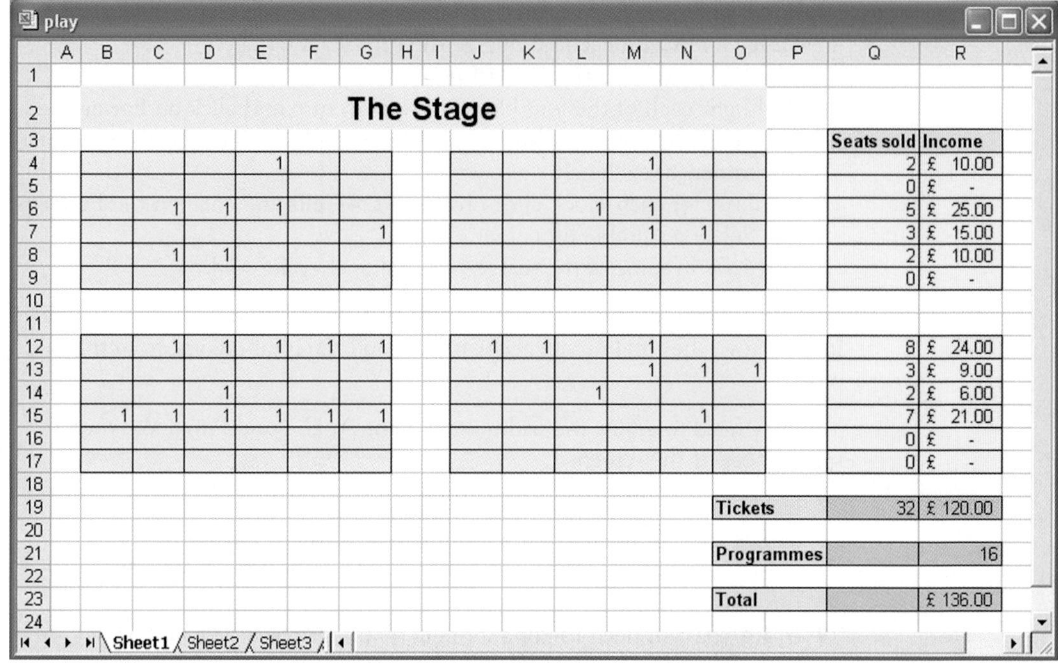

Figure 1. 25 ▲

Conditional formatting

You can use conditional formatting to make cells stand out if they meet certain criteria. For example, we can colour seats that are sold with a red background.

1 Highlight all the seats.

Hint: To do this, highlight one block of seats in the normal way. Then hold the CTRL key down and highlight another block. Repeat this until all four blocks are highlighted.

2 Click on **Format > Conditional Formatting**.

3 Choose **equal to** from the drop-down list and set the value to **1**.

Figure 1. 26 ▶

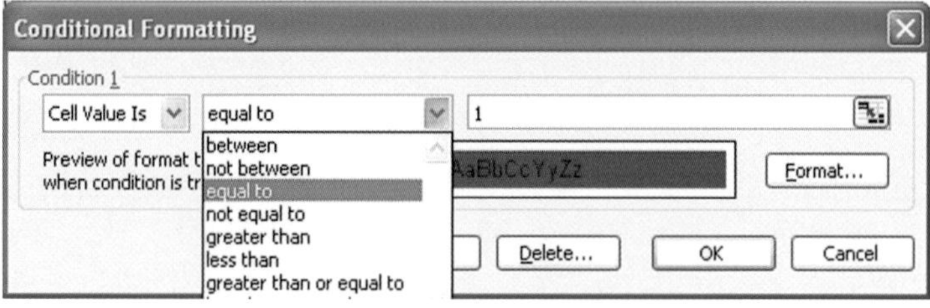

4 Click on **Format** and click on the **Patterns** tab to set the fill colour to red.

Figure 1. 27 ▶

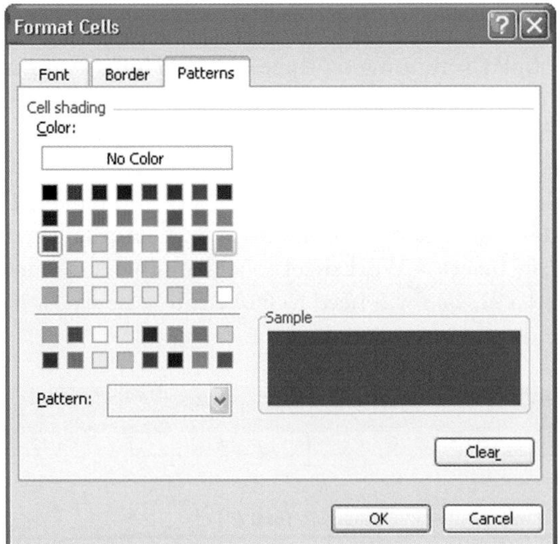

Figure 1. 28 ▼ You can quickly see which seats have been sold.

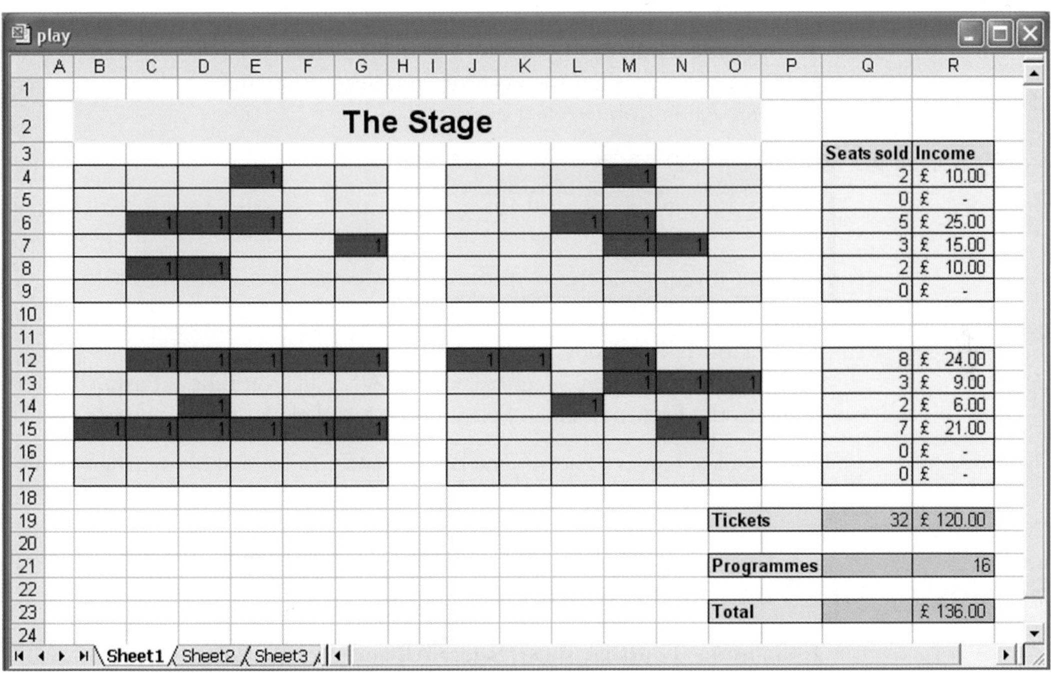

Note: Sometimes it is hard to tell where you have applied conditional formatting.

- Click on **Edit > GoTo > Special** and check **Conditional Formats**.
- Click on **OK**.
- The cells with conditional formatting will be highlighted.

Multiple worksheets

The school play is running on three nights, Thursday, Friday and Saturday. We will use a different worksheet for each performance to store details of ticket sales and a fourth sheet to store the total sales.

1 Double click on the sheet tab for Sheet1 and rename the sheet **Thursday**.
2 Rename Sheet2 as **Friday** and Sheet3 as **Saturday**.
3 Click on **Insert > Worksheet** to add another sheet and name it **Total** (see Figure 1.29). You will need to move it to a new position by holding the mouse down button and dragging.

Figure 1. 29 ▶

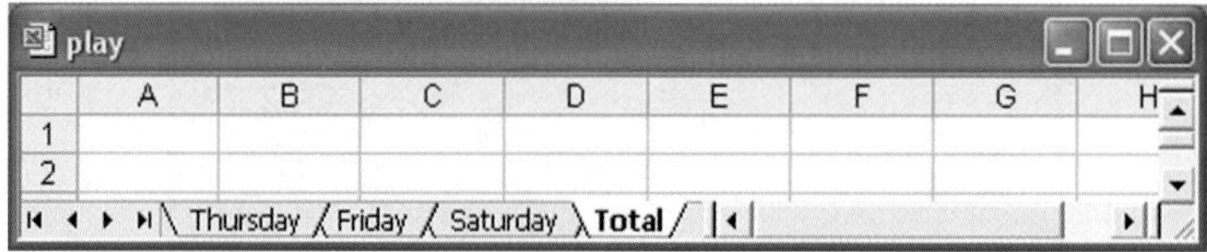

The next step is to copy all the detail on the Thursday worksheet including the formulas to both Friday and Saturday worksheets.

4 Go to the **Thursday** worksheet by clicking on the Sheet tab.
5 Press CTRL and **A** on the keyboard to select all or click on the **Select All** button to select every cell.

Figure 1. 30 ▶

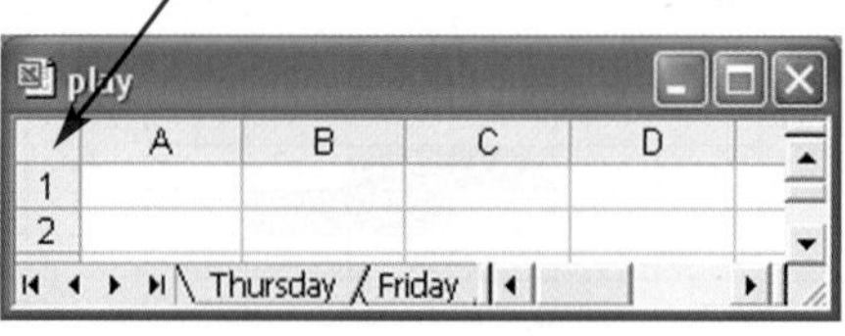

6 Click on **Edit > Copy.**
7 Switch to the **Friday** sheet. Select cell **A1**. Click on **Edit > Paste**.
8 Go to the **Saturday** sheet. Select cell **A1** and click on **Edit > Paste** again.

The formulas, borders, background colours and conditional formatting will all be copied. We now have a sales system for each performance.

Setting up the Total spreadsheet

1 Go to the **Thursday** sheet, **Select All** and click on **Edit > Copy**.
2 Switch to the **Total** sheet, select cell **A1** and click on **Edit > Paste**.

We now need to add formulas to the Total worksheet that will sum across the worksheets Thursday, Friday and Saturday.

3 In cell **B4**, type in **=Thursday!B4+Friday!B4+Saturday!B4**
This is adding up the values of cell B4 on the Thursday sheet, B4 on the Friday sheet and B4 on the Saturday sheet. If it has been sold on all three nights it should say 3.

Alternatively in cell **B4** of the Total worksheet:

- Enter =
- Switch to the Thursday worksheet and click on **B4**.
- Enter +
- Switch to the Friday worksheet and click on **B4**.
- Enter + again.
- Switch to the Saturday worksheet, click on **B4** and press ENTER. The formula builds as you go. (See Figure 1.31.)

Figure 1.31 ▼

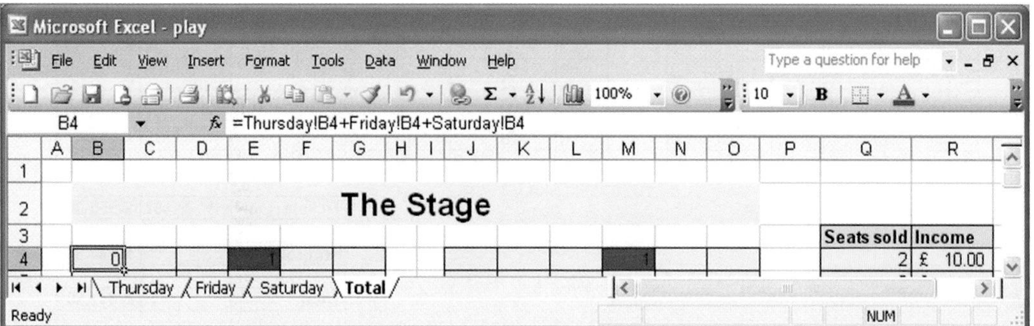

4. Remove the conditional formatting from cell **B4** by clicking on **Format > Conditional Formatting**. Click on **Delete** and delete **Condition 1.**
5. On the Total worksheet select cell **B4** and click on **Copy**. Select cells **B9** to **G9** and click on **Paste**.

You should see the totals for the first block of seats. (See Figure 1.32.)

Figure 1.32 ▶

play

	A	B	C	D	E	F	G	H	I
1									
2							The St		
3									
4		1	0	0	3	0	0		
5		0	0	1	0	0	0		
6		0	3	2	2	0	0		
7		0	0	0	1	0	2		
8		0	2	3	0	0	0		
9		0	0	0	0	0	0		
10									

Thursday

We now need to copy across to the other three blocks.

6. Highlight cells **B4** to **G9** and click on **Copy.**
7. Select in turn **B12**, **J12** and **J4** and click on **Paste**.
8. The spreadsheet will now show you how many times each seat has been sold as in Figure 1.33.

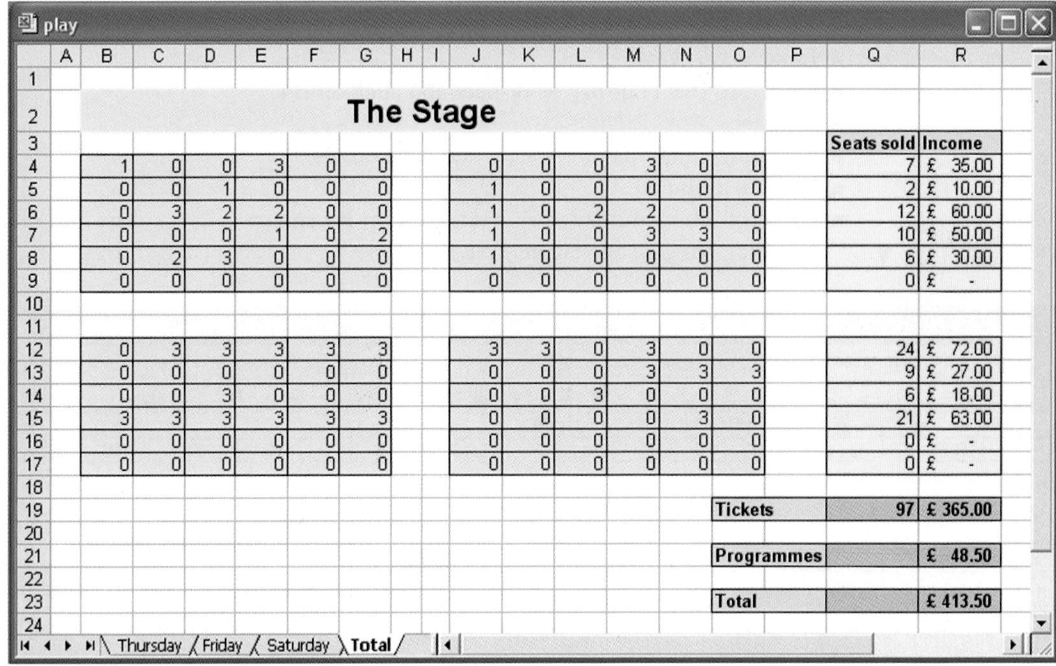

play

The Stage

	B	C	D	E	F	G	J	K	L	M	N	O	Q	R
3													Seats sold	Income
4	1	0	0	3	0	0	0	0	0	3	0	0	7	£ 35.00
5	0	0	1	0	0	0	1	0	0	0	0	0	2	£ 10.00
6	0	3	2	2	0	0	1	0	2	2	0	0	12	£ 60.00
7	0	0	0	1	0	2	1	0	0	3	3	0	10	£ 50.00
8	0	2	3	0	0	0	1	0	0	0	0	0	6	£ 30.00
9	0	0	0	0	0	0	0	0	0	0	0	0	0	£ -
12	0	3	3	3	3	3	3	3	0	3	0	0	24	£ 72.00
13	0	0	0	0	0	0	0	0	0	3	3	3	9	£ 27.00
14	0	0	3	0	0	0	0	0	3	0	0	0	6	£ 18.00
15	3	3	3	3	3	3	0	0	0	0	3	0	21	£ 63.00
16	0	0	0	0	0	0	0	0	0	0	0	0	0	£ -
17	0	0	0	0	0	0	0	0	0	0	0	0	0	£ -
19												Tickets	97	£ 365.00
21												Programmes		£ 48.50
23												Total		£ 413.50

Thursday / Friday / Saturday / Total

Figure 1. 33 ▲

9 Save your file.

Viewing multiple sheets

To view more than one sheet from the same workbook at a time, open a new window for each sheet that you wish to view.

1. Click on **Window > New Window.** Nothing appears to happen yet but it has created another window with your file in.
2. Click on the **Friday** tab.
3. Click on **Window > New Window** again and click on the **Saturday** tab.
4. Click on **Window > New Window** again and click on the **Total** tab.

Four windows are now open, each showing a different sheet.

5. Click on **Window, Arrange** to display the dialogue box (Figure 1.34).

Figure 1. 34 ▶

Choose the way you wish to view your worksheets. Figure 1.35 is tiled.

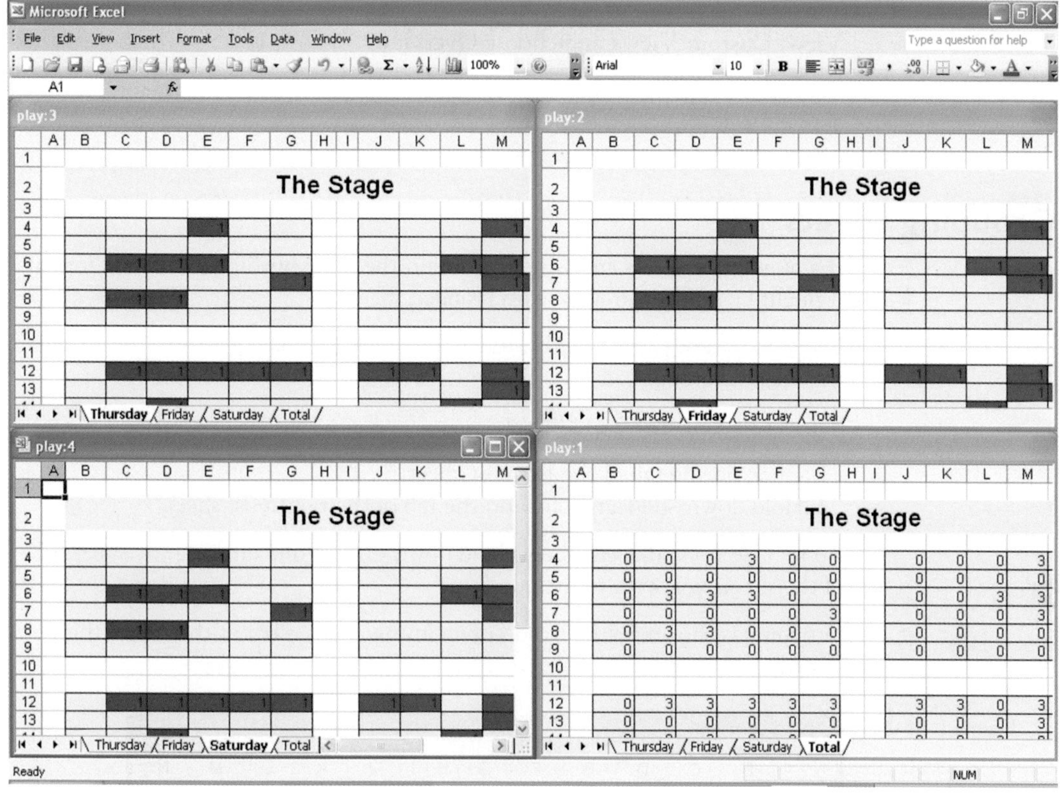

Figure 1. 35 ▲

Using Custom Views

You may wish to return regularly and quickly to the tiled view previously used.

1 Click on **View, Custom Views**.

Figure 1. 36 ▶

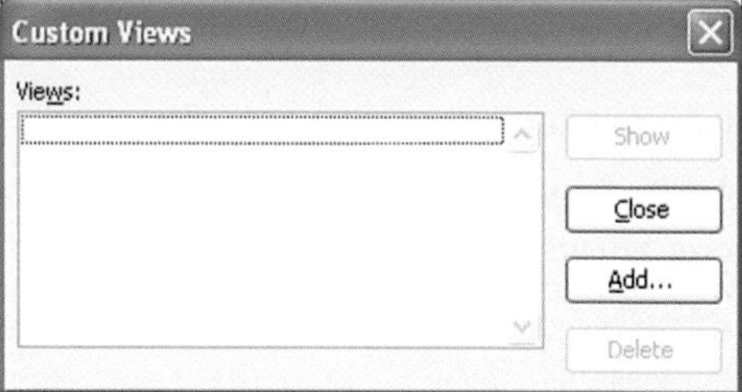

2 Click on **Add** and call the view **Overview.**

Figure 1. 37 ▶

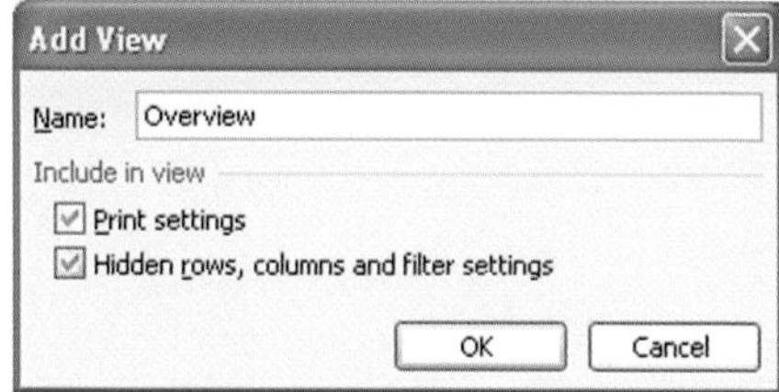

Whenever you wish to return to the custom view, from the menu click on **View, Custom Views** and choose **Overview.**

To return to the view showing one sheet, click on the Maximise icon on the active sheet.

Grouping sheets

If a number of sheets are going to contain the same headings, data and format it might be quicker to work with grouped sheets.

Every operation carried out on the active sheet is copied across to the sheets in the selected group.

Select adjacent sheets as follows:

1 Click on the tab of the leftmost sheet.
2 Hold down SHIFT and click on the tab of the rightmost sheet.

To include non-adjacent sheets hold down CTRL while clicking the sheet tab of the sheets you wish to include.

Grouping is shown by the word *Group* in the caption bar at the top of the screen.

Figure 1. 38 ▶

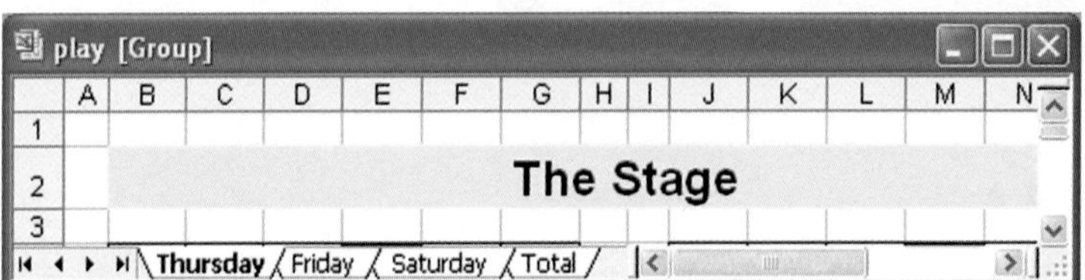

Be careful because it is easy to overtype data in another sheet by accident when the sheets are grouped.

If you print when several sheets are selected, they will all be printed at once, but each sheet starts on a new page.

To turn off sheet grouping:

3 Right click the sheet tab of the sheet you wish to become active.
4 Select **Ungroup Sheets** from the short cut menu.

Spreadsheet starter 4: The dice experiment

Features used:

- INT
- RAND
- COUNT
- COUNTIF
- SUM
- AVERAGE
- MEDIAN
- MODE
- Charts
- Absolute references

Katie Lewis is conducting an experiment with random numbers. She wants to roll a dice 100 times and count up how many times each number appears.

Rather than actually rolling the dice, she wants to conduct the experiment on computer using the **RAND()** function in Excel.

=RAND() gives a random number between 0 and 1

=RAND() * 6 gives a random number between 0 and 6

=RAND() * 6 + 1 gives a random number between 1 and 7

=INT() takes the whole number part of a number e.g. 8.73 becomes 8

=INT(RAND() * 6 + 1) gives a random whole number between 1 and 6

1. Type **=INT(RAND() * 6 + 1)** into cell **A1**. You will get a random whole number between 1 and 6.
2. Copy this formula down to **A10** by dragging the fill handle of this cell down to cell **A10**.
3. Copy this formula across to column J by dragging the fill handle across with cells **A1** to **A10** highlighted.

You will have 100 random numbers like this.

Figure 1. 39 ▶

Book1

	A	B	C	D	E	F	G	H	I	J
2	5	2	1	1	3	2	4	5	4	2
3	5	6	1	4	5	1	3	5	2	3
4	1	4	1	4	4	2	2	2	6	3
5	4	3	5	5	2	2	2	6	5	1
6	2	5	4	5	3	3	6	4	4	5
7	4	2	5	3	3	2	5	5	2	1
8	2	4	5	6	5	3	1	1	1	2
9	4	4	6	4	5	4	2	6	4	1
10	5	2	5	1	6	3	4	5	3	2

Sheet1 / Sheet2 / Sheet3

4. We now want to count how many 1s there are. Enter **1** into cell **A12**, **2** into **B12**, up to **6** in **F12**. Do not worry if the random numbers change when you enter data.
5. In cell **A13** type in **=COUNTIF($A$1:$J$10,A12)**

This formula counts the number of cells in **A1** to **J10** that are equal to the value of **A12**.

The formula uses absolute references so that when you copy the formula to other cells, it always looks in the table from **A1** to **J10**.

6 Drag this formula over to cell **F13**.
7 In cell **G12** enter **Total.**
8 In cell **G13** enter **=SUM(A13:F13)** This should display 100.
9 Format the borders of cells **A12** to **G13** to make the table stand out.

Figure 1. 40 ▶

Book1

	A	B	C	D	E	F	G	H	I	J
2	2	5	3	2	2	1	2	2	6	3
3	2	2	4	2	1	3	6	2	6	4
4	1	2	5	3	4	2	3	3	6	3
5	1	5	3	6	3	5	4	1	6	2
6	3	2	2	6	5	1	1	2	2	3
7	4	6	5	4	1	3	5	6	2	6
8	5	1	3	6	3	2	4	1	4	6
9	1	6	6	3	5	6	6	4	4	6
10	1	4	5	5	3	2	6	6	2	3
11										
12	1	2	3	4	5	6	Total			
13	13	22	19	11	15	20	100			

Sheet1 / Sheet2 / Sheet3

10 Highlight cells **A12 to F13** and click on the Chart Wizard icon.

Figure 1. 41 ▶

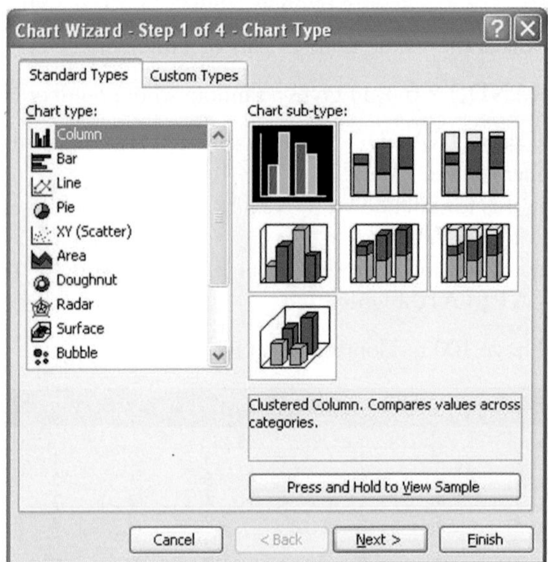

11 We want a column graph so click on **Next**.

Figure 1. 42 ▶

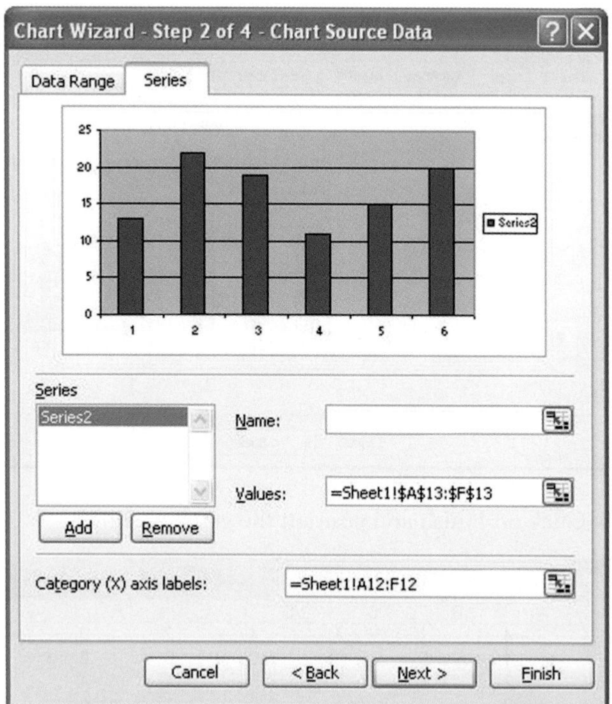

12 This is not the graph we want. The blue columns headed Series 1 are not required. Click on the **Series** tab, click on **Series1** and click on **Remove**.

13 Enter **=Sheet1!A12:F12** in the Category (x) axis labels box. This labels the x-axis. Click on **Next.**

Figure 1. 43 ▶

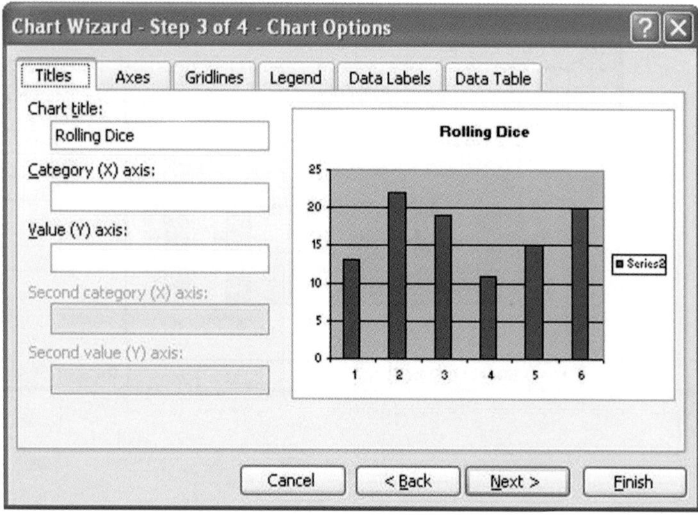

14 Add a title **Rolling Dice** in the Chart title box.

15 Click on the **Legend** tab and uncheck the tick box by **Show legend**.

Figure 1. 44 ▶

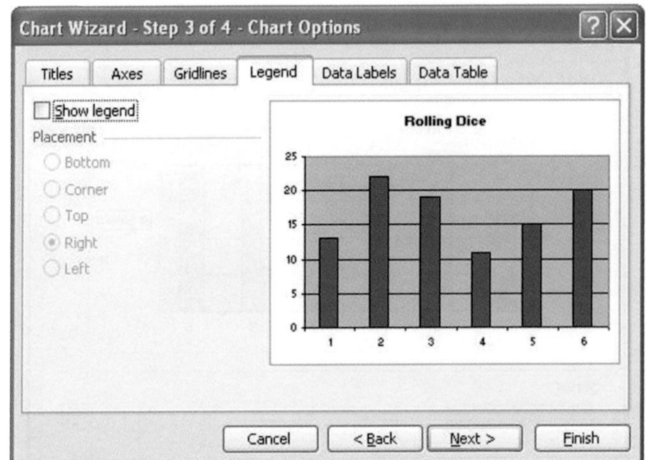

16 Click on **Finish** and position the graph as shown.

Figure 1. 45 ▶

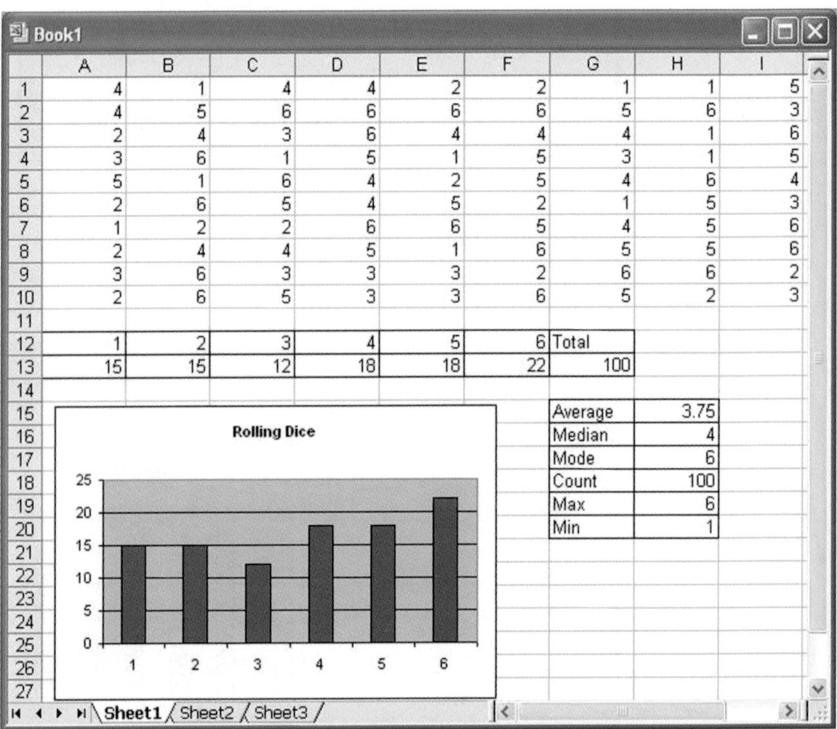

Book1

	A	B	C	D	E	F	G	H	I
1	4	1	4	4	2	2	1	1	5
2	4	5	6	6	6	6	5	6	3
3	2	4	3	6	4	4	4	1	6
4	3	6	1	5	1	5	3	1	5
5	5	1	6	4	2	5	4	6	4
6	2	6	5	4	5	2	1	5	3
7	1	2	2	6	6	5	4	5	6
8	2	4	4	5	1	6	5	5	6
9	3	6	3	3	3	2	6	6	2
10	2	6	5	3	3	6	5	2	3
11									
12	1	2	3	4	5	6	Total		
13	15	15	12	18	18	22	100		
14									
15							Average	3.75	
16							Median	4	
17							Mode	6	
18							Count	100	
19							Max	6	
20							Min	1	

17 In cells **G15** to **G20** enter the headings **Average**, **Median**, **Mode**, **Count**, **Max** and **Min**. In cells **H15** to **H20** enter the formulas:
=AVERAGE(A1:J10)
=MEDIAN(A1:J10)
=MODE(A1:J10)
=COUNT(A1:J10)
=MAX(A1:J10)
=MIN(A1:J10)

Format the cell range as shown. If you press the F9 key, you will get a different set of random numbers. The totals and the graph will adjust automatically.

Extension exercise

Extend your spreadsheet to include the sum of two dice rolled at the same time. Can you roll the dice 1000 times?

Figure 1. 46 ▶

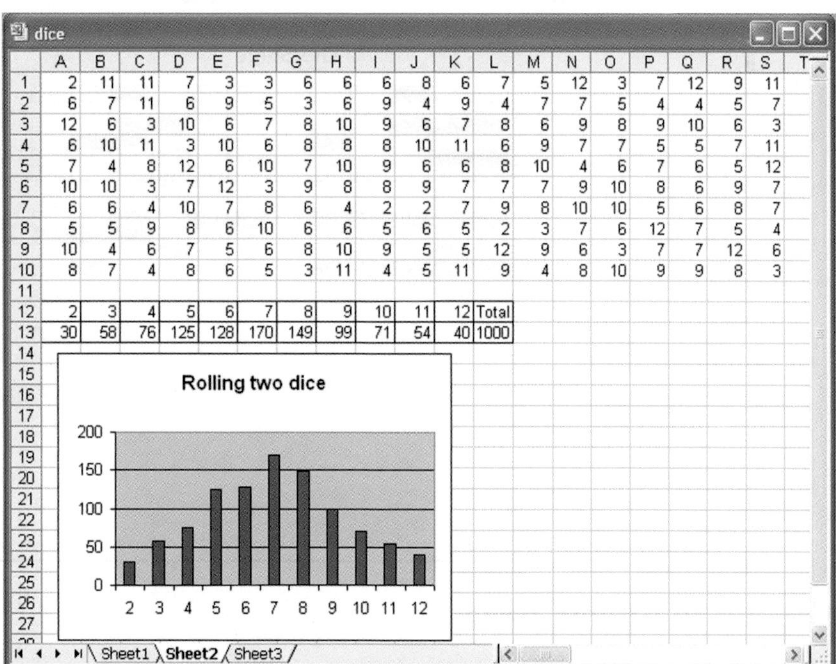

dice

	A	B	C	D	E	F	G	H	I	J	K	L	M	N	O	P	Q	R	S
1	2	11	11	7	3	3	6	6	6	8	6	7	5	12	3	7	12	9	11
2	6	7	11	6	9	5	3	6	9	4	9	4	7	7	5	4	4	5	7
3	12	6	3	10	6	7	8	10	9	6	7	8	6	9	8	9	10	6	3
4	6	10	11	3	10	6	8	8	8	10	11	6	9	7	7	5	5	7	11
5	7	4	8	12	6	10	7	10	9	6	6	8	10	4	6	7	6	5	12
6	10	10	3	7	12	3	9	8	8	9	7	7	7	9	10	8	6	9	7
7	6	6	4	10	7	8	6	4	2	2	7	9	8	10	10	5	6	8	7
8	5	5	9	8	6	10	6	6	5	6	5	2	3	7	6	12	7	5	4
9	10	4	6	7	5	6	8	10	9	5	5	12	9	6	3	7	7	12	6
10	8	7	4	8	6	5	3	11	4	5	11	9	4	8	10	9	9	8	3
11																			
12	2	3	4	5	6	7	8	9	10	11	12	Total							
13	30	58	76	125	128	170	149	99	71	54	40	1000							

Hint: You will need the formula:
=INT(RAND()* 6 + 1) + INT(RAND()* 6 + 1).

Spreadsheet starter 5: Printing in Excel

Features used:

There are many options available to us when printing in Excel. We can use features such as the following to customise our output:

- Print areas
- Landscape print
- Headers and footers
- Page breaks
- Fitting a printout to a page

Our aim is to produce a professional printout for the ticket sales, using colour and the whole of the page.

Figure 1. 47 ▶

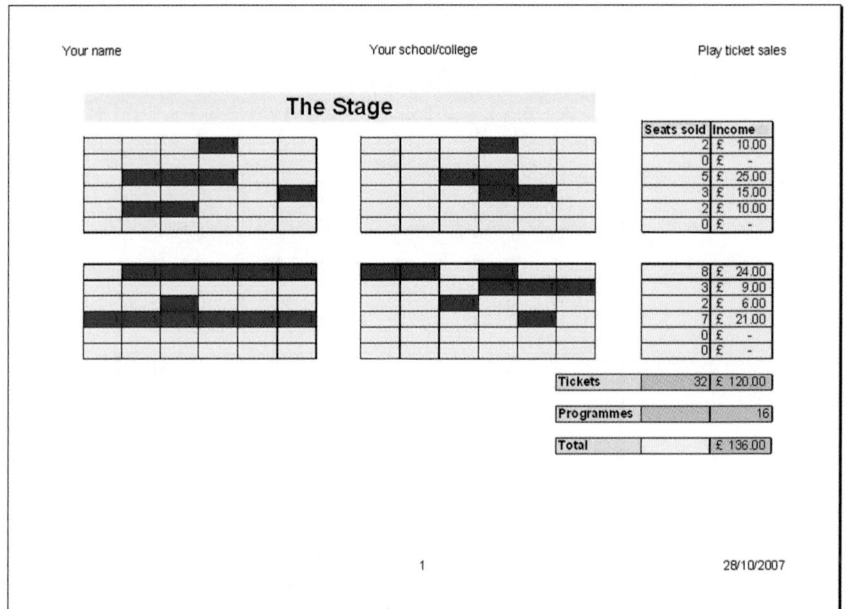

Setting the Print Area

1 Load the file **play.xls** from Spreadsheet Starter 3 – the School Play. Select the sheet called **Thursday**.

The first thing to do is to decide what area you want to print.

2 Highlight the area to be printed, cells **A1** to **R23**.

3 Click **File > Print Area > Set Print Area**.

Only the selected area will be printed. A dashed line should appear around your print area. To clear click **File > Print Area > Clear Print Area**.

Landscape or portrait printing

Printing in landscape mode is often more suitable in Excel as it reflects the shape of the screen. Set the Orientation to landscape as follows:

1 Click on **File > Page Setup** and click on the **Page** tab.
2 Select **Landscape** and then click on **OK.**

Adding a header and footer to your printouts

The header and footer are useful because they appear on every page of your printout, not just the first page. The sort of things that headers and footers are used for are:

- title of documents or sections of documents
- the name of the creator of the document
- their email address
- page numbers
- the date of creation

1 Click on **View > Header and Footer.** You will see the **Page Setup** dialogue box shown in Figure 1.48.

Figure 1. 48 ▶

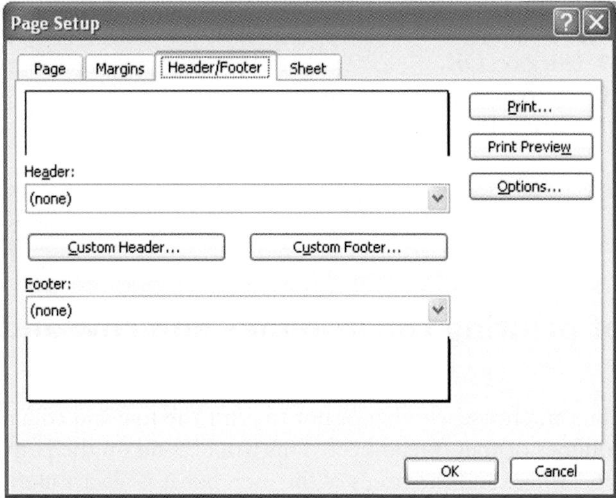

2 Click on **Custom Header**.

Figure 1. 49 ▶

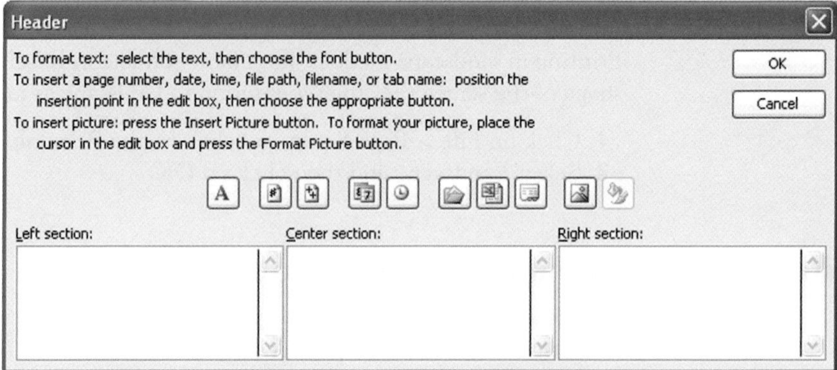

The header is in three sections, Left, Centre and Right.

3 Enter your name in the left section. Put the name of your school or college in the middle section.
4 In the right section type in **Play ticket sales.**
5 Click on **OK.**
6 Click on **Custom Footer.**
7 In the middle section set up the page numbering by clicking on the second (#) icon. It appears on screen as **&[Page].**
8 In the right section enter the date by clicking on the fourth (calendar) icon. It appears on screen as **&[Date].**
9 Click on **OK.**
10 Customise the header and footer further if you wish.
11 Choose **Print Preview** to see the effect.

Hint:
- You can use the built-in drop-down list to choose a header.
- You can insert an image into a header or footer using the second icon from the right.

Printing or not printing the gridlines and row and column headings

You can choose whether or not to print the row and column headings and the gridlines of your spreadsheet. This will depend on the purpose of your spreadsheet and the needs of the user, but it is always useful to show them when printing your formulas.

1 Use CTRL and back tick (the key next to the 1 key) to show your formulas, and click on **File > Page Setup**.
2 Click on the **Sheet** tab.
3 Check **Gridlines** and **Row and column headings** as in Figure 1.50.
4 Choose **Print Preview** to see the effect.

Figure 1. 50 ▶

Note: If you want some gridlines to print and not others, you will need to place a border around your cells. Click **Format > Cells** and click the **Border** tab and choose from a range of types, styles and colours.

To remove borders highlight the cells, click on the Borders Icon drop-down and choose **No Border.**

Adjusting the size of your spreadsheet

You can make your printout bigger or smaller to fit onto your page.

1. Open the **Page Setup** dialogue box by clicking on **File > Page Setup.**
2. Click on the **Page** tab.
3. The spreadsheet is a little smaller than the page so you can set the scaling to 125% and it should still fit on the page. The printout will now be a quarter bigger than the normal size.

Figure 1. 51 ▶

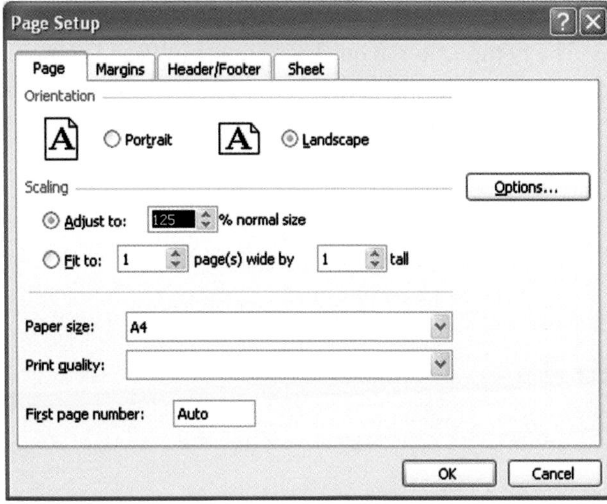

Check that it fits on one page using the **Print Preview** button. If you choose 130%, it doesn't fit.

Automatically scaling the page

1 If your spreadsheet is slightly too big to fit on the page, you can select the **Fit to** option, **1 wide by 1 tall.** Excel will reduce the worksheet by whatever percentage is needed to fit everything to the page.

Figure 1. 52 ▶

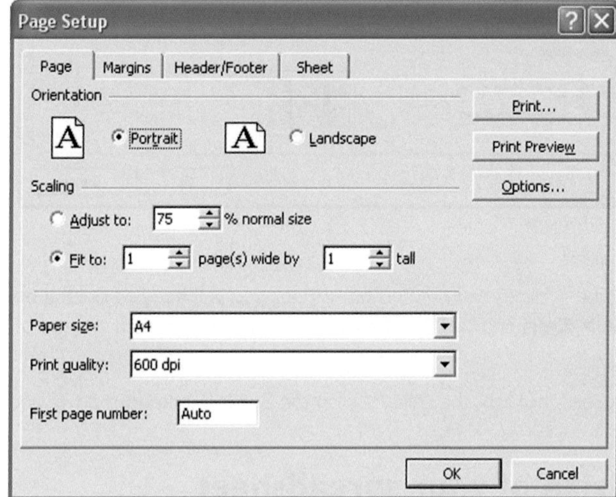

Print preview

Always preview before you print. It will save a lot of paper. You can check what will print by clicking on **File > Print Preview.**

1 Check that your printout will be what you expect using Print Preview.
2 Try the **Margins** icon in the Preview. You will see lines around the area to be printed, and small handles at the top of each column. Now you can adjust the column widths and the margins to improve the printout.
3 The **Setup** icon is a quick way to get to Page Setup.
4 Print the page showing evidence of landscape printing, colour printing, headers, footers and resizing as in Figure 1.47.

2 Building a solution in Microsoft Excel

In this part we will look at some more features of Excel that you might want to include in your spreadsheet through the scenario of the *Denton Gazette*.

The *Denton Gazette* is a weekly newspaper in the small town of Denton. Dozens of local businesses know that an advert in the *Gazette* gets a good response. Advertisements can be in colour or black and white and they can be a full page, a half page, a quarter page, an eighth of a page or a twelfth of a page.

The cost of an advertisement will depend on:

- the size of the advertisement; a table of prices is given below
- whether the advertisement is in black and white or in colour
- the page on which the advertisement will be printed.

SIZE	COST
Full page	£560.00
Half page	£300.00
Quarter page	£160.00
Eighth page	£ 85.00
Twelfth page	£60.00

This is the cost of a black and white advertisement on an inside page. A colour advertisement costs 30 per cent more.

If an advertisement is on the front page, it costs an extra 50 per cent. If the advertisement is on the back page it costs an extra 40 per cent. Advertisements on either the front page or the back page cannot be bigger than a quarter of the page.

Advertisers can book for up to 26 weeks. If they book for between four and nine consecutive weeks they get a discount of 10 per cent. If they book for ten or more consecutive weeks they get a discount of 20 per cent.

At present when someone places an order for an advertisement in the newspaper, the cost of the advertisement is calculated manually.

The owner of the *Denton Gazette*, Janice Peters would like an easy-to-use computer system that will calculate the price of placing advertisements in the newspaper.

The system must use:

- the company's house font Verdana
- the company logo of a dove
- the company's house colour scheme of:
  - background – pale green: Red 200, Green 237, Blue 234
  - alternative background – mid green: Red 176, Green 220, Blue 216
  - text – dark green: Red 75, Green 112, Blue 105

Figure 2. 1 ▶

Janice would like to have an easy-to-use system, where the user is able to:

- adjust prices easily
- store the name and address of the customer
- clear the screen for the next customer as required
- print the quotation at the touch of a button
- file the quotation away for future reference
- prevent full-page and half-page advertisements on the front page or the back page
- protect the file from accidental deletion of formulas
- create an automatic and user-friendly front end for the system.

Unit 1: Named areas

In this unit you will learn how to name areas of your spreadsheet. It is not necessary to name these areas but it is good practice to name data in a table.

The first task is to enter the price data into a table.

1 Open a new file in Excel.
2 Set the width of column B to 12 by clicking in **B1** and clicking on **Format > Column > Width** and type in **12.**
3 Enter the data as shown in Figure 2.2 into Sheet1.

Figure 2. 2 ▶

Newspaper

	A	B	C	D
1		Size	Cost	
2	1	Full page	£560.00	
3	2	Half page	£300.00	
4	3	Quarter page	£160.00	
5	4	Eighth page	£85.00	
6	5	Twelfth page	£60.00	

Sheet1 / Sheet2

4 Format the numbers in cells **C2** to **C6** to currency.
5 Rename the sheet **Prices** by double clicking on the name on the Sheet tab.

Figure 2. 3 ▶

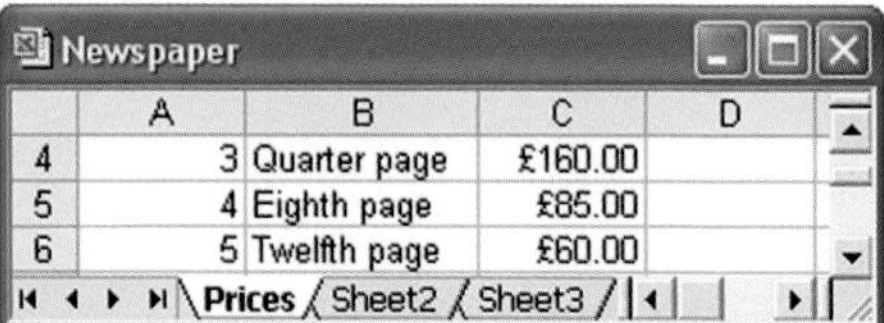

Newspaper

	A	B	C	D
4	3	Quarter page	£160.00	
5	4	Eighth page	£85.00	
6	5	Twelfth page	£60.00	

Prices / Sheet2 / Sheet3

6 Highlight the cells **A2** to **C6**. Click on **Insert > Name > Define** and type in **Prices** and click on **OK**.
7 Save your file as **Newspaper.xls**

Below the toolbars on the left of the screen is the Name box, which normally shows the reference of the selected cell, for example in the image below the selected cell is A1.

Figure 2. 4 ▶

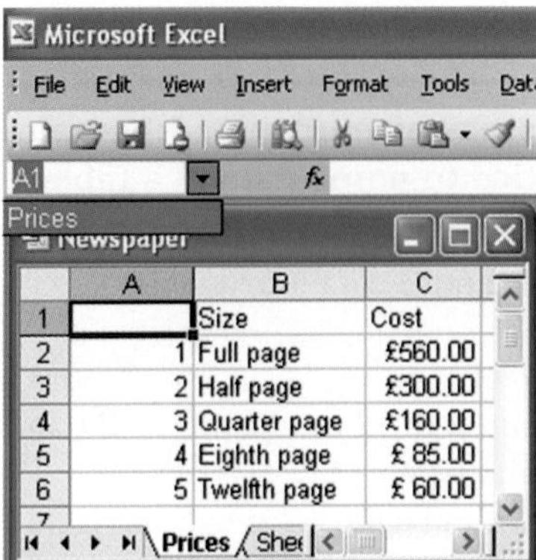

If you click on the little arrow to the right of the Name box, you will get a list of all the named areas. At present there is only one named area in the list.

Click on the name **Prices** and the named area will be selected.

Unit 2: Check Boxes

In this unit you will learn how to set up and use check boxes. A check box is a small square on the screen. If you click on this square, a tick appears in the square. If you click again the tick disappears. Use a check box to turn an option on or off.

We will use a check box to show whether an advertiser wishes to have a colour advertisement or not.

1. Load Excel and open the spreadsheet **Newspaper.xls** from Unit 1 if it is not already loaded.
2. Go to Sheet2 and rename the sheet **Quotation.**
3. Use **Format > Column > Width** to adjust the widths of each of these columns in turn:

Column A:	5
Column B:	16
Column C:	45
Column D:	5
Column E:	19
Column F:	6
Column G:	11
Column H:	5

4. Turn on the Forms toolbar: **View > Toolbars > Forms**

Figure 2. 5 ▶

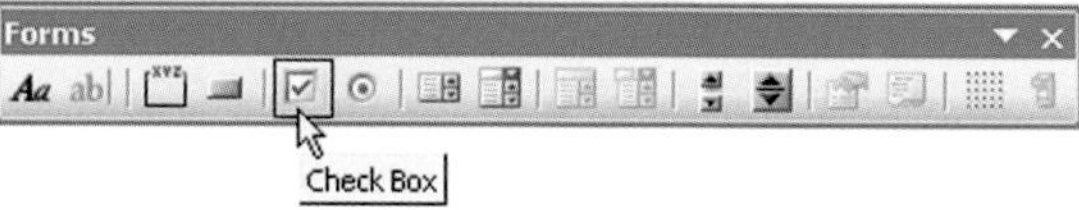

5. Click on the **Check Box** icon.
6. Drag out a rectangle on the worksheet over cell **E11**. It will look like this:

Figure 2. 6 ▶

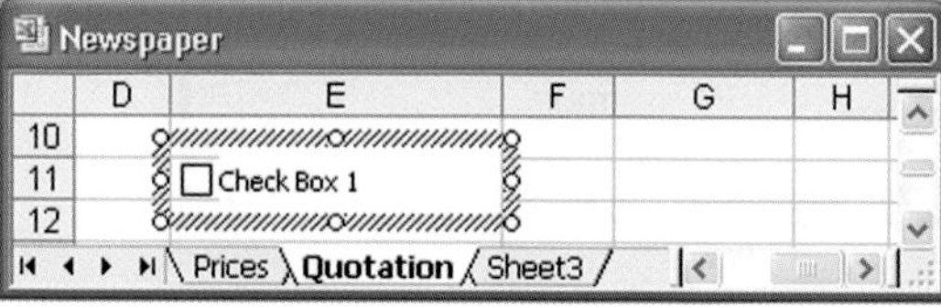

7. Right click on the check box. Choose **Edit Text** and delete the text that says Check Box 1 and replace it with the word **Colour**.

Figure 2. 7 ▶

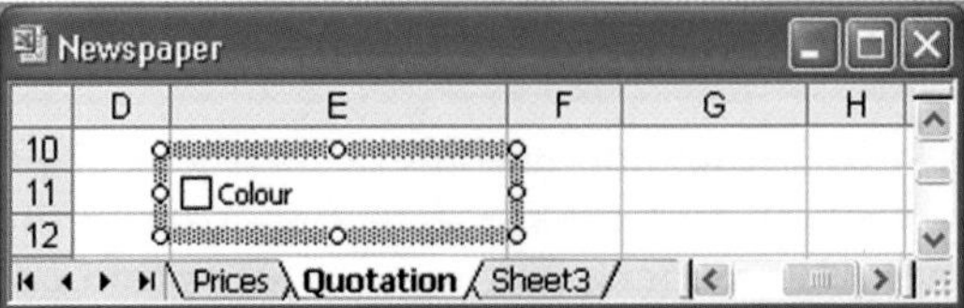

8 Right click again on the check box. Click on **Format Control**.
9 A dialogue box appears. Set the cell link to **F11** and click on **OK**.

Figure 2. 8 ▶

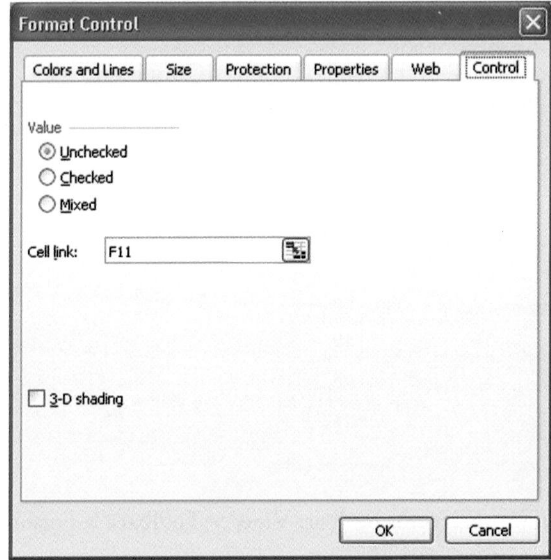

10 Click away from the check box.
11 Test the check box works. When you click on the box the tick appears and the word TRUE appears in F11. Click again and the tick is removed and the word FALSE appears in F11.

Figure 2. 9 ▶

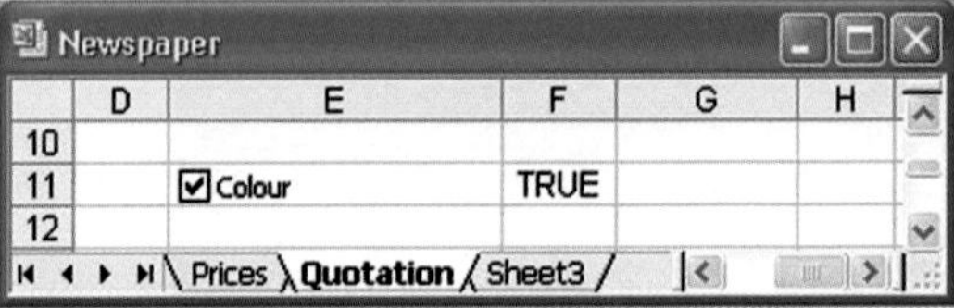

12 Save your work.

Unit 3: Using the IF function

In this unit you will learn how to set up and use the IF function. The IF function tests the value in a cell and does one thing if the test is true and another if the test is false.

IF statements are of the form:

=IF(A12=4,72,0)

Suppose this formula is in cell A10. If the value in cell A12 is 4, 72 will appear in cell A10. If the value in cell A12 is *not* 4, 0 will appear in cell A10.

A colour advertisement costs 30 per cent more than a black and white one. That means that if an advertisement is in colour, we must multiply the price of a black and white advertisement by 1.3.

If an advertisement is in black and white, we multiply by 1.

1 Enter this formula in cell G11 **=IF(F11=TRUE,1.3,1)**
2 Save your work and test that as you click on the check box the number in cell G11 changes from 1.3 to 1 and back again as shown in Figure 2.10 and Figure 2.11.

Figure 2. 10 ▶

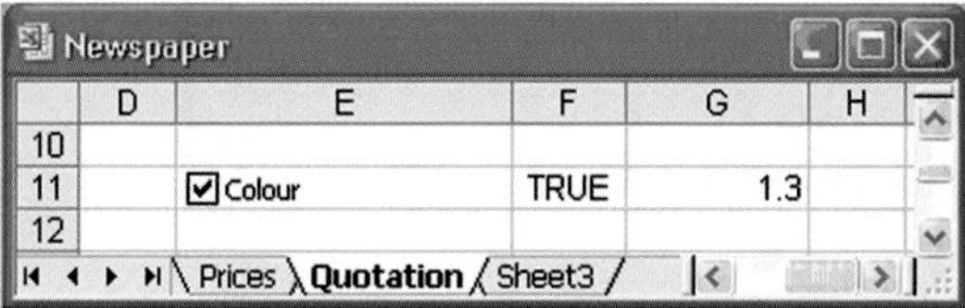

Figure 2. 11 ▶

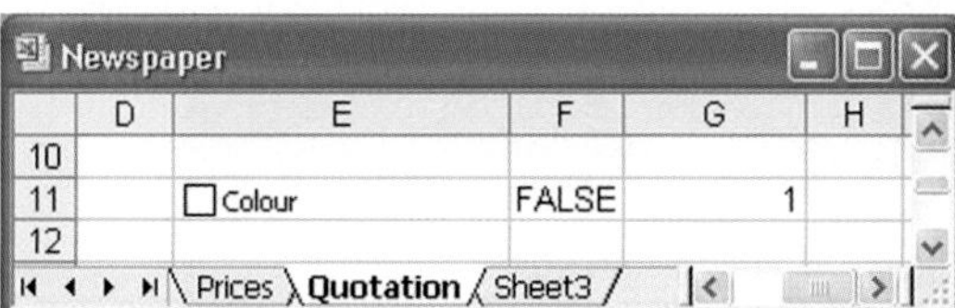

Unit 4: Option buttons

In this unit you will learn how to set up and use option buttons. Option buttons, sometimes called radio buttons, allow you to select one from a group of options.

We will use option buttons to make the choice of the front page, the back page or the inside pages as this affects the price of an advertisement.

1 Click on the **Option Button** icon on the **Forms** toolbar.

Figure 2. 12 ▶

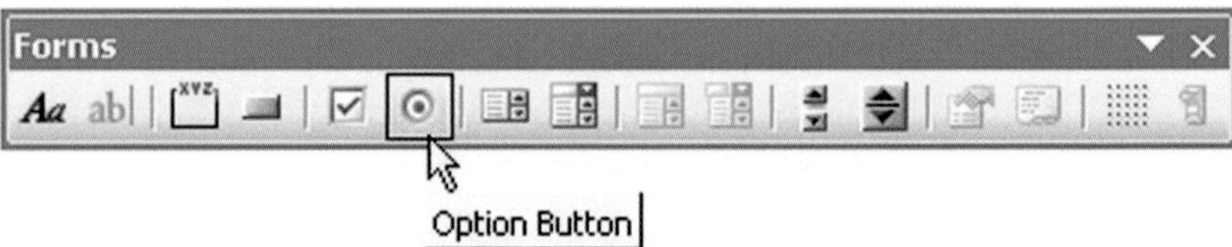

2 Drag out a rectangle over cell **E13**.

Figure 2. 13 ▶

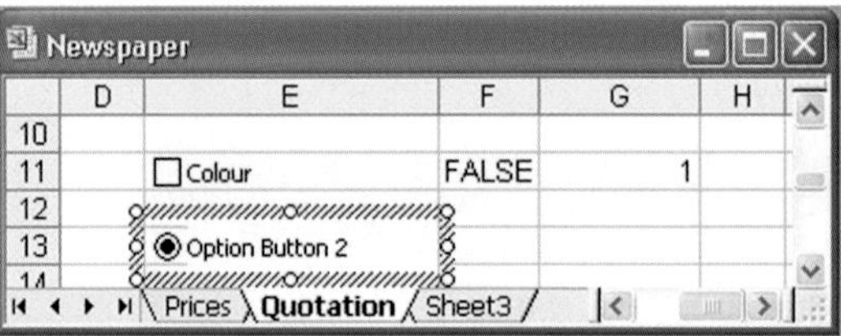

3 Right click on the option button. Choose **Edit Text** and delete the text which says Option Button 2 and replace it with **Front page**.

Figure 2. 14 ▶

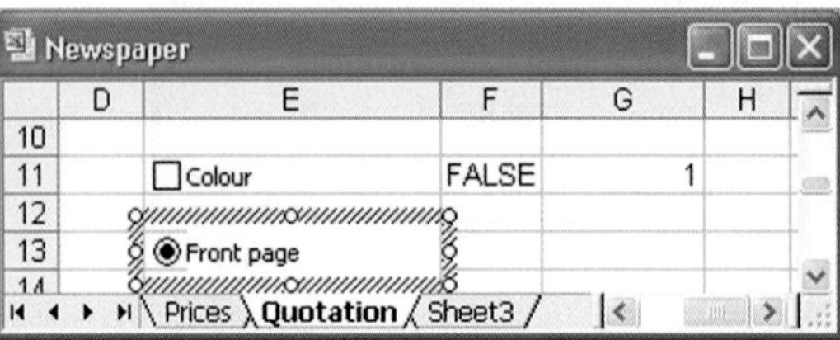

4 Right click again on the option button. Choose **Format Control**.
5 Set the cell link to **F15**.
6 Click on the Option Button icon again and drag out a rectangle over cell **E15**. Change the label of this button to **Back page.** You do not need to set the cell link again.
7 Then add a third option button over cell **E17** and label this one **Inside pages**.
8 Test that as you click on the option buttons, F15 changes from 1 to 2 to 3.
9 Save your work.

Hint: To make sure that all three buttons are in a neat straight line.

(a) Right click on one of the option buttons

(b) Hold down the CTRL key and click on the other two option buttons in turn to select all three option buttons.

(c) Click on **Draw** on the Drawing toolbar **> Align or Distribute > Align Left**

Figure 2. 15 ▶

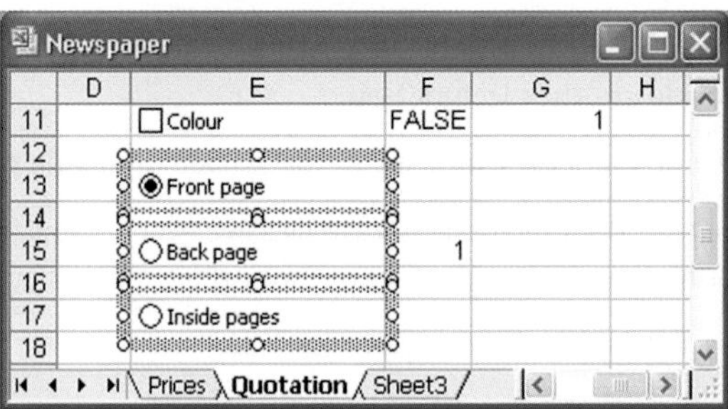

Note: All option buttons on one sheet will link by default to the same cell. If you want two or more groups of option buttons, select the **Group Box** on the Forms toolbar and draw a box round each group of option buttons.

If you want to practise setting up option buttons, check boxes and IF statements, look at Dynamic Learning Exercise 2.

Unit 5: Nested IF statements

In this unit we will look at how you can use the nested IF function.

With an IF statement such as **=IF(F11=TRUE,1.3,1)** you have only two choices TRUE and FALSE.

Nested IF increases the number of possible outcomes by placing one IF function inside another IF function.

We want three choices, **Front page**, **Back page** or **Inside pages**.

Inside pages are the cheapest. Back pages are 40 per cent more. The front page is much more expensive, 50 per cent more than inside pages.

So if F15 is 1 the price is multiplied by 1.5.

If F15 is 2 the price is multiplied by 1.4.

If F15 is 3 the price is the same (multiply by 1).

The formula for this is: **=IF(F15=1,1.5,IF(F15=2,1.4,1))**.

Here we have nested one IF function inside another. You can have more nested IFs up to a maximum of 7.

1. Enter this formula in cell **G15**.
   This formula checks if F15 is 1. If it is G15 is set to 1.5. If not, it checks if F15 is 2. If it is G15 is set to 1.4. If not, it is set to 1.
2. Test that the IF statement is working correctly by clicking on each option button in turn.
3. Save your work.

Figure 2. 16 ▶

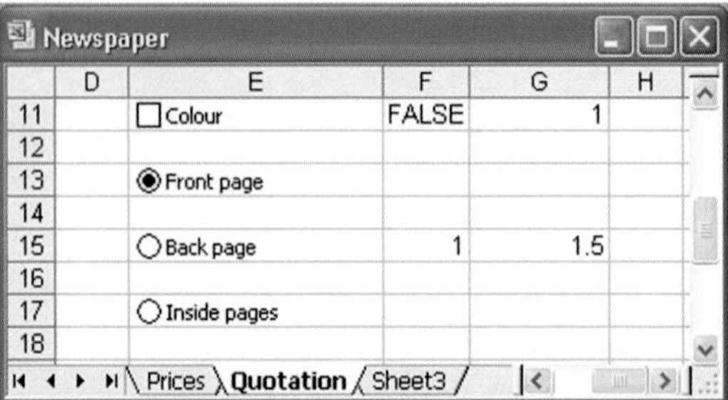

If you want to practise setting up nested IF statements, look at Dynamic Learning Exercise 3.

Unit 6: Combo boxes

In this unit we will look at using drop-down boxes to make a choice from a list.

Combo box is the term used in Excel for a drop-down box. You need to ensure that the **Forms** toolbar is visible. If it is not, click on **View > Toolbars > Forms.**

1 Click on the **Combo Box** icon in the Forms toolbar.

Figure 2. 17 ▶

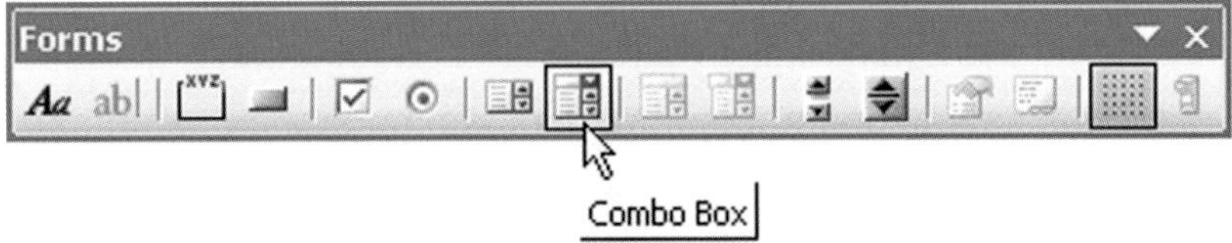

2 Drag out a rectangle over cell **E9**. A combo box will appear as shown in Figure 2.18.

Figure 2. 18 ▶

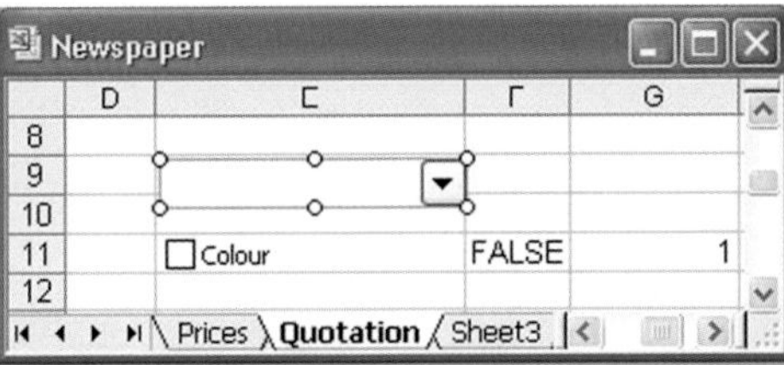

3 Right click on the combo box and choose **Format control.** A dialogue box appears on the screen.

4 Click in the **Input range** box. Click on the **Prices** tab to switch to the Prices worksheet and highlight cells **B2** to **B6**.

5 Click in the **Cell link** box on the dialogue box and enter **F9**.
The dialogue box should look like this:

Figure 2. 19 ▶

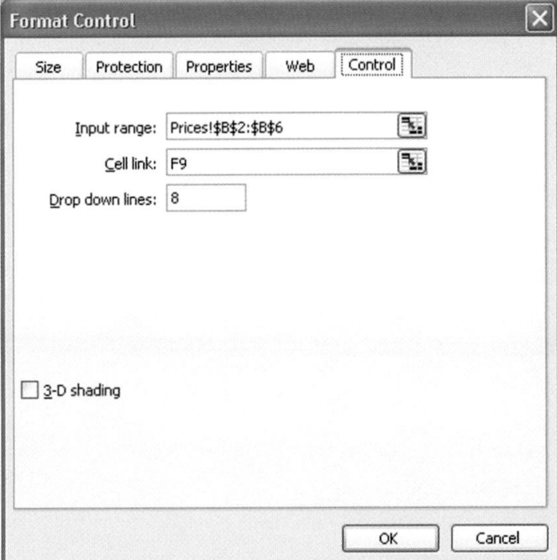

6 Click on **OK**.

7 Test that the choices on the combo box are as shown in Figure 2.20.

Figure 2. 20 ▶

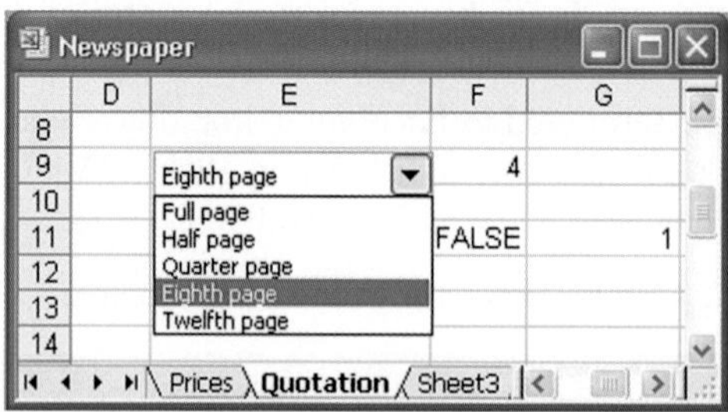

8 If you select the first item in the combo box, a number 1 will appear in cell F9 and so on. Check that as you choose a different selection from the combo box, the correct data appears in cell F9.

Note: If you type a value such as 2 into cell F9, it changes the information displayed in the combo box.

9 Save the file.

Unit 7: The VLOOKUP function

In this unit we will look at how to use the VLOOKUP function to look up data in a table. We will link the VLOOKUP to the combo box set up in Unit 6 to look up the price of an advertisement for the size chosen.

There are three lookup functions, **LOOKUP, VLOOKUP** and **HLOOKUP.** We will concentrate on the most commonly used function, VLOOKUP (Vertical lookup).

HLOOKUP (Horizontal lookup) and LOOKUP are very similar and may be worth investigating further later.

We will put the price of the advertisement in cell G9.

1 Select cell **G9** and format it to **currency**.
2 In this cell, enter the formula **=VLOOKUP(F9,Prices,3)**

You should now see that as you select a different size advertisement using the combo box, you get the appropriate price in cell G9. For example, the price of one-eighth of a page is £85.

Figure 2. 21 ▶

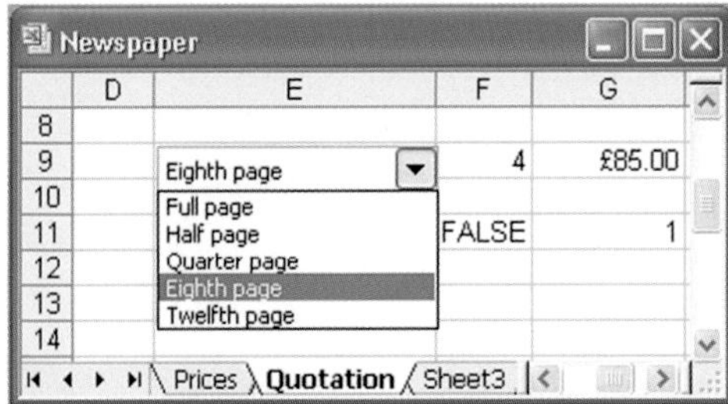

3 Test that it works by choosing different advertisement sizes using the combo box.

How does the formula work?

- **F9** is the cell whose value is to be looked up.
- **Prices** is the named area storing the price data set up in Unit 1.
- **3** is the number of the column in the table from which we want to take the data.

Figure 2. 22 ▶

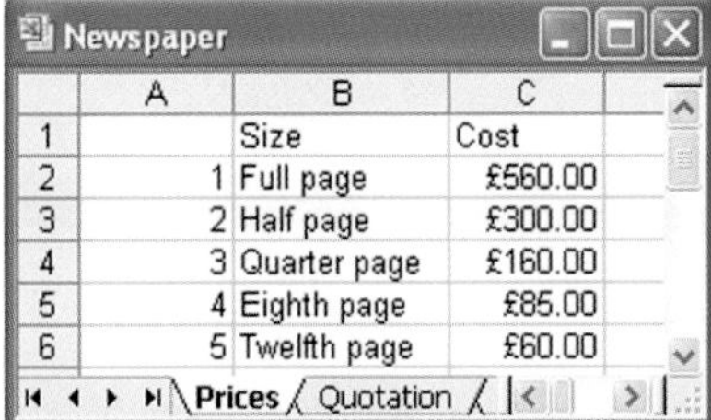

Newspaper

	A	B	C
1		Size	Cost
2	1	Full page	£560.00
3	2	Half page	£300.00
4	3	Quarter page	£160.00
5	4	Eighth page	£85.00
6	5	Twelfth page	£60.00

Prices / Quotation

The software will look in cell F9 and find the value 4. It will then look in the first column of the prices table (Column A) until it finds 4. Then it goes to the right until it reaches the third column (Column C). The value it finds here (£85) will be displayed in cell G9.

Note: This will only work if the data in the first column is in ascending order.

4 Save the file.
5 You might want to experiment with typing impossible values such as 0, 4.5 and 6, into cell F9 to see what happens.

If you want to practise setting up lookups and combos, look at Dynamic Learning Exercises 4 and 5.

Dynamic Learning Exercise 6 offers the challenge of setting up a small Excel solution that will calculate the cost of sending an air-mail letter, given the weight and the destination country.

Unit 8: Spinners

In this unit you will learn how to set up and use spinner controls.

A **spinner** or spin button is a button, with small up and down arrows, that enables you to increase or decrease the value of a number in a cell by clicking on the arrows.

1. Enter **Number of weeks** into cell **E19**.
2. If the Forms toolbar is not visible, turn it on with **View > Toolbars > Forms**.
3. Select the **Spinner** icon in the **Forms** toolbar.

Figure 2. 23 ▶

4. Drag out a small rectangle over cells **F19** and **F20**. A spinner will appear as shown in Figure 2.24.

Figure 2. 24 ▶

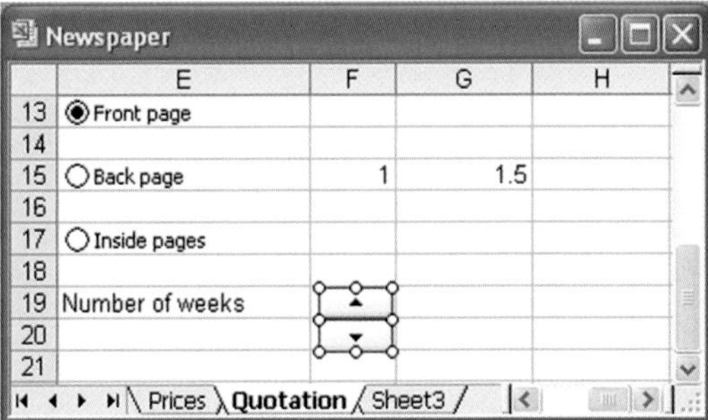

5. Right click on the spinner and choose **Format Control**.
6. A dialogue box appears. Set the minimum value to 1, the maximum value to 26, leave the incremental change at 1 and set the cell link to G19 as shown in Figure 2.25.

Figure 2. 25 ▶

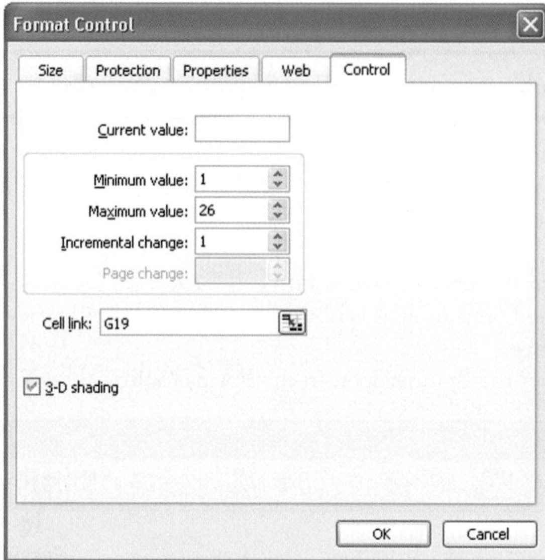

7 Click on **OK** and click on the spinner to test that the spinner works.
8 Save your work.

If you want to practise setting up spinners, look at Dynamic Learning Exercises 7 and 8.

Unit 9: Layout

In this unit you will learn to use Merge and Center to merge cells and improve the layout of the page.

Figure 2. 26 ▶

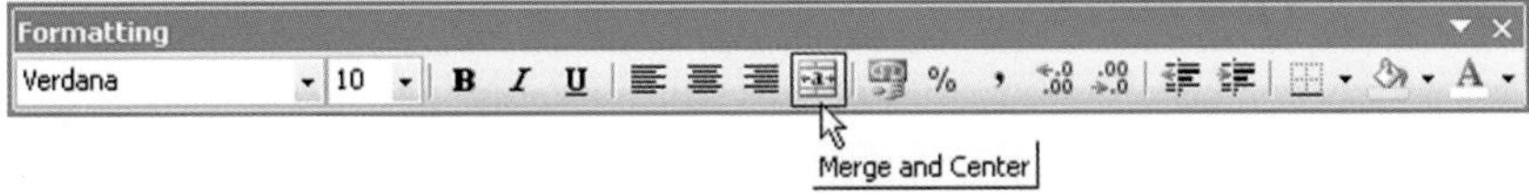

1 Highlight cells **B2** to **G5**.
2 Click on the **Merge and Center** icon on the Formatting toolbar.
3 Set the font to size **48**.
4 Insert the title **Denton Gazette**.

Figure 2. 27 ▶

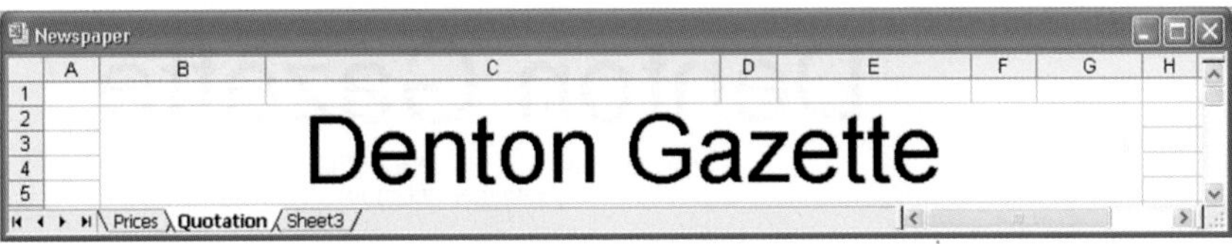

5 Merge cells **B6** to **G6**.
6 Enter the address and phone number, **25 High Street, Denton, DN6 9AA (01976) 434343**.
7 Merge cells **B7** to **G7**.
8 Enter the company's website address, **www.dentongazette.co.uk.** If Excel formats the web address as a hyperlink click on **Edit > Undo**.
9 Format that cell to **Bold**.
10 Save the file.

We are now ready to link all the information on the spreadsheet together to work out the price.

11 In cell **E22** enter the wording **Basic price**.
12 In cell **G22** enter the formula **=G9*G11*G15*G19**.

This simply works out the price of the advertisement including colour and the page selected for the number of weeks chosen.

13 In cell **E24** enter the word **Discount**.
14 In cell **G24** you need to enter a nested IF statement. If cell G19 is more than or equal to 10, there is a 20 per cent discount. If cell G19 is less than 4 there is no discount. Otherwise the discount is 10 per cent.

If you can't work it out, the formula is given at the end of the unit.

15 Format cell **G24** to percentage with the **Percent Style** icon on the Formatting toolbar.
16 In cell **E26** enter the wording **Final price**.
17 Enter a formula in cell **G26** to work out the price minus the discount. Again this is at the end of the unit if you can't work it out.
18 Format cell **G26** to **Bold** so that it stands out.
19 In cell **B11** enter **Customer Details**. Format this cell to **Bold**.

20 Enter the headings in **B13**, **B15**, **B17**, **B19** and **B21** as shown in Figure 2.28 and format these cells to **Bold**. The customer's name and address will be entered next to these cells.
21 Format cells **E22**, **E24** and **E26** to **Bold**.

Adding the date

A quotation like this will normally include the date.

22 Select cell **B9**.
23 Enter =TODAY()

Your spreadsheet should look as shown in Figure 2.28.

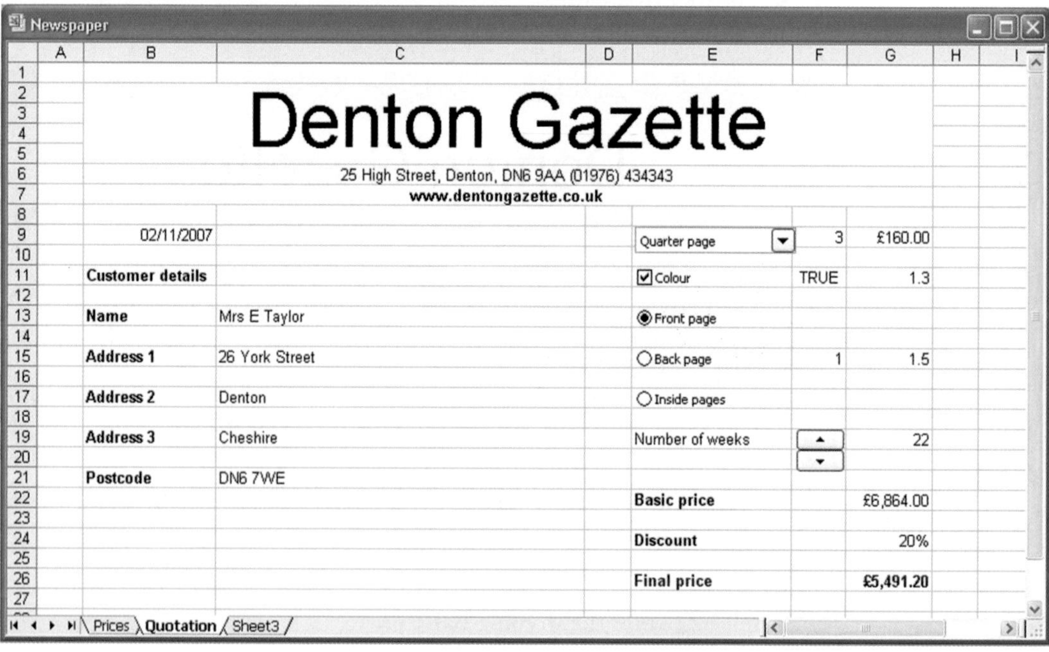

Figure 2. 28 ▲

24 Save your work.

Testing your spreadsheet

It is important that you test your spreadsheet thoroughly. If a spreadsheet is not accurate it will be of little use.

The best way to check your spreadsheet is to test it for a number of different scenarios. You should work out the cost in your head or with a calculator and then check that the spreadsheet gives the correct amount.

For example you might choose the following scenarios:

1 Quarter page, colour, front page, 22 weeks
2 Full page, no colour, inside page, 3 weeks
3 Eighth page, colour, back page, 8 weeks

For each scenario you must work out the cost. So for scenario 1, the price of the advertisement is £160. Colour is 30 per cent more. 30 per cent of £160 is £48. This gives £208.

The front page is 50 per cent more. 50 per cent of £208 is £104. This adds up to £312.

22 weeks will cost 22 times £312 = £6864.

Figure 2. 29 ▶

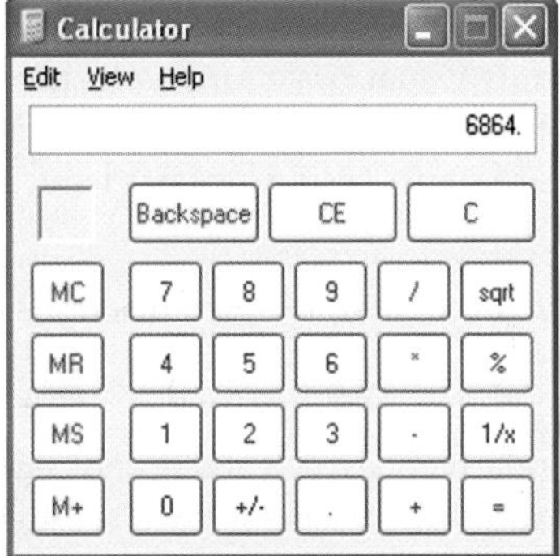

22 weeks qualifies for a 20 per cent discount. 20 per cent of £6864 = £1372.80.

£6864 minus £1372.80 = £5491.20.

Figure 2. 30 ▶

As you can see in Figure 2.28, the spreadsheet gave the expected answer.

Hints:
- The formula for cell G24 is: =IF(G19>=10,0.2,IF(G19<4,0,0.1)).
- The formula for cell G26 is: =G22-G24*G22.

Unit 10: Macros

In this unit you will learn about macros, why they are useful and how to create them.

An Excel macro is a set of instructions. You use macros to automate common procedures. It means that you can replace several clicks with just one click and so save time. Macros can also make the spreadsheet more user-friendly for someone who is not an IT professional.

In Excel, macros are written in Visual Basic for Applications (VBA) often shortened to Visual Basic or VB. For those who cannot write VBA code, Excel allows you to record a series of steps – using keyboard and mouse – that Excel then converts into VBA.

You can then set up a button or an icon to run a macro.

You can:

1. Record macros. This is relatively easy as you do not need to know about Visual Basic coding. Most of the macros we will set up will be recorded in this way.
2. Write the macros yourself in Visual Basic. This is more difficult, as you need to know the various VB coding commands. However some macros can *only* be set up in this way. (See Unit 13.)
3. Edit the Visual Basic in macros you have recorded. Again it is necessary to know about VB coding. We will edit a few macros in this way.

Recording macros

There are three common procedures that we want to automate using a macro:

1. switching to the Prices worksheet (e.g. to change prices)
2. switching back to the Quotation sheet
3. clearing the data for the next customer.

We will start by recording a macro to switch to the Prices worksheet. Make sure that you are on the Quotation sheet.

1. Click on **Tools > Macro > Record New Macro**
2. Call the macro **Prices** and click on **OK**

Figure 2. 31 ▶

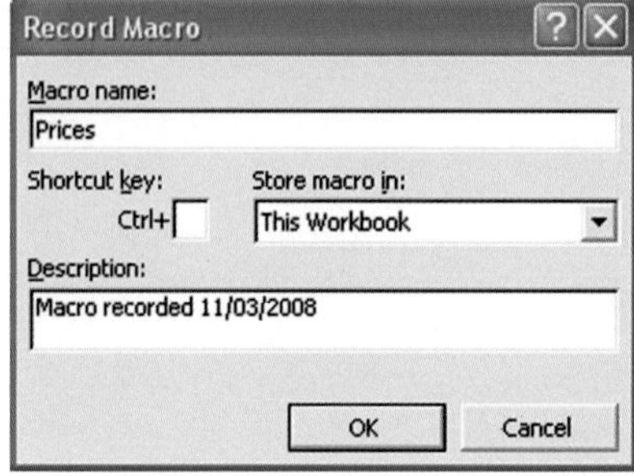

You will notice a small toolbar on the screen like this:

Figure 2. 32 ▶

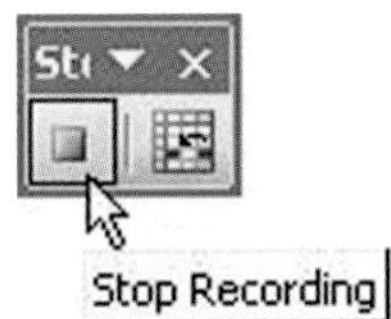

You may also notice the word **Recording** appears in the Status Bar at the bottom left of the spreadsheet.

Figure 2. 33 ▶

1 Click on the Sheet tab to select the **Prices** sheet.
2 Click on the **Stop Recording** icon or click on **Tools > Macro > Stop Recording**

That's it.

You can see the Visual Basic coding of the macro by clicking on: **Tools > Macro > Macros > Prices > Edit.**

Note: The Prices macro is sometimes labelled as **Module1.Prices**. However it will still work properly.

It looks something like this:

Figure 2. 34 ▶

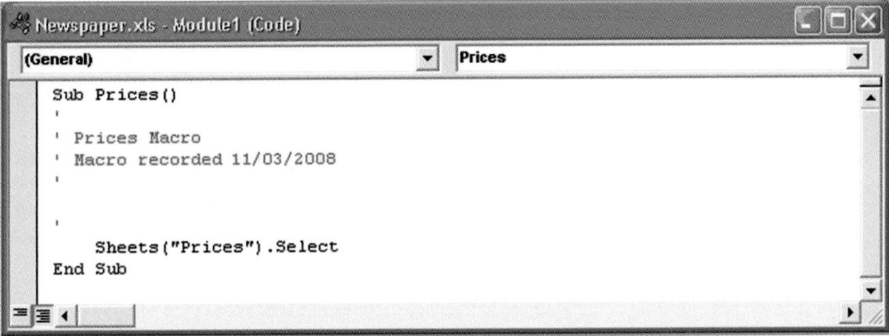

It is easy to see what is happening. The first line says the name of the macro. The next five lines begin with a ' and are in green. They are just for information. The next line switches to the sheet Prices. All macros end with End Sub.

3 Return to Excel by clicking on the **View Microsoft Excel** icon.
4 Record a similar macro called **Quotation** to take you back to the Quotation sheet.
5 Don't forget to stop recording and save your work.

You should now test your macros.

6 Test the Prices macro by clicking on **Tools > Macro > Macros > Prices > Run.** It should take you to the Prices sheet.
7 Test that the Quotation macro takes you back to the Quotation sheet.

Security settings

Figure 2. 35 ▶

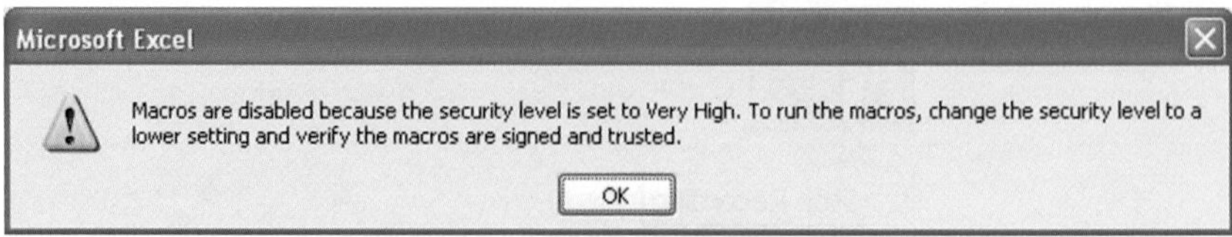

If you get the error message in Figure 2.35 when you try to run a macro, the security settings on your computer have been set so that macros cannot run. This is done to prevent viruses.

1 To allow macros to run, click on **Tools > Macro > Security**
2 If the security level is set to **Very High** or **High**, set it to **Low**

Figure 2. 36 ▶

3 Save your work and exit from Excel. Reload Excel and reload your file.

It should now work.

Unit 11: Macro buttons

In this unit you will learn how to set up buttons to run macros. This means that you can run a macro with just one click.

We will now add two buttons, one to run each of the macros.

1 Go to the **Quotation** sheet of the Newspaper.xls file if you are not already on it.
2 Click on the **Button** icon on the **Forms** toolbar.

Figure 2. 37 ▶

3 Drag out a rectangle over cells **B24** and **B25**, about half the width of column B as shown in Figure 2.38.

Figure 2. 38 ▶

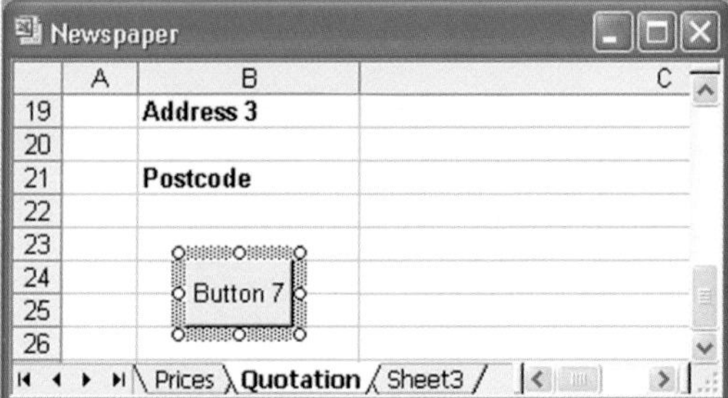

The Button will be given a name like Button 7.

4 The Assign Macro dialogue box will open. Assign the macro **Prices** (which may be called **Module1.Prices**) and click on **OK**.
5 Right click on the button. Choose **Edit Text**. Delete the text on the button and replace it with **Prices** as in Figure 2.39.

Figure 2. 39 ▶

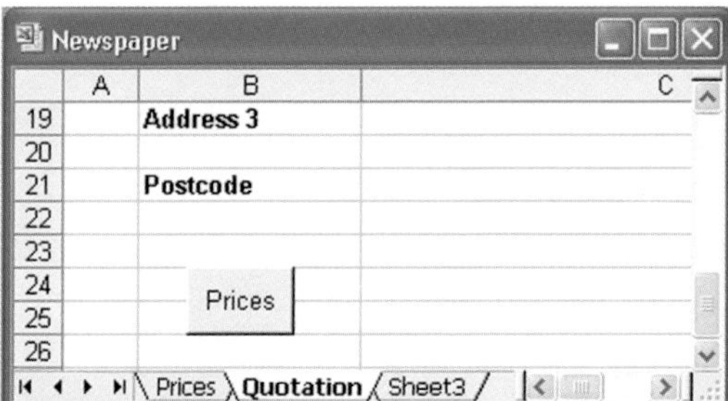

6 Click anywhere away from the button and then click on the button to test that it works.
7 Add a similar button on the **Prices** sheet to run the **Quotation** macro.
8 Save your work.

It is now easy to switch to the Prices sheet to adjust prices.

If you want to look at alternative buttons for running macros, look at Dynamic Learning Exercise 8.

Unit 12: A macro to clear data

In this unit you will set up a macro to clear the sheet ready for the next customer.

The user needs to clear all the data after one quotation has been made so that another quotation can be given. This can also be done with a macro and a button.

1. Starting on the **Quotation** sheet, start to record a macro called **Clear (Tools > Macro > Record New Macro).**
2. Select cell **F9** and press the **Delete** key on the keyboard.
3. Select cell **F11** and press the **Delete** key.
4. Select cell **F15** and press the **Delete** key.
5. Select cell **G19** and press the **Delete** key.
6. Select cell **C13** and press the **Delete** key.
7. Select cell **C15** and press the **Delete** key.
8. Select cell **C17** and press the **Delete** key.
9. Select cell **C19** and press the **Delete** key.
10. Select cell **C21** and press the **Delete** key.
11. Click on **C13** to make this cell the active cell.
12. Stop recording.

All the data has now been removed, although in some cases we have the error message #N/A. We will learn how to remove these in Unit 16.

We want a button to run the Clear macro to the right of the Prices button. To make it exactly the same size as the first button:

13. Right click on the **Prices** button and choose **Copy**.
14. Click on **Edit > Paste**.
15. Slide the new button down so that it is exactly to the right of the first button.

You can align the buttons in exactly the same way as you aligned the option buttons in Unit 4.

16. Right click on the second button. Choose **Edit Text** and change the text to **Clear**.
17. Right click again. Choose **Assign Macro** and choose the **Clear** macro.

Figure 2. 40 ▲

18 Enter some data and test that the clear button works.
19 Save your work.

A print macro

One of the client's original requirements was to print the quotation at the touch of a button.

1 Set the page to Landscape (use **File > Page Setup**).
2 Highlight the area from **A1** to **H30**. Click on **File > Print Area > Set Print Area.** (The print area will be shown by a dotted line as in Figure 2.41.)
3 Use **View > Header and Footer** to add your name, the date and the page number.
4 Record a macro called **PrintQuote** to print page 1 of the quotation sheet.
5 Add another button to run this macro and label this button **Print** as in Figure 2.41.

Figure 2. 41 ▶

Unit 13: Message boxes

In this unit you will learn how to set up macros to display message boxes on the screen.

As explained in Unit 10 some macros can only be created by writing them yourself in Visual Basic or by editing the Visual Basic of an existing macro.

You need to know a little Visual Basic to put a message box on the screen like the one in Figure 2.42. Fortunately the code is not too difficult.

Figure 2. 42 ▶

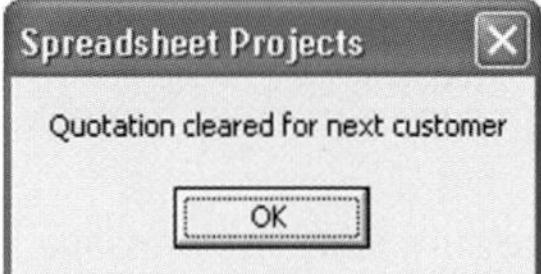

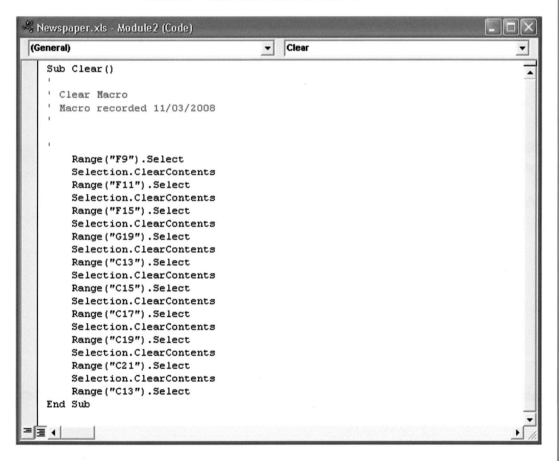

1 Click on **Tools > Macro > Macros > Clear > Edit**.
2 This loads up the Visual Basic coding of the macro in the Visual Basic Editor. Your code will be similar to that in Figure 2.43. You will learn more about the Visual Basic Editor in Unit 21.

Newspaper.xls - Module2 (Code)

(General) | Clear

```
Sub Clear()
'
' Clear Macro
' Macro recorded 11/03/2008
'


'
    Range("F9").Select
    Selection.ClearContents
    Range("F11").Select
    Selection.ClearContents
    Range("F15").Select
    Selection.ClearContents
    Range("G19").Select
    Selection.ClearContents
    Range("C13").Select
    Selection.ClearContents
    Range("C15").Select
    Selection.ClearContents
    Range("C17").Select
    Selection.ClearContents
    Range("C19").Select
    Selection.ClearContents
    Range("C21").Select
    Selection.ClearContents
    Range("C13").Select
End Sub
```

Figure 2. 43 ▲

3 Click at the end of the line above End Sub. Press **Enter** and type in the following code as shown in Figure 2.44. Remember that the coding has to be spelt exactly right for it to work.

```
response = MsgBox("Quotation cleared for next customer ", ,"Spreadsheet Projects")
```

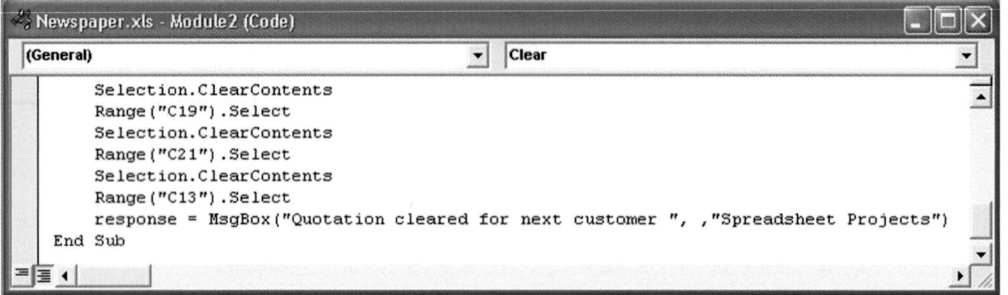

Figure 2. 44 ▲

4 Close the Visual Basic Editor program in the normal way or press ALT and **F11**.
5 Run the Clear macro and make sure that the message box appears.
6 Test it and save your work.

Sometimes people exit from a program in error. We can use a macro and a message box as a double check.

1 Load the Visual Basic code for the Clear macro as before. **Tools > Macro > Macros** > **Clear** > **Edit**.
2 Scroll down to the bottom and type in this code which creates a new macro called Quit.

```
Sub Quit()
response = MsgBox("Are you sure you want to quit?",
vbYesNo)
If response = vbYes Then Application.quit
End Sub
```

Hint: The computer will put the **End Sub** line in for you.

What does this macro do?

Line 1 says the macro is called **Quit.**

Line 2 displays the message box with the message and Yes and No buttons (see Figure 2.45).

Line 3 checks if the response is Yes and if it is exits from Excel.

Line 4 ends the macro.

Figure 2. 45 ▶

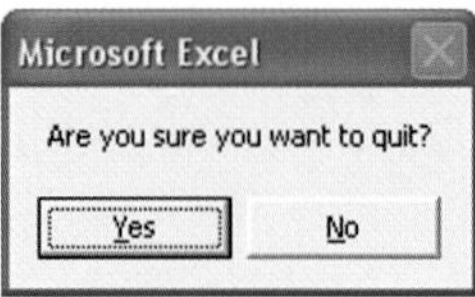

3 Save your file.
4 Close the Visual Basic Editor (press ALT and **F11**) and test that the macro works for both the Yes button and the No button.
5 Add a button to run the **Quit** macro.

Unit 14: Further macros

In this unit you will learn how to set up a macro to file away quotation details.

In the original requirements, the client requested that the user should be able to file the quotation away for future reference.

We will do this by using a macro to copy data to a file in a different sheet.

1 Switch to **Sheet3** and rename the worksheet **QuoteFile** as shown in Figure 2.46.

Figure 2. 46 ▼

Hint: Although it is possible to have a space in the name of a worksheet, it is easier when using certain features to avoid spaces.

2 Highlight columns A to K and set the column width to 10 using **Format > Column > Width**.
3 Enter the column headings as shown in Figure 2.47.

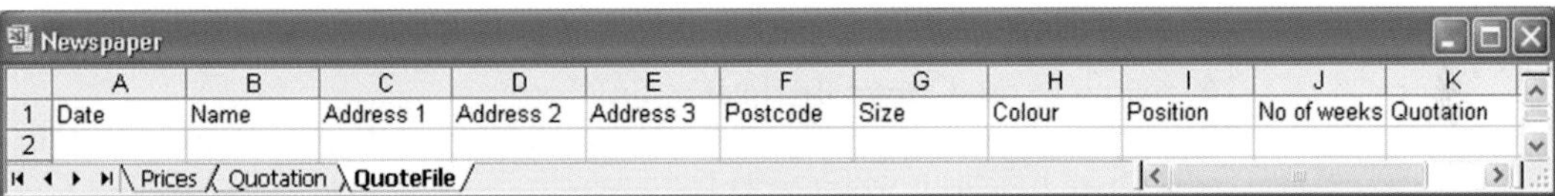

Figure 2. 47 ▲

4 Highlight column A and format to date using **Format > Cells.** Click on the **Number tab > Date > OK.**
5 Highlight column K and format to currency using the **Currency** icon.
6 Switch back to the **Quotation** sheet.

You are now going to make a copy of all the data in row 31 at the bottom of the screen, ready to file.

7 Scroll down to cell **A31**. Enter the formula **=B9.** (Do not worry if the date does not fit in the cell and you see #######.)
8 In **B31** enter the formula **=C13**
9 In **C31** enter the formula **=C15**
10 In **D31** enter the formula **=C17**
11 In **E31** enter the formula **=C19**
12 In **F31** enter the formula **=C21**
13 In **G31** enter the formula **=VLOOKUP(F9,Prices,2)**
14 In **H31** enter the formula **=IF(F11=TRUE,"Colour","Not colour")**

15 In I31 enter the formula **=IF(F15=1,"Front Page",IF(F15=2,"Back page","Inside pages"))**
16 In J31 enter the formula **=G19& "weeks"**

This is called concatenation where two or more pieces of text are joined together in a cell.

17 In K31 enter the formula **=G26**

It will look something like Figure 2.48. If the details don't fit in the cells, it does not matter.

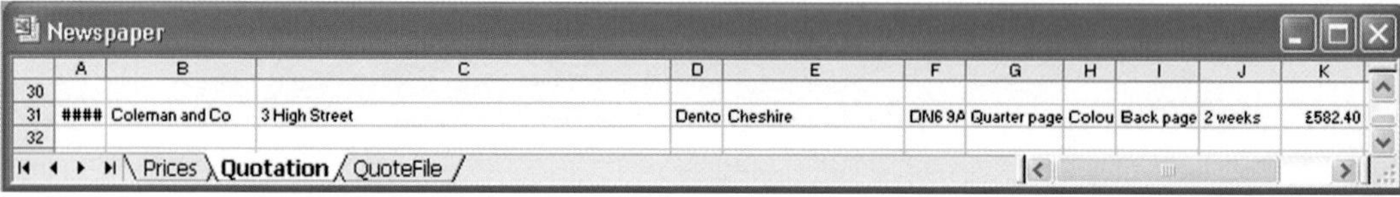

Figure 2. 48 ▲

We are now ready to record the macro. It is quite complicated and you have to get all the commands in the right order. You may want to practise the sequence of tasks before you record the macro.

18 Switch to the **Quotation** sheet.
19 Start to record a macro called **FileQuote. Tools > Macro > Record New Macro.**
20 Switch to the **QuoteFile** sheet.
21 Highlight cells A2 to K2.
22 Click on **Insert > Cells > Shift cells down > OK** (this makes a space to store the quotation).
23 Switch back to the **Quotation** sheet.
24 Highlight cells **A31** to **K31**.
25 Click on **Edit > Copy**.
26 Switch to the **QuoteFile** sheet again.
27 Click on **Edit > Paste Special > Paste Values > OK** (you cannot use **Edit > Paste** here as it won't work).
28 Switch back to the **Quotation** sheet again. Click on cell **C13** and press the ESCAPE key on the keyboard.
29 Stop recording.
30 We don't need to see the data in cells A31 to K31, so highlight these cells and set the font colour to be white.
31 Add a button to run the FileQuote macro on the right of the other four buttons.

Align the tops of all the five buttons and space them out evenly as follows.
32 Right click on one button.
33 Hold down the CTRL key and select the other four buttons.
34 Display the Drawing Toolbar if it is not showing (**View > Toolbars > Drawing**).
35 Click on **Draw > Align or Distribute > Align Top**.
36 Click on **Draw > Align or Distribute > Distribute Horizontally**.

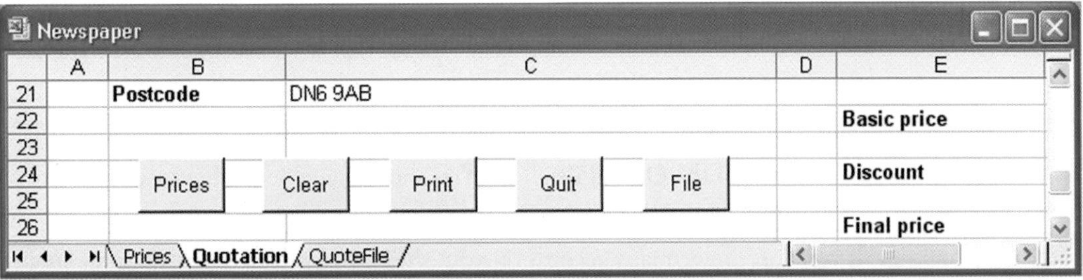

Figure 2. 49 ▲

37 Test that the macro works by filing four or five additional quotations as shown in Figure 2.50.

Newspaper

	A	B	C	D	E	F	G	H	I	J	K
1	Date	Name	Address 1	Address 2	Address 3	Postcode	Size	Colour	Position	No of weeks	Quotation
2	31/10/2007	Denton Unite	The Stadium	Denton	Cheshire	DN6 9AZ	Full page	Colour	Inside pages	26 weeks	£15,142.40
3	31/10/2007	Healey's Un(	41 Station S	Denton	Cheshire	DN6 9AU	Twelfth page	Not colour	Front Page	1 weeks	£90.00
4	31/10/2007	Denton Boro	82 High Stre	Denton	Cheshire	DN6 9AP	Half page	Colour	Back page	14 weeks	£6,115.20
5	31/10/2007	Gibbs and G	7 High Stree	Denton	Cheshire	DN6 9AB	Full page	Colour	Inside pages	14 weeks	£8,153.60
6	31/10/2007	Sandra's Hai	5 High Stree	Denton	Cheshire	DN6 9AB	Half page	Not colour	Front Page	7 weeks	£2,835.00
7	31/10/2007	Coleman an(	3 High Stree	Denton	Cheshire	DN6 9AB	Quarter page	Colour	Back page	2 weeks	£582.40

Prices / Quotation / QuoteFile

Figure 2. 50 ▲

Unit 15: Data Forms

In this unit you will learn how to use data forms to view previous quotations

1 Switch to the **QuoteFile** sheet. You should have several quotations as in Figure 2.50.

If you don't have many records on your sheet, you will need to add some more quotations.

2 Click on any of the cells in the table.
3 Click on **Data > Form.**

A form will appear on the screen like Figure 2.51.

Figure 2. 51 ▶

You can scroll through the records using the scrollbar.

Suppose you wanted to find the quotation for Gibbs and Gibbs (or a company you have entered).

4 Click on the **Criteria** button.
5 Enter the first few letters such as **Gibbs** in the Name box.
6 Click on **Find Next**.

You should find the record for Gibbs and Gibbs (or your company).

7 Record a macro called **Quotes** that will take you from the Quotation sheet to the QuoteFile sheet and display the data form. You will have to close the data form before you can stop recording, but the Close operation won't be recorded.
8 Add a button to the Quotation sheet to run this macro. You now should have six macro buttons and you will probably need to re-align them as in Figure 2.52.

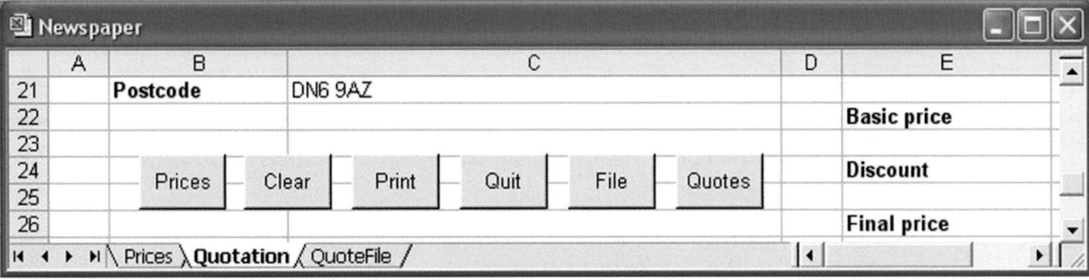
Newspaper
A
B
C
D
E
21
Postcode
DN6 9AZ
22
Basic price
23
24
Discount
25
26
Final price
Prices
Clear
Print
Quit
File
Quotes
Prices
Quotation
QuoteFile

Figure 2. 52 ▲

Unit 16: Error trapping

In this unit you will learn various ways of removing the #N/A error message.

If you run the Clear macro you get the #N/A error message in cells G9, G22 and G26.

This occurs because a value in a formula is missing. In this case, it is missing because we have cleared the data.

For example, the formula in G9 is **=VLOOKUP(F9,Prices,3)**. The VLOOKUP function is trying to look up the value in cell F9 but there is no data in cell F9 so there is nothing to look up.

The #N/A is unsightly and unfriendly. We can remove it as follows:

1 Replace the formula in **G9** with: **=IF(F9="","", VLOOKUP(F9,Prices,3))**

This formula checks the value of F9. If it is blank (""), then G9 is also blank. Otherwise it looks up the value as before.

2 Test that the formula works. If you run the Clear macro, G9 is blank. If you choose a value from the combo box, the price appears in G9.
3 There are also errors in cells G22 and G26. Enter the formulas to prevent these errors based on checking if F9 is blank.
If you can't work them out for yourself, the formulas are given in the hint below.
4 The error messages have now been removed.
5 Save your work.

Figure 2. 53 ▲

Hints: The formula in G22 should be **=IF(F9="","", G9*G11*G15*G19).**
The formula in G26 should be **=IF(F9="","", G22-G24*G22).**

Error trapping: using the ISERROR function

An alternative method is to use the **ISERROR** function in Excel. The ISERROR function tests if an error has occurred.

Again we use the IF function and the command is even longer.

1 Replace the formula in G9 with:
=IF(ISERROR(VLOOKUP(F9,Prices,3)),"",VLOOKUP(F9,Prices,3))

This formula checks if there is an error in the VLOOKUP formula. If there is, it returns a blank. If not, it returns the VLOOKUP value.

2 Test that the formula works. If you run the Clear macro, G9 is blank. If you choose a value from the combo box, the price appears in G9.
3 There are also errors in cells G22 and G26. Use ISERROR functions to prevent these errors based on checking if there is an error in the calculation: G9*G11*G15*G19.

Unit 17: Using Visual Basic to validate data

In this unit you will learn more about using Visual Basic to create a macro.

In the original requirements, the client said that you can't have full-page and half-page advertisements on the front page or the back page.

How it will work

Cell F9 has the value 1 for a full page and 2 for a half page. Cell F15 has the value 1 for a front page, 2 for the back page and 3 for inside pages.

If the value of F9 is 1 or 2 then the value of F15 must be 3.

We can set up a macro to set F15 to 3 if the value of F9 is 1 or 2 as follows:

1. Edit any macro with **Tools > Macro > Macros > Edit**.
2. The Visual Basic Editor will load with the macro coding shown. Scroll down to the bottom of the box with the code in it.
3. Enter the code as shown in Figure 2.54.

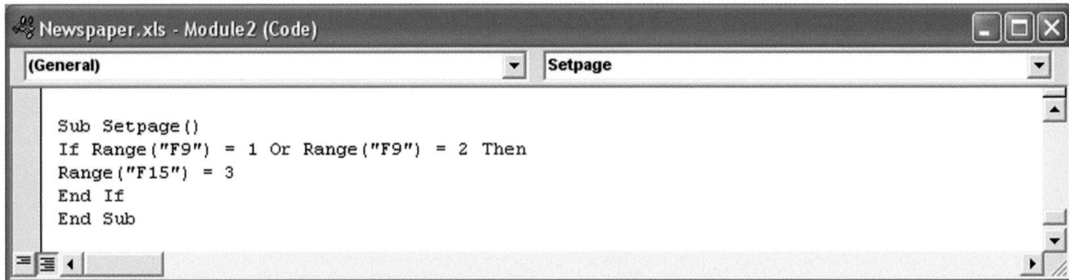

Newspaper.xls - Module2 (Code)
(General)
Setpage
Sub Setpage()
If Range("F9") = 1 Or Range("F9") = 2 Then
Range("F15") = 3
End If
End Sub

Figure 2. 54 ▲ This macro checks if the value of cell F9 is either 1 or 2. If it is, the value of F15 is set to 3 (Inside pages).

4. Switch back to Excel by pressing ALT and **F11**.
5. Select the combo box. Right click on it and choose **Assign macro**. Choose the **Setpage** macro and click on **OK**.
6. Test that the macro works.

We have set up this macro so that if a full page or half page is selected, then *Inside Pages* is automatically selected too. However there is nothing to stop the user now choosing Front Page or Back page so we need another macro to prevent this.

7. Edit any macro with **Tools > Macro > Macros > Edit**.
8. The Visual Basic Editor will load with the macro coding shown. Scroll down to the bottom of the box with the code in it.
9. Enter the code as shown in Figure 2.55.

Newspaper.xls - Module2 (Code)

(General) | Impossible

```
Sub Impossible()
If (Range("F9") = 1 Or Range("F9") = 2) And (Range("F15") = 1 Or Range("F15") = 2) Then
MsgBox ("This is an impossible combination.")
Range("F9") = ""
Range("F15") = ""
End If
End Sub
```

Figure 2. 55 ▲ This prevents the impossible combination of 1 or 2 in cells F9 and F15. If impossible data has been entered, a message box will appear and the values will be reset to blank.

10 Switch back to Excel by pressing ALT and **F11**.
11 Select the option button Front page. Right click on it and choose **Assign macro**. Choose the **Impossible** macro and click on **OK**.
12 Do the same for the option button Back page.
13 Test that the macro works. You need to test both possible and impossible combinations.

Figure 2. 56 ▶

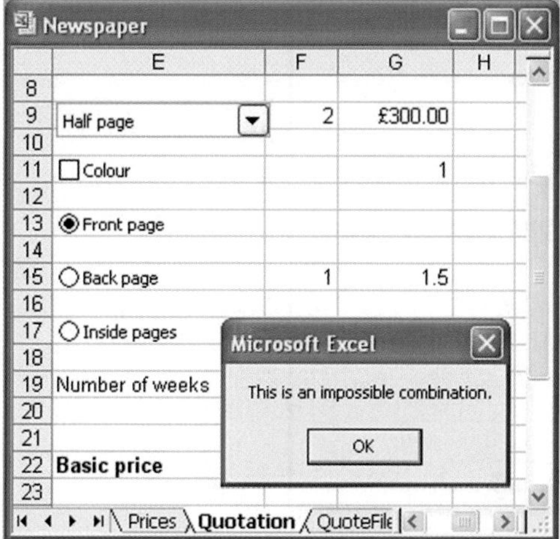

Unit 18: Cell protection

Having set up the spreadsheet it is important to protect it from alteration using the sheet protection feature described in Part 1.

On the Quotation sheet, the user will need to change these cells: C13, C15, C17, C19, C21, F9, F11, F15 and G19.

All the other cells contain formulas or text that doesn't change.

Protecting a whole worksheet

1 Highlight the nine cells, **C13**, **C15**, **C17**, **C19**, **C21**, **F9**, **F11**, **F15** and **G19**. (Select one, then hold down the CTRL key and select the others.)
2 Click on **Format > Cells** and click on the **Protection** tab, uncheck the **Locked** box and click on **OK**.
3 Click on **Tools > Protection > Protect Sheet.** You will see the box as shown in Figure 2.57.

Figure 2. 57 ▶

4 It is not a good idea to use a password – you may forget it and then you won't be able to complete the spreadsheet.
5 Make sure that only the **Select unlocked cells** box is checked as in Figure 2.57 and click on **OK.**

Users won't even be able to select locked cells.

6 Test the protection. You should now be able to change the data, use the spinner, combo box, option buttons, and the check box, file a quote and clear a quote but not be able to click in other cells.
7 To turn off protection, click on **Tools > Protection > Unprotect Sheet...** If you have used a password, you will be prompted to type it in now.

If you want to practise setting up sheet protection, look at Dynamic Learning Exercise 10.

Unit 19: Customising the spreadsheet and the screen

Now that our spreadsheet is nearly complete, there are a variety of things we can do to make the screen tidier and more friendly for the user.

1 Turn off any sheet protection. **Tools > Protection > Unprotect Sheet...**

First you need to set up your foreground and background colours.

2 Click on **Tools > Options** and choose the **Color** tab.
3 Select one of the colours on the bottom row and click on **Modify**.
4 Click on the **Custom** tab and choose the first house colour of the *Denton Gazette*, pale green: Red 200, Green 237, Blue 234 and click on **OK**.

Figure 2. 58 ▶

5 Select two more colours from the bottom row and modify them so that they are the other two house colours of the *Denton Gazette*:

- mid green: Red 176, Green 220, Blue 216
- dark green for the text: Red 75 Green 112 Blue 105

6 Click on **OK**.
7 Format the background colours and borders as shown in Figure 2.58. (You will need to click on **Format > Cells** and click on the **Patterns** tab as the customised colours are not available if you click the Fill Color icon.)

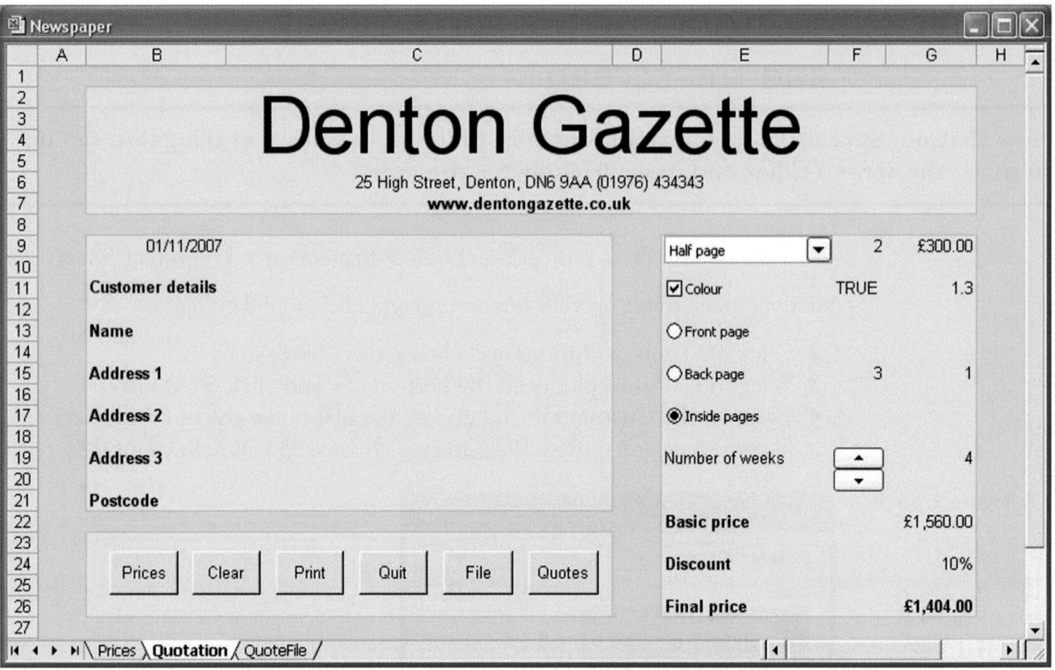

Figure 2. 59 ▲

8 Format the text colour to **dark green** and format the font to **Verdana**.

9 Column G is not wide enough to show every price so format the width of this column to 15.

10 Hiding the working. The data in these cells does not need to be shown: F9, G9, F11, G11, F15 and G15. Set the font colour for these cells to be the same as the background colour, using **Format > Cells > Font > Color**.

11 Select all the macro buttons and click on **Format > Control** and select the **Font** tab. Set the font colour to dark green, the font weight to bold and the font to Verdana.

12 Add the company logo as in Figure 2.60.

There are many items on the screen which help us create the spreadsheet but which are not required by the user. It is possible to customise the screen to remove these features that might distract the user.

These features include:

- icons and toolbars
- status bar
- formula bar
- row and column headings
- scrollbars
- sheet tabs

13 Record a macro called **Auto_open** to remove all these features. Remove the toolbars using **View > Toolbars**. Use **Tools > Options** and click on the **View** tab to remove all the other features – gridlines, status bar, sheet tabs, formula bar, scrollbars and row and column headers.

It's a good idea to practise what you will record first before recording the macro.

This macro will run automatically when the spreadsheet loads.

Newspaper

Denton Gazette

25 High Street, Denton, DN6 9AA (01976) 434343
www.dentongazette.co.uk

13/11/2007

Customer details

Name

Address 1

Address 2

Address 3

Postcode

Prices Clear Print Quit File Quotes

Full page

Colour

Front page

Back page

Inside pages

Number of weeks 4

Basic price £1,560.00

Discount 10%

Final price £1,404.00

Figure 2. 60 ▲ The macro coding will look like the coding shown below in Figure 2.61.

Figure 2. 61 ▶

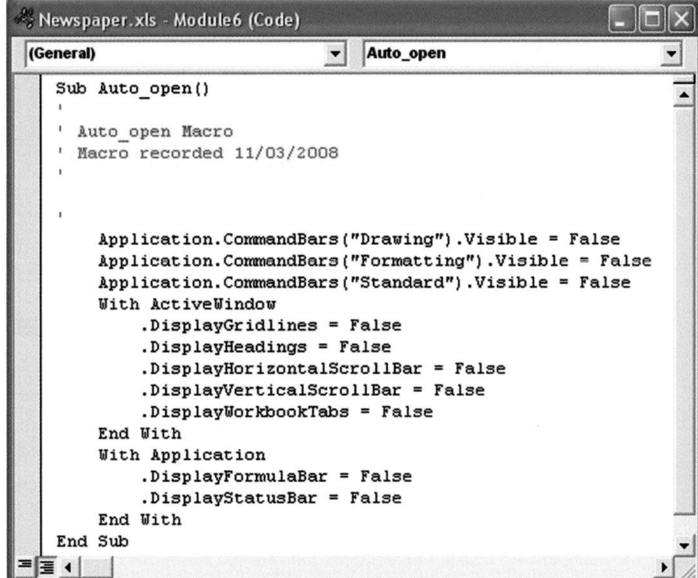

Newspaper.xls - Module6 (Code)

(General) Auto_open

```
Sub Auto_open()
'
' Auto_open Macro
' Macro recorded 11/03/2008
'


'
    Application.CommandBars("Drawing").Visible = False
    Application.CommandBars("Formatting").Visible = False
    Application.CommandBars("Standard").Visible = False
    With ActiveWindow
        .DisplayGridlines = False
        .DisplayHeadings = False
        .DisplayHorizontalScrollBar = False
        .DisplayVerticalScrollBar = False
        .DisplayWorkbookTabs = False
    End With
    With Application
        .DisplayFormulaBar = False
        .DisplayStatusBar = False
    End With
End Sub
```

14 Record another macro called **Auto_close** to put all these features back when you close the spreadsheet.
15 Test both macros work as expected.
16 Turn on the sheet protection. **Tools > Protection > Protect Sheet...**
17 Save the file.

Unit 20: Templates

In this unit you will learn how to make the system reusable using templates.

A template is an Excel spreadsheet that has been set up for a specific purpose, into which you can enter data. It is easy to convert your completed worksheet into a template. It then can be loaded easily.

To save your spreadsheet as a template:

1 Start on the **Quotation** sheet.
2 Run the **Clear** macro to remove any data.
3 Click on cell **C13**.
4 Click on **File > Save As…**
5 Click on the drop-down arrow by the **Save as type** box and select **Template (*.xlt)**.

Figure 2. 62 ▶

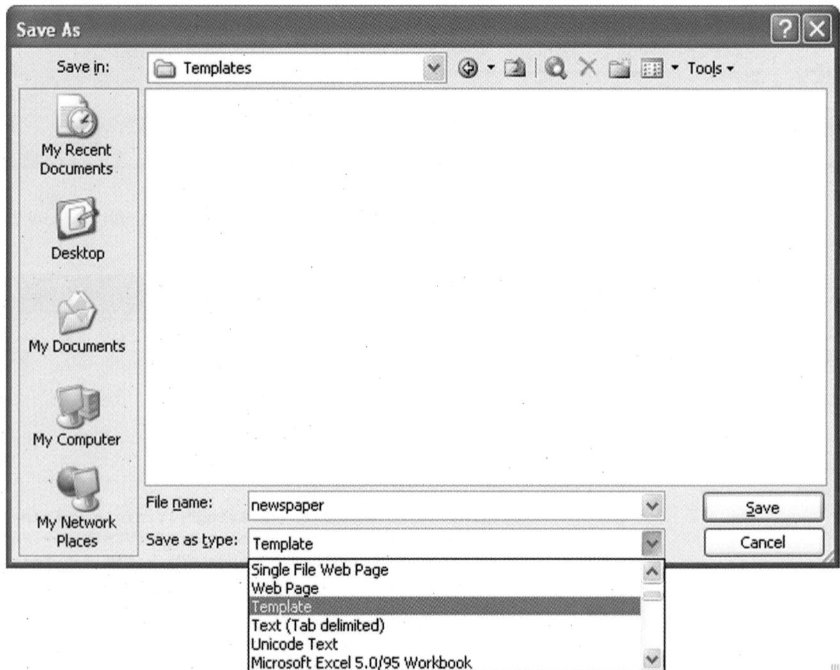

Your file will be saved as **Newspaper.xlt**. It will be saved in your templates folder.

6 Close the file.

Loading a blank document

1 To load a document based on the template click on **File > New.** A menu appears on the right of the screen as shown in Figure 2.63.

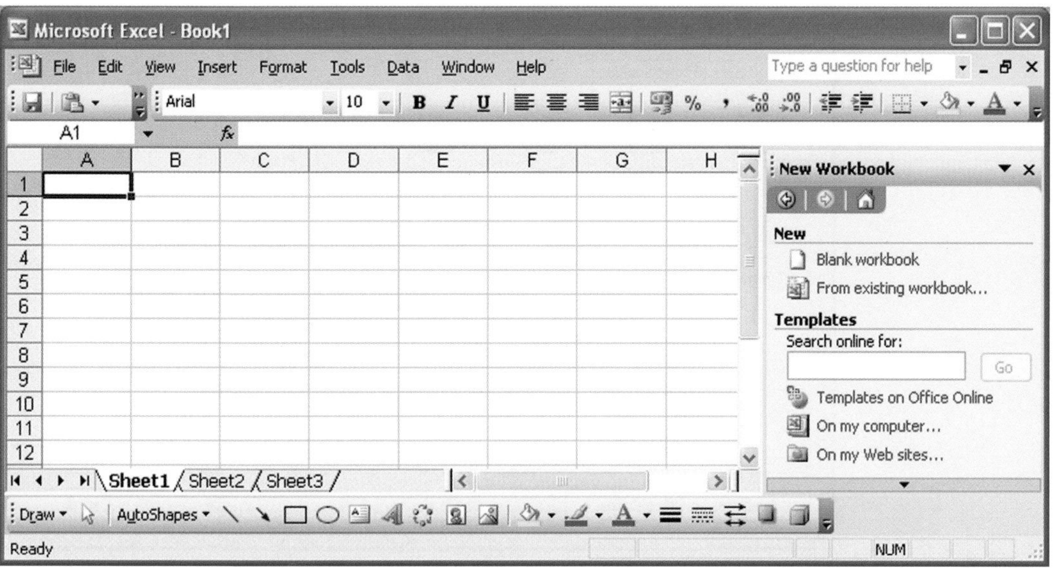

Figure 2. 63 ▲

2 Click on **On my computer…**

Figure 2. 64 ▶

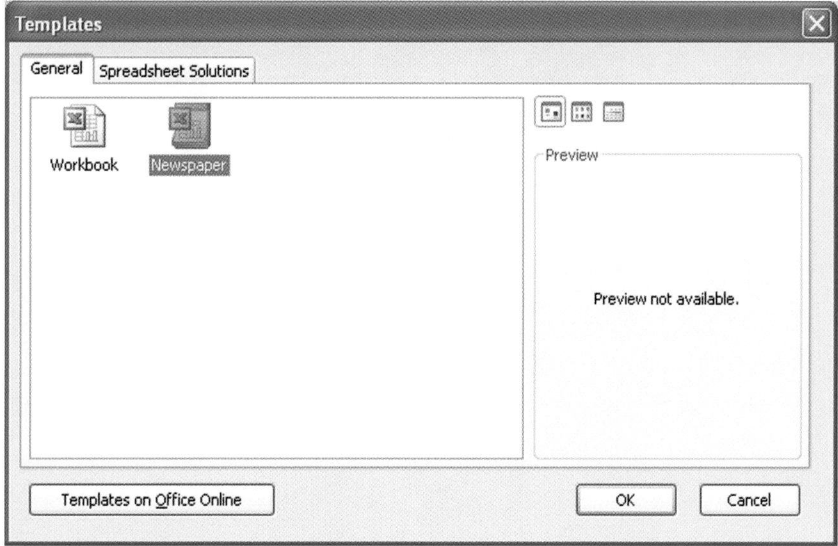

3 A dialogue box appears. Click on **Newspaper** and then **OK**.

Why use templates?

It is a good idea to use templates because when you start a document based on the template, it is a new file called Newspaper1, Newspaper2, etc. This means that each quotation is stored separately using different filenames.

Excel comes with some templates already installed. Click on the **Spreadsheet Solutions** tab to see these. Others are available online.

Figure 2. 65 ▶

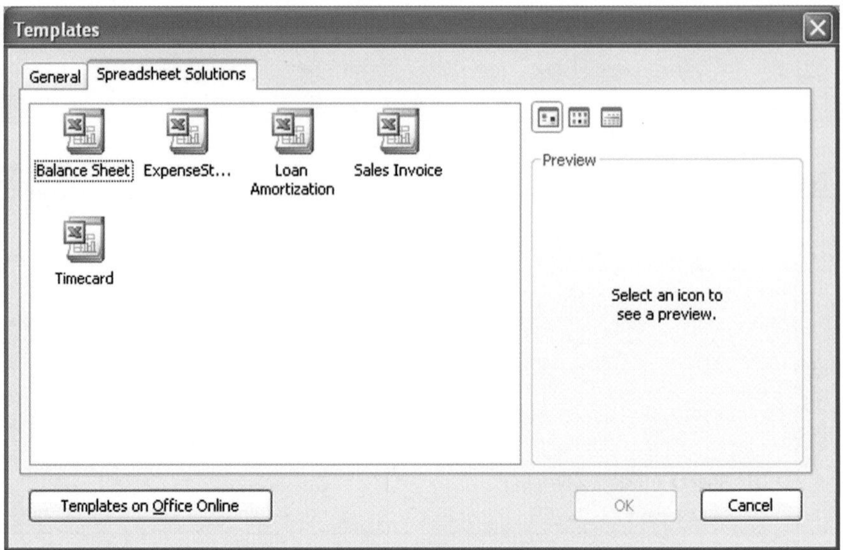
Templates
General
Spreadsheet Solutions
Balance Sheet
ExpenseSt...
Loan Amortization
Sales Invoice
Timecard
Preview
Select an icon to see a preview.
Templates on Office Online
OK
Cancel

Unit 21: The Visual Basic Editor

In this section you will learn how to use the Visual Basic Editor to customise more features in Excel.

The Visual Basic Editor Window is used for entering commands in Excel's programming language Visual Basic, sometimes called VBA (Visual Basic for Applications).

We have already used the Visual Basic Editor to set up macros such as to display a message box. We will also use the Visual Basic Editor to set up UserForms.

Before we do this you need to familiarise yourself with the Visual Basic Editor.

1 Still using the newspaper file, load the **Visual Basic Editor** by clicking on **Tools > Macro > Visual Basic Editor** or pressing ALT and F11.

The screen will look something like the one shown in Figure 2.66.

Figure 2. 66 ►

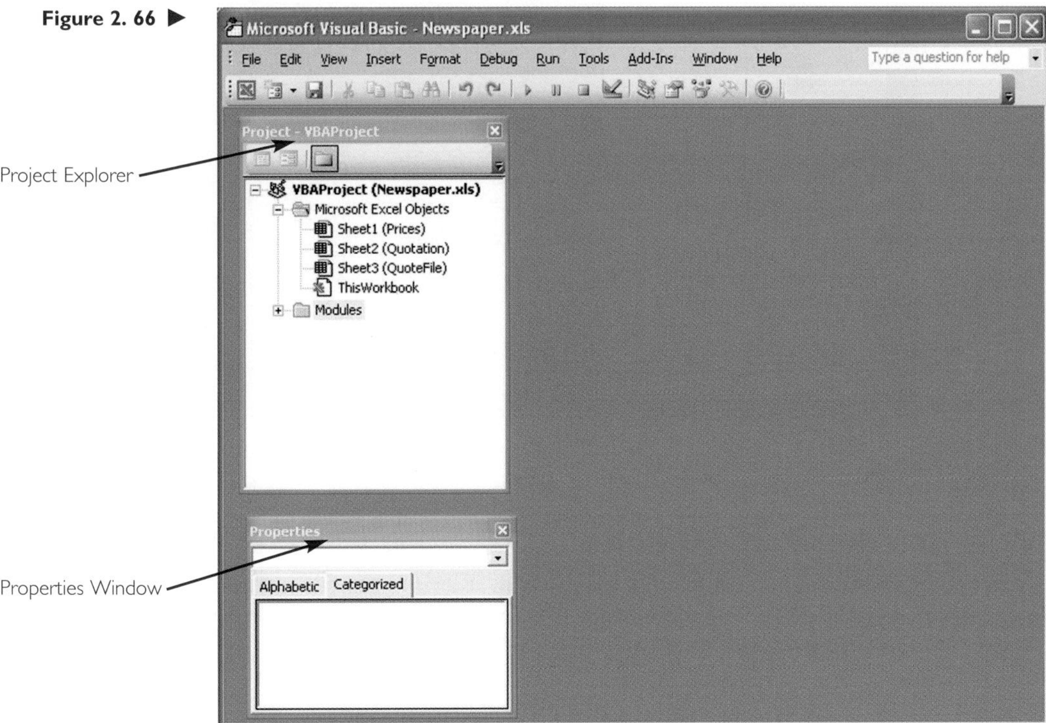

In the top left of the screen is the **Project Explorer.**

2 If the Project Explorer is not visible, click on **View > Project Explorer**. In the bottom left of the screen is the **Properties Window**.
3 If the Properties Window is not visible click on **View > Properties Window**.

You can adjust the size of the windows and move them around the screen by dragging in the normal way.

The Project Explorer displays a list of the projects. Any open workbook is a project consisting of worksheets, modules (where macros are stored) and UserForms.

4 Click on the + sign to the left of the word Modules in the Project Explorer to display a list of all your modules. In this example there are six modules.

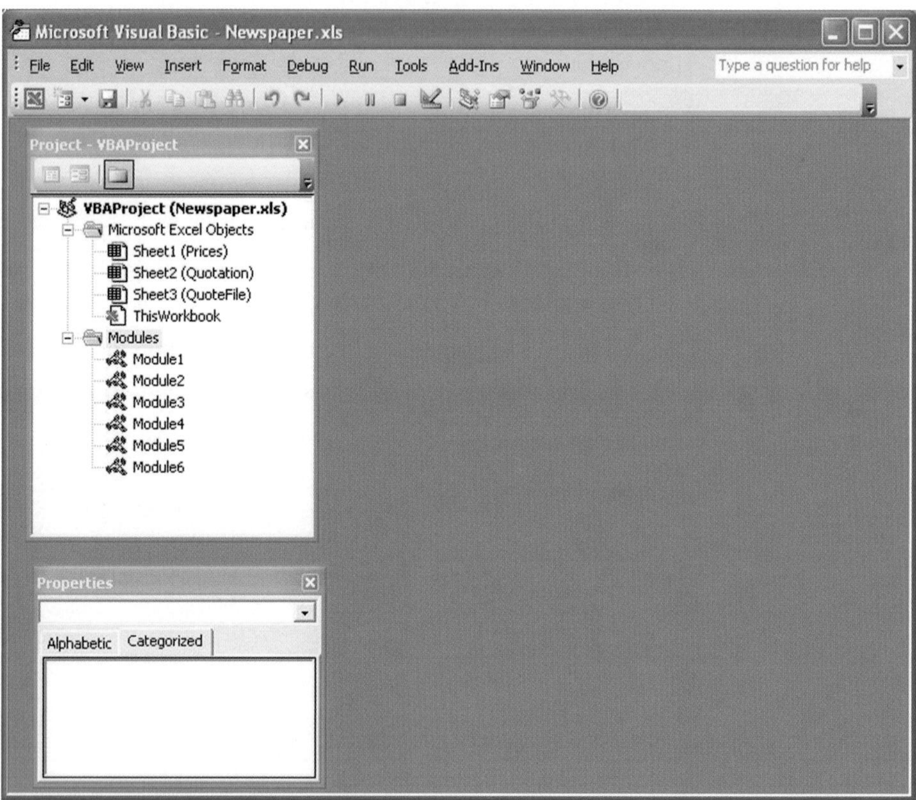

Figure 2. 67 ▲

Why are there six modules?

When you first record macros in a file they will be stored in Module1. If you log off and log back on again later and record some more macros, they will be stored in Module 2 and so on. It will not affect the user wherever the macros are stored.

5 Double click on **Module1** in the Project Explorer. The coding for all the macros stored in Module 1 will appear in a new window on the right of the screen.

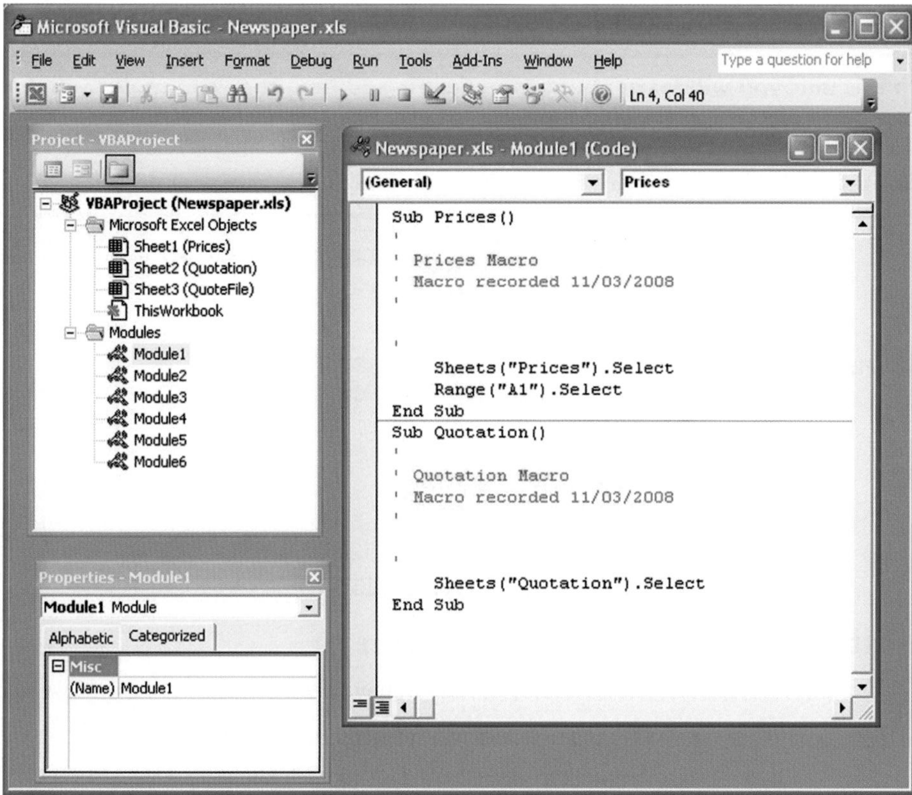

Figure 2. 68 ▲ The **Properties Window** displays the properties for the objects that make up the project, e.g. UserForms, Worksheets, etc.

6 Close the Module1 Window ready for the next unit.

Unit 22: UserForms

In this unit you will learn about UserForms and how they can make a user-friendly front end for an Excel worksheet.

Sometimes UserForms are called dialogue boxes.

A UserForm is a way of providing a customised user interface for your system. A UserForm might look like the one shown in Figure 2.69 which we will set up in this unit.

Figure 2. 69 ▶

Setting up a front end UserForm

We will set up a front end (a menu system) that:

- loads automatically when the file is opened
- gives a choice of making a quotation, changing prices or looking at the quotation file

1 Open the file **Newspaper.xls** and load the **Visual Basic Editor** by clicking on **Tools > Macro > Visual Basic Editor** or pressing ALT and **F11**.
2 Click on **Insert > UserForm** or click on the **Insert UserForm** icon.

A blank UserForm as shown in Figure 2.70 will appear in the main Visual Basic Editor window on the right-hand side.

Figure 2. 70 ▶

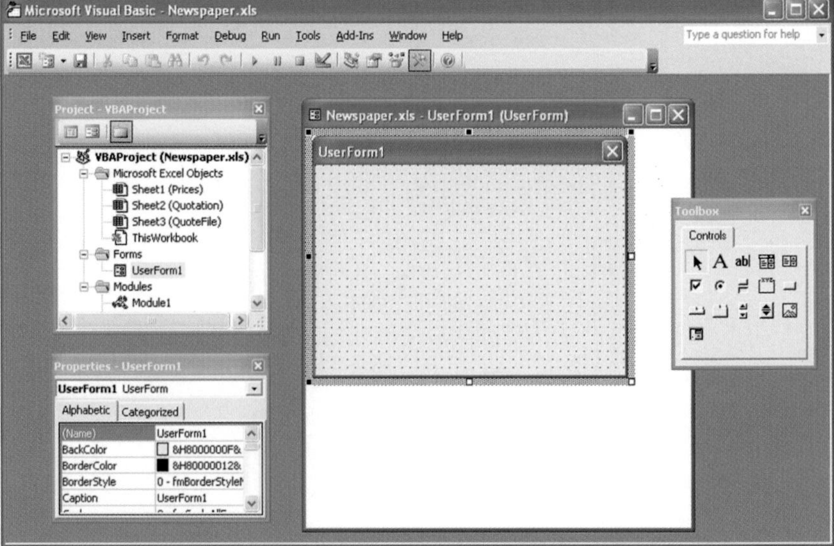

A set of icons called the Toolbox will also appear as shown in Figure 2.71.

3 If it is not visible, click on the blank UserForm and click on **View > Toolbox**.

Figure 2. 71 ▶

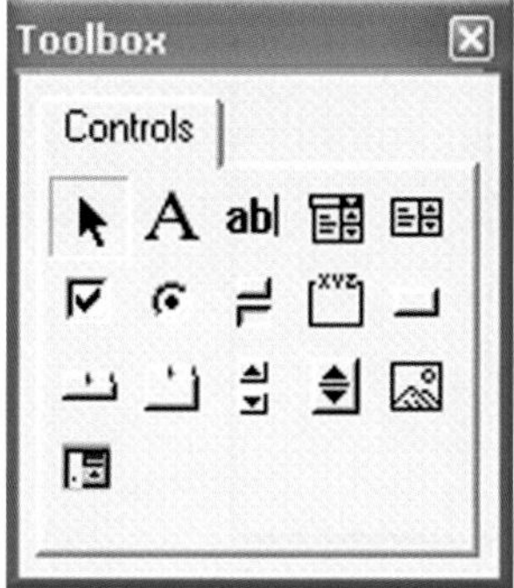

4 Click in the Properties Window in the bottom left-hand corner of the screen.
The Toolbox will disappear.

5 In the Properties Window, set the Height of the UserForm to **120** and set the width to **190**.

Figure 2. 72 ▶

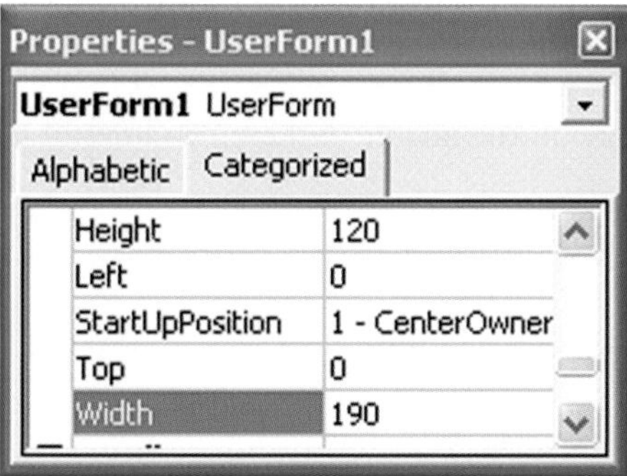

6 Click on the blank UserForm. The toolbox will reappear.

7 In the Toolbox, click on the **CommandButton** icon and drag out a rectangle near the bottom left of the UserForm as shown in Figure 2.73.

Figure 2. 73 ▶

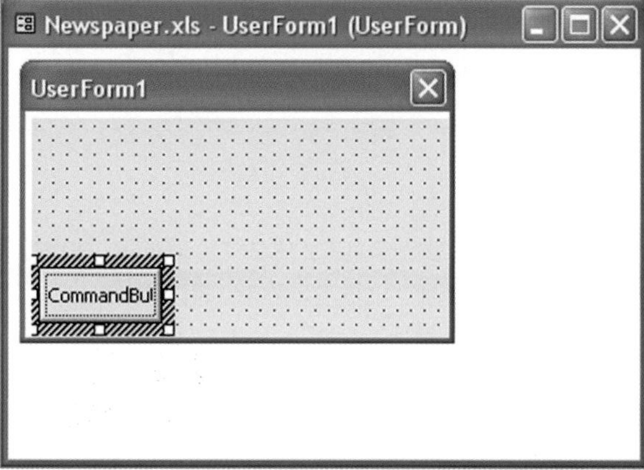

8 The text on the button will say **CommandButton1**. Edit this by clicking once on the button. Delete and change to **Quotation** as in Figure 2.74.

Figure 2. 74 ▶

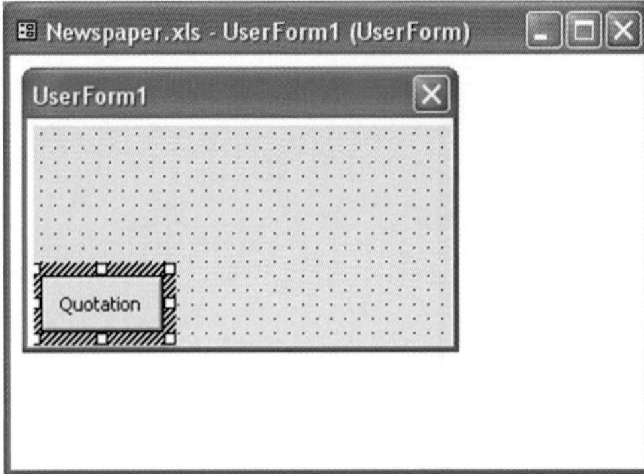

9 Double click on the button. You will see the code shown in Figure 2.75.

Figure 2. 75 ▶

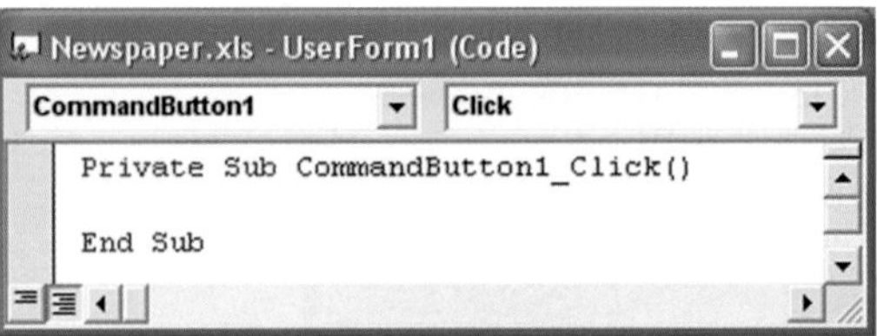

The cursor should be in the middle of these two lines. If it is not, click between the two lines.

10 Enter this text:

```
Sheets("Quotation").Select
UserForm1.Hide
```

It will now look like Figure 2.76.

Figure 2. 76 ▶

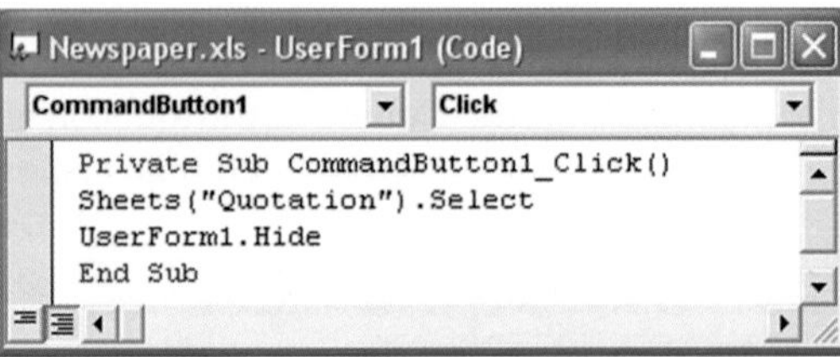

What the code means

Sheets("Quotation").Select moves to the sheet called **Quotation**.

The command **UserForm1.Hide** removes the UserForm from the screen.

Note: The spelling and the punctuation must be exactly as above or it won't work. There are no spaces in the above commands.

11 Click on **View > Object** or click on the **View Object** icon in the Project Explorer Window (top left of screen) shown in Figure 2.77 to go back to the plan of the UserForm.

Figure 2. 77 ▶

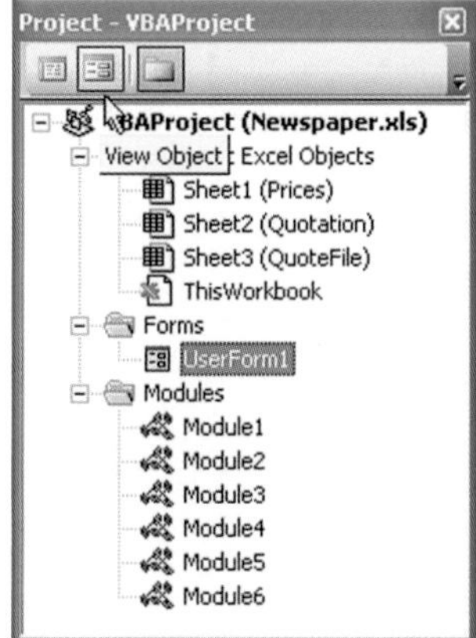

12 Add another button to the right of the first and the same size as shown in Figure 2.78. The command here is exactly the same except it loads the **Prices** sheet (Figure 2.79).

Figure 2. 78 ▶

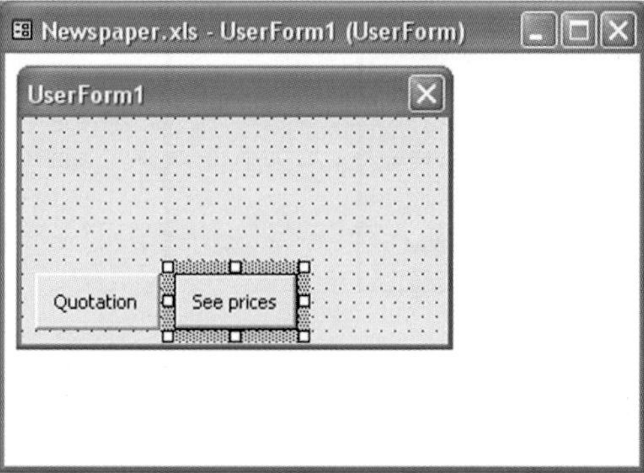

Figure 2. 79 ▶

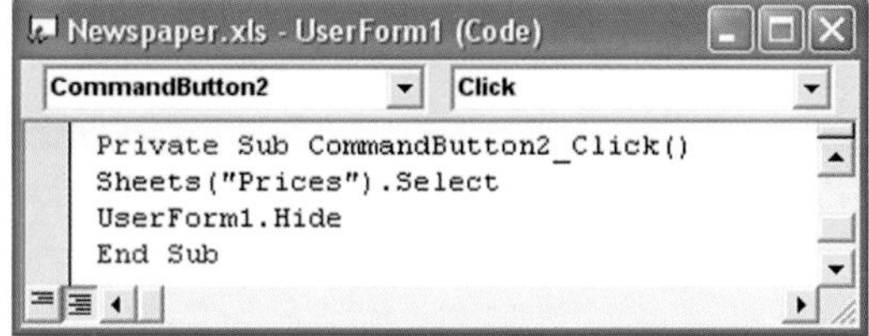

13 Repeat this for a third button that will take you to the **QuoteFile** worksheet.

Figure 2. 80 ▶

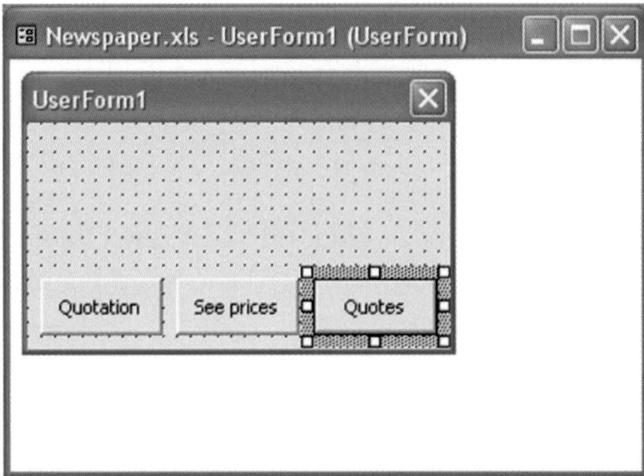

14 Click on the **Label** icon in the Toolbox.

Figure 2. 81 ▶

15 Drag out a rectangle near the top left of the UserForm and enter **Denton Gazette**. The UserForm will now look like this:

Figure 2. 82 ▶

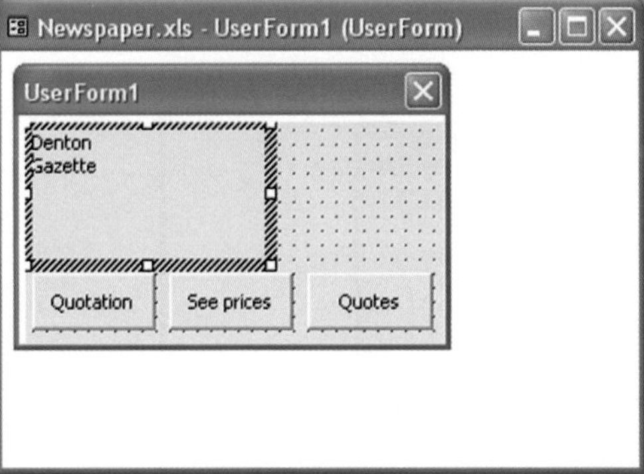

Hint: Use CTRL and ENTER to insert a line break.

Using the Properties Window

The Properties Window at the bottom left-hand corner of the screen is used to set the properties of the UserForm and its controls. For example it is used to set the caption, the size, the colour, the font and any links to cells in the spreadsheet.

1 Select the label **Denton Gazette**. In the **Properties Window** scroll down to **Font.** Click on the three dots icon and set the font to **Verdana** and the size to 22.
2 Scroll down to the **Text Align** property and select **2-fmTextAlignCenter** to centre the text as shown in Figure 2.83.

Figure 2. 83 ▶

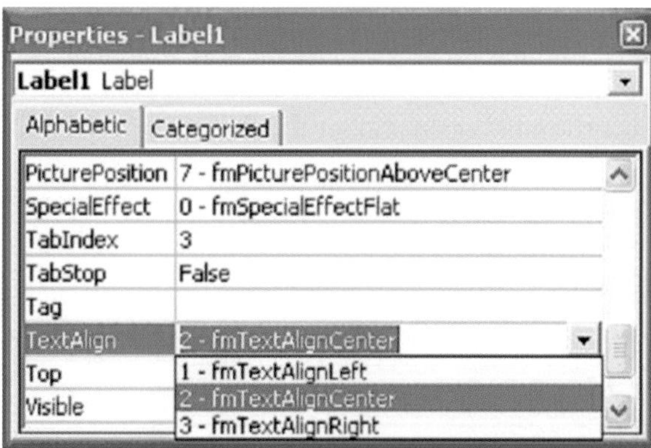

To edit the text colour, you would normally click on **ForeColor** in the Properties Window. Click on the drop-down arrow and choose **Palette**. You have a variety of colours to choose from.

Figure 2. 84 ▶

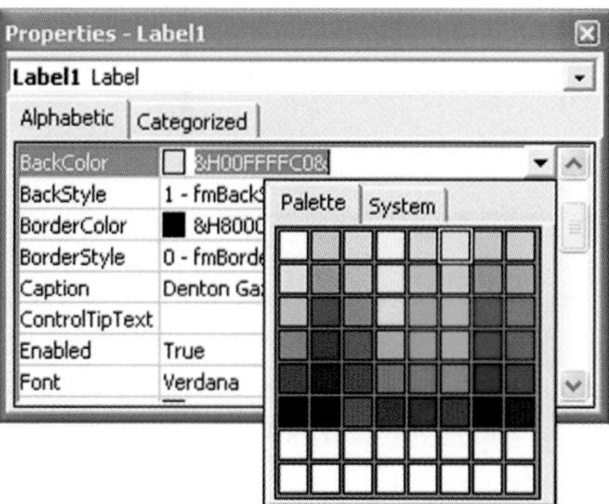

3 The green colour that we require is not on the palette so select ForeColor and enter this code as in Figure 2.85. **&H0069704A&**

Figure 2. 85 ▶

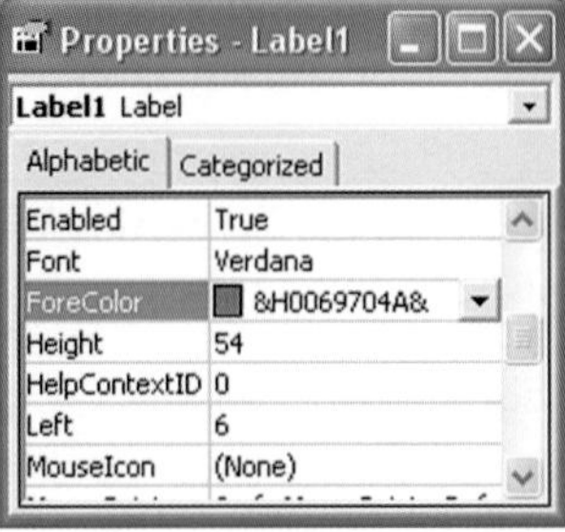

4 Select all three buttons and set the text to Verdana font with the same ForeColor.
5 Select the label again and set the BackColor to: **&H00EAF1C8&**

These numbers are in Hexadecimal form.

6 Select the whole UserForm by clicking on its title bar, and set the BackColor to the same as the label.

The UserForm will look like this:

Figure 2. 86 ▶

7 Select the **Caption** property to set the Caption to **Denton Gazette**. Use the **Image** icon in the Toolbox to add the image to your UserForm.
8 Click on the Image icon and drag out a rectangle on the UserForm.
9 Use **Picture** in the Properties Window to select the image.
10 Use **PictureSizeMode** to set the picture size (choose 1 - fmPictureSizeModeStretch).
11 Set the **BorderStyle** to 0 (No border).
12 Set the **BackStyle** to 0 (Transparent).
13 Save your file.

Figure 2. 87 ▶

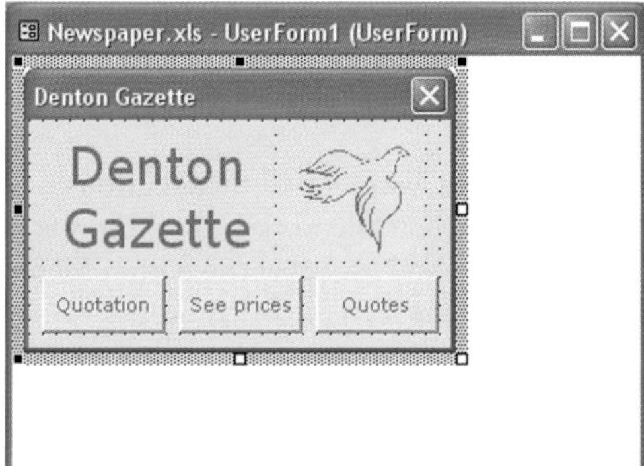

The UserForm is now set up. The finished UserForm is shown in Figure 2.69 at the beginning of this unit.

14 Test the UserForm by selecting the UserForm and clicking on the **Run Sub/UserForm** icon or by pressing **F5**. The UserForm will load. Test the three buttons in turn.

Note: If when you are in the Visual Basic Editor, you insert a second UserForm by mistake, you can delete it by clicking on **File > Remove UserForm.**

Setting up a macro to display your UserForm

Once you have created a UserForm, you will need to set up a macro to display it. The macro will be set up in Visual Basic.

1 If you are not already in the Visual Basic Editor, load the **Visual Basic Editor** by clicking on **Tools > Macro > Visual Basic Editor** or pressing ALT and **F11**.
2 Double click on **Module1** in the Project Explorer Window, shown in Figure 2.77.

Note: If Module1 is not visible click on the + sign next to **VBA project** in the Project Explorer Window. Then double click on Module1.

A new window opens with the coding of the macros you have already set up.

3 Scroll down to the bottom and underneath the last macro text, enter the following:

```
Sub Box()
Load UserForm1
UserForm1.Show
End Sub
```

- This sets up a macro called **Box**.
- The two middle lines of code load the UserForm and display it on the screen.
- You will not need to type in the **End Sub** part as when you enter a line beginning with Sub, the End Sub line is automatically inserted below.

4 Click on **File > Close and Return to Microsoft Excel** or press ALT and **Q** to close the Visual Basic Editor and go back to Excel.
5 Check the macro works using **Tools > Macro > Macros** and click on **Box > Run**.
6 Test that the UserForm works for all three buttons.
7 Add a button on the QuoteFile worksheet to run the Box macro. Put the button over columns L and M. Label the button **Menu**.
8 Copy this button and add it to the Prices worksheet.

When you are confident that the UserForm and Box macro are fully working, you can include Box in the Auto_open macro that runs when you load the file.

1 Click on **Tools > Macro > Macros**. Select **Auto_open** and click on **Edit**. This displays the Visual Basic coding of the macro.
2 Put the cursor at the beginning of the last line (End Sub).
3 Press ENTER.
4 Go up a line and enter the word **Box** as shown in Figure 2.88.

Figure 2. 88 ▶

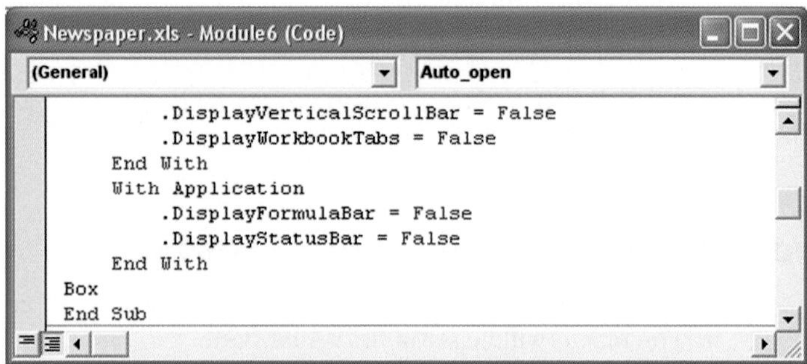

5 Save your file and close the Visual Basic Editor.
6 Close the Excel file.
7 Reload the Excel file and test that the UserForm loads as expected.

3 Further Excel features

In this part we will look at some other useful features of Excel. It is not necessary to use these features but you might find some of them useful in completing a project. These features include financial functions, scenarios, pivot tables and database functions.

Unit 23: Financial functions

In this unit you will learn about financial functions, PMT, FV and RATE.

There are a number of useful financial functions in Excel.

One example is PMT function. PMT is short for payment. This function works out the monthly repayments for a loan given the amount of the loan, the interest rate and the term of the loan.

The formula is
=PMT(rate,nper,pv)

rate is the interest rate
nper is the total number of payments
pv is the amount of the loan.

You need to be careful because normally repayments are made monthly. In which case, the interest rate must also be a monthly rate. This is roughly but not exactly one twelfth of the annual rate.

Example: A loan repayment calculator

Figure 3.1 ▶

Unit 23

	A	B	C
1		**Loan repayment**	
2			
3		Price of car	£10,000
4		Downpayment	£4,000
5		Loan	£6,000
6		Monthly interest rate	0.49%
7		Number of payments	36
8		**Amount**	-£182.21
9			

Sheet1 / Sheet2 / Sh

1 Start a new spreadsheet.
2 Enter the row headings as shown in Figure 3.1
3 Enter the data into cells **C3**, **C4**, **C6** and **C7**.
4 In **C5** enter the formula **=C3–C4**
5 In **C8** enter the formula ***=PMT(C6,C7,C5)***

The monthly repayment is shown as a negative as it is being paid back. The repayment is £182.21.

Exercise 1

Add a spinner to your spreadsheet to adjust the interest rate in steps of 0.01%.

Exercise 2

Add a scrollbar to your spreadsheet to adjust the down payment in steps of £1000.

Note: The scrollbar works in a similar way to the spinner. Use the Scrollbar icon on the Forms toolbar to add a scrollbar.

Figure 3. 2 ▶

Your finished spreadsheet should appear as in Figure 3.3

Figure 3. 3 ▶

Unit 23

	A	B	C	D	E	F
1		**Loan repayment**				
2						
3		Price of car	£10,000			
4		Downpayment	£4,000			
5		Loan	£6,000			
6		Monthly interest rate	0.49%			49
7		Number of payments	36			
8		**Amount**	-£182.21			
9						

Sheet1 / Sheet2 / Sheet3

Save your file as ***Unit 23.xls***

The Future Value (FV) function
This function returns the Future value of an investment assuming constant periodic payments and a constant interest rate.
Suppose you invest £100 per month for 2 years at 5% interest per annum.
This is roughly 0.42% per month.
The formula to calculate the value of your money after 2 years is: =FV(0.42%,24,-100)

- **0.42% is the interest rate**
- **24 is the number of payments**
- **-100 means a monthly payment of £100. It is negative because it is a payment.**

Exercise 3

Add a future value calculator to your spreadsheet using a spinner to adjust the interest rate in steps of 0.01% and a scrollbar to adjust the payments in steps of £20.

The Rate function

The ***Rate*** function works out the interest rate given the amount borrowed, the number of payments and the amount of each payment.

The formula ***=RATE(24,-230,5000)*** works out the interest rate for a loan of £5000, repaid at £230 a month for 24 months.

The result (which is the monthly interest rate) is **0.81%**. If your computer gives this as 1%, click on the ***Increase decimal*** icon.

Multiply by 12 for a rough annual interest rate. The result is **9.7%**.

Exercise 4

Add a rate calculator to your spreadsheet using a spinner to adjust the number of payments and a scrollbar to adjust the amount of payments in steps of £20 and the loan in steps of £1000.

Note that if you get a negative interest rate, this means you have not paid enough to cover the loan.

Exercise 5

Use Excel's built-in online Help to investigate other financial functions.

Unit 24: Scenarios

In this unit you will learn how to use scenarios to save different versions of the same worksheet.

The Hotel Manhattan wants to plan their cash flow. Their occupancy rates are around 70–80 per cent in summer and 50–60 per cent in winter. They can store various predictions for their income using **Scenarios.**

Figure 3. 4 ▶

Unit 24

	A	B	C	D	E
1		Hotel Manhattan			
2	**Type of room**	**Price per night**	**No of rooms**	**Income if full**	
3	Single room	£67.00	42	£2,814.00	
4	Double room	£87.00	31	£2,697.00	
5	Suite	£125.00	3	£375.00	
6	Penthouse	£250.00	1	£250.00	
7				**£6,136.00**	
8					
9	**Season**	**Month**	**Number of days**	**Forecast occupancy**	**Forecast revenue**
10	High season	May to September	153	70%	£657,165.60
11	Low season	October to April	212	70%	£910,582.40
12					**£1,567,748.00**
13					

Sheet1 / Sheet2 / Sheet3

1 Load the spreadsheet **Unit24.xls**

Cells B3 to B6, D3 to D7 and E10 to E12 are formatted as currency. Cells D10 to D11 are formatted as percentages.

The hotel has decided to save predictions based on:

- 70 per cent occupancy all year round
- 60 per cent occupancy all year round
- 50 per cent occupancy all year round
- 70 per cent occupancy in high season and 50 per cent occupancy in low season.

We can set up four different **scenarios** to help them. To set up scenarios:

2 Click on **Tools > Scenarios**. You will see the Scenario Manager shown in Figure 3.5.

Figure 3. 5 ▶

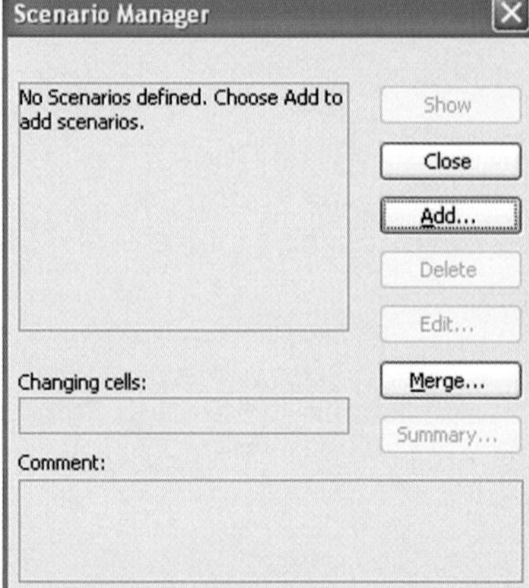

3 No scenarios exist at present so we need to add some. Click on **Add...**

4 Enter the name of the scenario, **70 per cent occupancy** and the names of the two changing cells into the dialogue box as in Figure 3.6.

Figure 3. 6 ▶

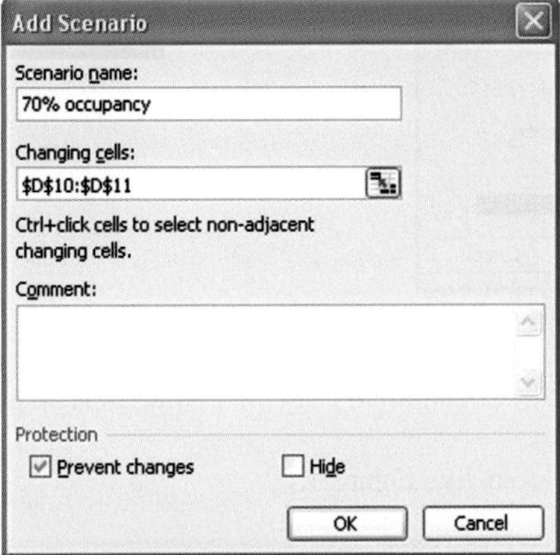

5 Click on **OK**.

Figure 3. 7 ▶

6 Enter the value **0.7** for each of the changing cells as in Figure 3.7 and click on **OK**.

7 Add three more scenarios with the appropriate data.

Figure 3. 8 ▶

8 If you click on **Summary…** you will set up a new worksheet with a summary of all the scenarios. First the scenario summary box appears as in Figure 3.9.

Figure 3. 9 ▶

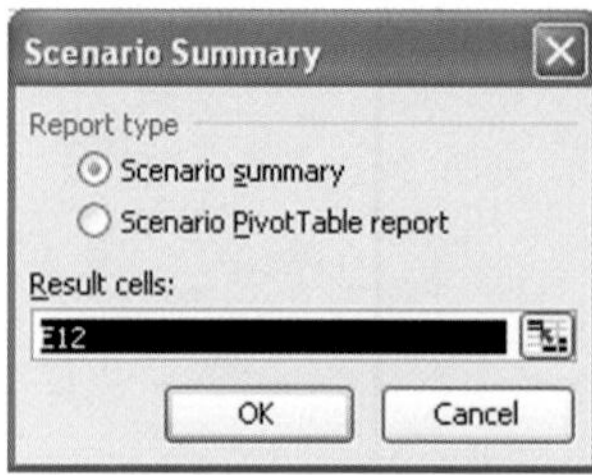

9 E12 is the cell with the total amount of the bill stored in it. This is the figure we want in our summary but we could click on any cell. Click on **OK**.

10 The summary looks like Figure 3.10.

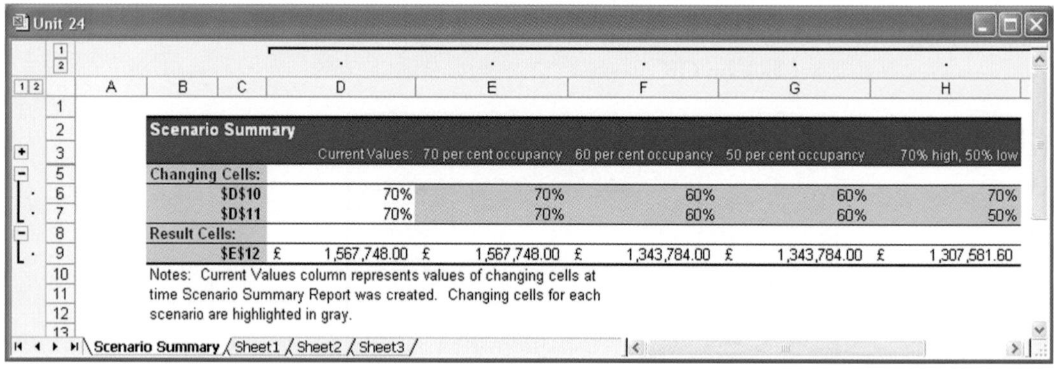

Scenario Summary

		Current Values:	70 per cent occupancy	60 per cent occupancy	50 per cent occupancy	70% high, 50% low
Changing Cells:						
	$D$10	70%	70%	60%	60%	70%
	$D$11	70%	70%	60%	60%	50%
Result Cells:						
	$E$12	£ 1,567,748.00	£ 1,567,748.00	£ 1,343,784.00	£ 1,343,784.00	£ 1,307,581.60

Notes: Current Values column represents values of changing cells at time Scenario Summary Report was created. Changing cells for each scenario are highlighted in gray.

Figure 3. 10 ▲

To load any of the scenarios:

- Go back to Sheet1
- Click on **Tools > Scenarios**
- Click on the scenario required
- Click on **Show**
- Click on **Close**

11 Go back to Sheet1 and alter the price of a single room to £77.

12 Switch back to the sheet called Scenario Summary and you will see that the figures have not been updated. You will need to go back to Sheet1, click on **Tools > Scenario** again and click on **Summary…** This will set up a new worksheet called **Scenario Summary 2**.

Unit 25: Pivot Tables

In this unit you will learn how to use Pivot Tables to group large amounts of data in an easy to read table. The Hotel Manhattan has a file of its employees, shown in Figure 3.11.

Unit 25

	A	B	C	D	E	F	G	H
1	EMPL NO	SURNAME	FORENAME	DEPT	SALARY	DOB	POST	M/F
2	000262	Bird	Linda	Accommodation	£ 18,600	17/02/1976	Chef	F
3	000159	Caulder	Fraser	Restaurant	£ 16,200	05/06/1941	Chef	M
4	000267	Clark	Sarah	Reception	£ 14,090	31/10/1942	Receptionist	F
5	000297	Cook	Sally	Accommodation	£ 11,200	17/06/1953	Cleaner	F
6	000141	Dyson	Angela	Restaurant	£ 10,600	19/02/1958	Waitress	F
7	000011	Green	Julie	Accommodation	£ 11,200	20/06/1961	Cleaner	F
8	000185	Johnson	Rebecca	Restaurant	£ 10,900	22/12/1949	Waitress	F
9	000118	Jones	Robert	Restaurant	£ 10,900	17/08/1969	Waiter	M
10	000367	Khan	Wahir	Restaurant	£ 16,700	31/12/1958	Chef	M
11	000034	Noble	Marie	Restaurant	£ 10,950	14/06/1962	Waitress	F
12	000281	Patel	Niru	Restaurant	£ 10,900	01/05/1978	Waitress	F
13	000245	Powell	Sharon	Reception	£ 16,000	11/01/1966	Receptionist	F
14	000444	Robertson	Richard	Reception	£ 17,125	18/07/1960	Security Officer	M
15	000555	Robinson	Damion	Reception	£ 14,075	14/04/1978	Doorman	M
16	000190	Sands	Elizabeth	Accommodation	£ 11,500	04/04/1967	Cleaner	F
17	000247	Sands	Elaine	Accommodation	£ 11,600	18/12/1962	Cleaner	F

Sheet4 | **Sheet1** | Sheet2 | Sheet3

Figure 3. 11 ▲

A Pivot Table will allow us to group this information by department, by post and by sex to analyse exactly where the hotel pays wages.

1 Open the file called **Unit 25.xls**. This saves you typing in the data.

Note:

- If you enter 000262 into a cell, it will appears as 262 unless you type in an apostrophe first – '000262.
- Note that a small green triangle appears in the top left-hand corner of the cell. This is because it recognises an error has occurred – a number is being stored as text. To remove the green triangle, highlight all the cells, click on the drop-down arrow and choose **Ignore Error** as shown in Figure 3.12.

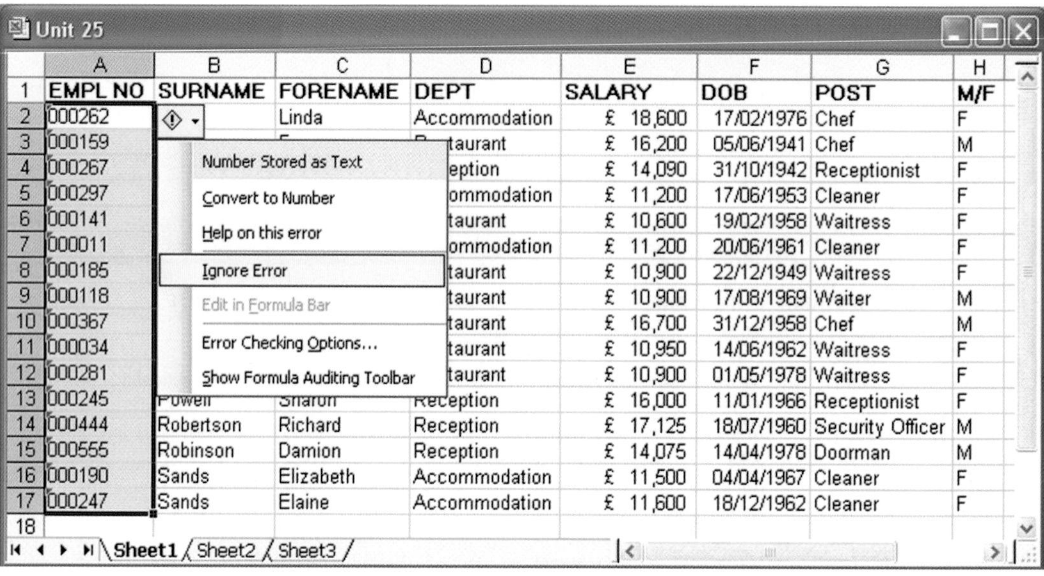

Figure 3. 12 ▲

2 Highlight the data (cells **A1** to **H17**) and click on **Data > Pivot Table and Pivot Chart Report**.

Figure 3. 13 ▶

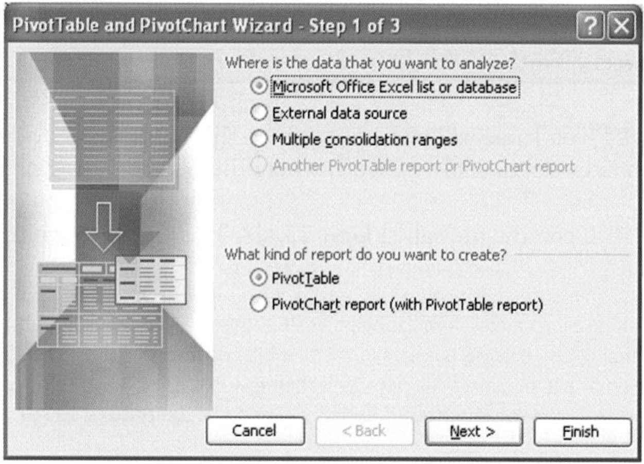

3 It loads a wizard. Select **Microsoft Excel list or database** if not already selected and click on **Next**.

Figure 3. 14 ▶

4 The next stage of the wizard asks where is the data that you want to use. Click on **Next**.

Figure 3. 15 ▶

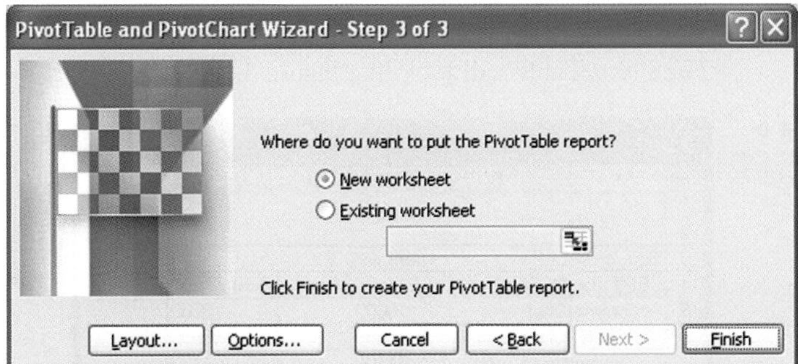

5 Click on **New worksheet** and click on **Layout**. The dialogue box shown in Figure 3.16 appears.

Figure 3. 16 ▶

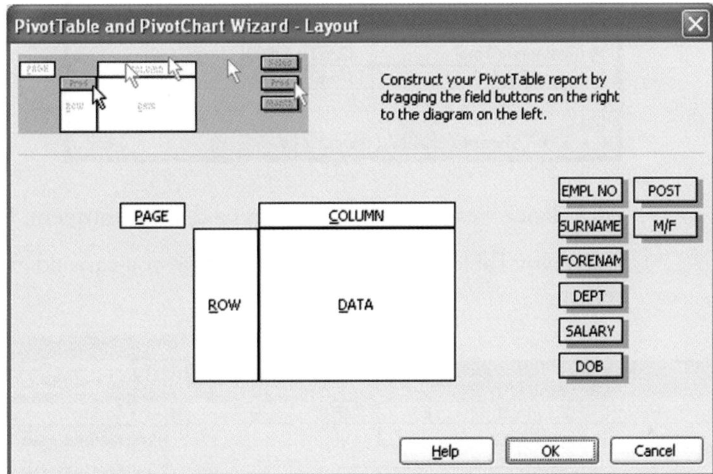

6 This is where you choose which data to group and display. Drag the fieldnames, **Dept** and **Post** to where it says ROW. Drag **M/F** to where it says COLUMN and drag **Salary** to where it says DATA. When you drag **Salary** onto the middle of the page it becomes **Sum of Salary**, as in Figure 3.17.

Figure 3. 17 ▶

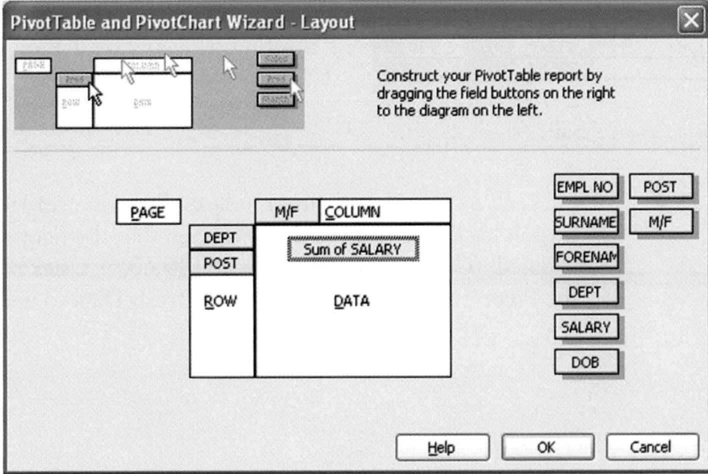

7 Click on **OK** and then click on **Finish**.

The Pivot Table will look like Figure 3.18.

Figure 3. 18 ▶

Unit 25

	A	B	C	D	E
1					
2					
3	Sum of SALARY		M/F		
4	DEPT	POST	F	M	Grand Total
5	Accommo	Chef	18600		18600
6		Cleaner	45500		45500
7	Accommodation Total		64100		64100
8	Reception	Doorman		14075	14075
9		Receptionist	30090		30090
10		Security Officer		17125	17125
11	Reception Total		30090	31200	61290
12	Restaurant	Chef		32900	32900
13		Waiter		10900	10900
14		Waitress	43350		43350
15	Restaurant Total		43350	43800	87150
16	Grand Total		137540	75000	212540
17					
18					

Sheet4 / Sheet1 / Sheet2

At a glance we can see total salaries paid, by department, by post and by sex.

The Pivot Table Field List is visible so that you can add extra fields to the report.

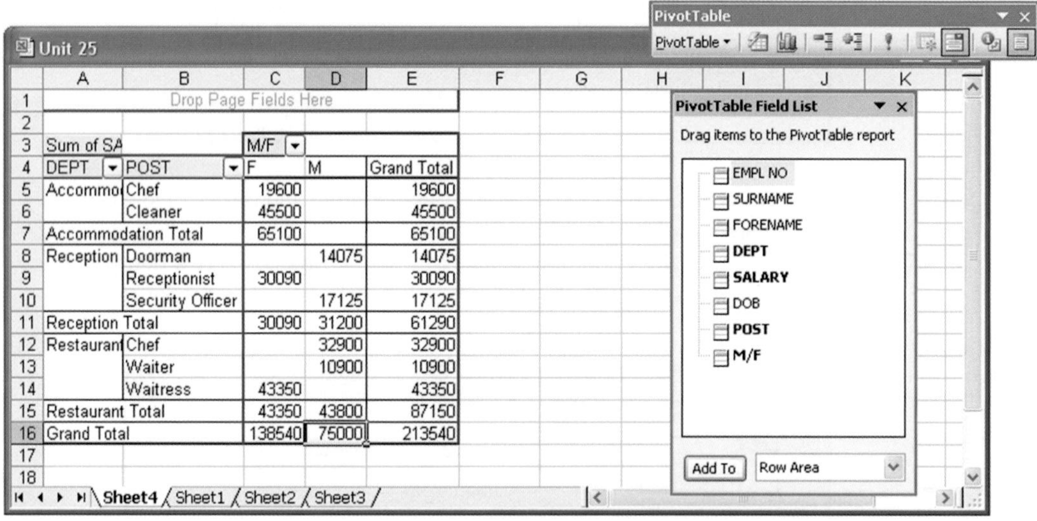

Unit 25

	A	B	C	D	E
1	Drop Page Fields Here				
2					
3	Sum of SA		M/F		
4	DEPT	POST	F	M	Grand Total
5	Accommo	Chef	19600		19600
6		Cleaner	45500		45500
7	Accommodation Total		65100		65100
8	Reception	Doorman		14075	14075
9		Receptionist	30090		30090
10		Security Officer		17125	17125
11	Reception Total		30090	31200	61290
12	Restaurant	Chef		32900	32900
13		Waiter		10900	10900
14		Waitress	43350		43350
15	Restaurant Total		43350	43800	87150
16	Grand Total		138540	75000	213540
17					
18					

Figure 3. 19 ▲

8 Go back to Sheet1 and alter Linda Bird's salary to **£19,600**.

9 Switch back to Sheet4 and you will see that the figures have not been updated. (Cell **C5** should now read £19,600.) Click on one of the cells in the Pivot Table. Click on **Data > Refresh Data** to update the Pivot Table.

Pivot Table exercise

The different departments of a company are charged on the basis of hours of internet use. The company has to distinguish between use for email and use for the World Wide Web. Load the file called ***Unit 25 exercise.xls*** as shown in Figure 3.20 and set up a Pivot Table to group the data, to show Internet, intranet and total use for each department split into www and email.

Figure 3. 20 ▶

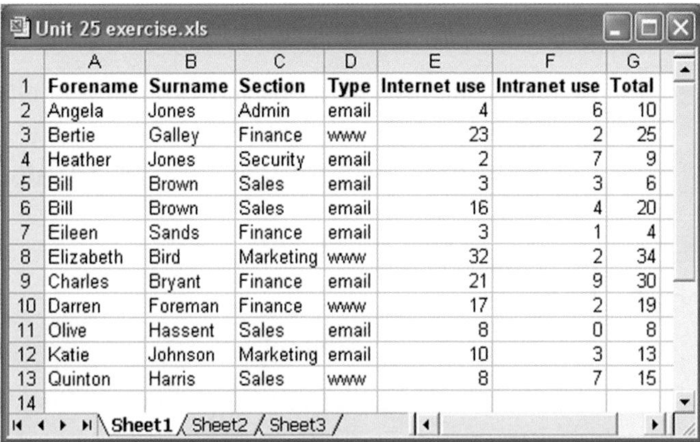

Unit 25 exercise.xls

	A	B	C	D	E	F	G
1	**Forename**	**Surname**	**Section**	**Type**	**Internet use**	**Intranet use**	**Total**
2	Angela	Jones	Admin	email	4	6	10
3	Bertie	Galley	Finance	www	23	2	25
4	Heather	Jones	Security	email	2	7	9
5	Bill	Brown	Sales	email	3	3	6
6	Bill	Brown	Sales	email	16	4	20
7	Eileen	Sands	Finance	email	3	1	4
8	Elizabeth	Bird	Marketing	www	32	2	34
9	Charles	Bryant	Finance	email	21	9	30
10	Darren	Foreman	Finance	www	17	2	19
11	Olive	Hassent	Sales	email	8	0	8
12	Katie	Johnson	Marketing	email	10	3	13
13	Quinton	Harris	Sales	www	8	7	15
14							

Sheet1 / Sheet2 / Sheet3

Unit 26: Using Excel to create a database

In this unit you will cover how Excel can be used to create a database including:

- Setting up, sorting and searching a database
- Using Data Forms
- Using AutoFilter
- Using the Advanced Filter
- Database functions

A spreadsheet lends itself to storing and sorting lists of information, such as employees, customers, cars, students and so on.

More commonly files or lists such as this are called databases, Excel calls them **lists**.

Creating a data list

We are going to use a simple **file** of properties for sale.

Each **record** in the file or row in the spreadsheet will hold details of a property.

The **fields** or columns in the spreadsheet will be Estate Agent, Area, Type, No of Bedrooms and Price as shown in Figure 3.21.

Figure 3. 21 ▶

Unit 26

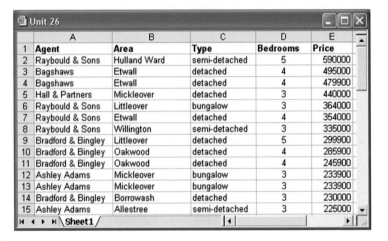

	A	B	C	D	E
1	**Agent**	**Area**	**Type**	**Bedrooms**	**Price**
2	Raybould & Sons	Hulland Ward	semi-detached	5	590000
3	Bagshaws	Etwall	detached	4	495000
4	Bagshaws	Etwall	detached	4	479900
5	Hall & Partners	Mickleover	detached	3	440000
6	Raybould & Sons	Littleover	bungalow	3	364000
7	Raybould & Sons	Etwall	detached	4	354000
8	Raybould & Sons	Willington	semi-detached	3	335000
9	Bradford & Bingley	Littleover	detached	5	299900
10	Bradford & Bingley	Oakwood	detached	4	285900
11	Bradford & Bingley	Oakwood	detached	4	245900
12	Ashley Adams	Mickleover	bungalow	3	233900
13	Ashley Adams	Mickleover	bungalow	3	233900
14	Bradford & Bingley	Borrowash	detached	3	230000
15	Ashley Adams	Allestree	semi-detached	3	225000

Sheet1

Sorting the file

Sorting can be done on the whole file or a named range of cells.

To produce a sorted list of houses by price:

1. Load the file **Unit 26.xls**.
2. Click on any cell in the table such as A2 and click on **Data > Sort**. The Sort dialogue box in Figure 3.22 appears.

Figure 3. 22 ▶

3 Click on the down arrow on the **Sort by** box, choose **Price** and click on **Descending**, click **OK**.

It is also possible to sort on more than one field, for example in agent order and then in price order.

4 Click on A2 or any cell in the table. From the menu choose **Data > Sort**.
5 Click on the down arrow on the Sort by box, choose **Agent** and click on **Ascending**.
6 Click on the down arrow on the next Sort by box, choose **Price** and click on **Descending** and click **OK**.

This should produce a list sorted by Agent and then by price.

Using a Data Form to search and edit a file

7 Click on **Data > Form**

Figure 3. 23 ▶

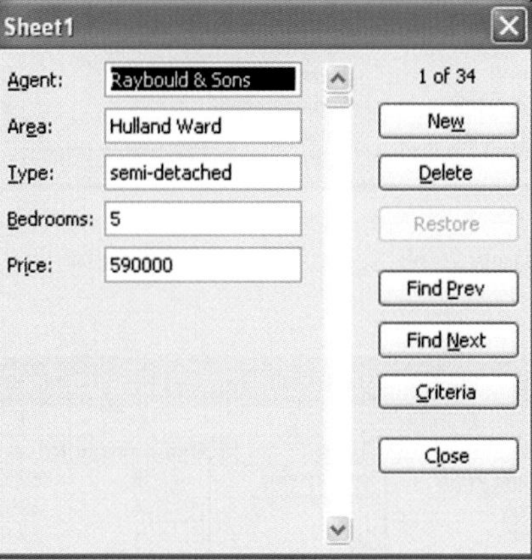

- Click on **Find Next** to take you to details of the next house.
- Click on **Find Prev** to take you to details of the previous house.
- Click on **Delete** to enable you to remove a house from file.
- Click on **New** to allow you to enter details of a new property (press Tab between entering fields).

You can use the Data Form to do simple searches

8 Click on Criteria and a blank form loads.
9 Enter **Etwall** in the field area and click on **Find Next** to scroll through the houses in Etwall.

You can narrow down the search.

10 Click on Criteria again and enter 3 in the **Bedrooms** field.
11 You can now scroll through the three bedroom houses in Etwall.

Data exercise 1

Use the Data Form to answer the following questions:

1 Produce details of all houses for sale in Oakwood. How many are there?
2 A customer wants details of detached houses for sale in Mickleover. How many are there and what price are they?
3 A customer wants to purchase a house with three bedrooms in Littleover. Search for details. How many are there and what price are they?

Using AutoFilter to search the database

1 Click on any cell in the data table, e.g. **A2**.
2 Click on ***Data > Filter > AutoFilter***.

Drop-down boxes appear by each field name as in Figure 3.24.

Figure 3. 24 ▶

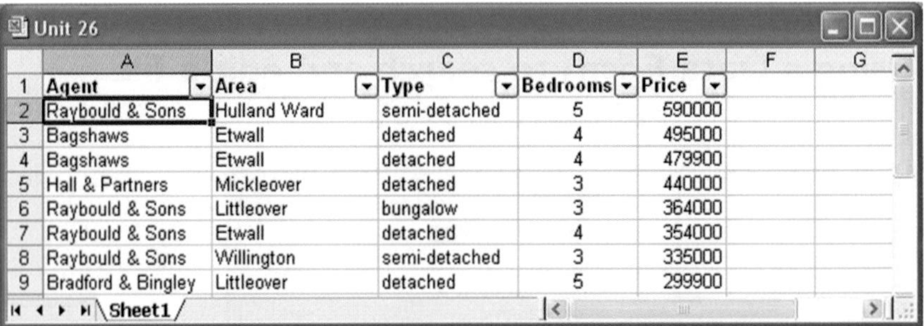
Unit 26

	A	B	C	D	E	F	G
1	Agent	Area	Type	Bedrooms	Price		
2	Raybould & Sons	Hulland Ward	semi-detached	5	590000		
3	Bagshaws	Etwall	detached	4	495000		
4	Bagshaws	Etwall	detached	4	479900		
5	Hall & Partners	Mickleover	detached	3	440000		
6	Raybould & Sons	Littleover	bungalow	3	364000		
7	Raybould & Sons	Etwall	detached	4	354000		
8	Raybould & Sons	Willington	semi-detached	3	335000		
9	Bradford & Bingley	Littleover	detached	5	299900		

Sheet1

If you click on the arrow it will give you a list of items in that field as in Figure 3.25.

Figure 3. 25 ▶

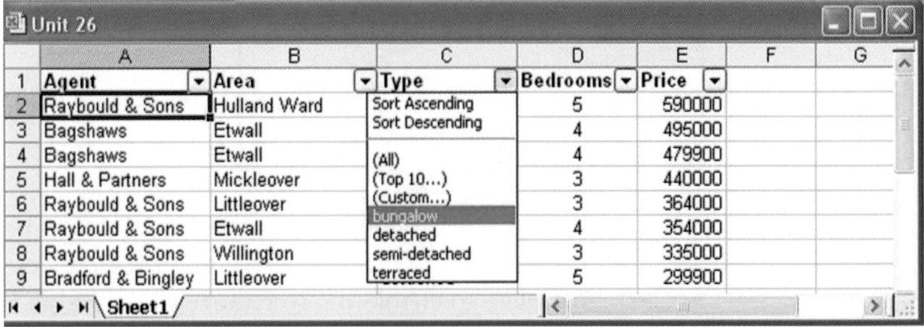
Unit 26

	A	B	C	D	E	F	G
1	Agent	Area	Type	Bedrooms	Price		
2	Raybould & Sons	Hulland Ward		5	590000		
3	Bagshaws	Etwall		4	495000		
4	Bagshaws	Etwall		4	479900		
5	Hall & Partners	Mickleover		3	440000		
6	Raybould & Sons	Littleover		3	364000		
7	Raybould & Sons	Etwall		4	354000		
8	Raybould & Sons	Willington		3	335000		
9	Bradford & Bingley	Littleover		5	299900		

It is easy to build up quick searches e.g. bungalows in Mickleover.

1 Click on the **Area** field drop-down and choose ***Mickleover***.
2 Then click on the **Type** field drop-down and choose ***terraced***.

You should get the results in Figure 3.26.

Figure 3. 26 ▶

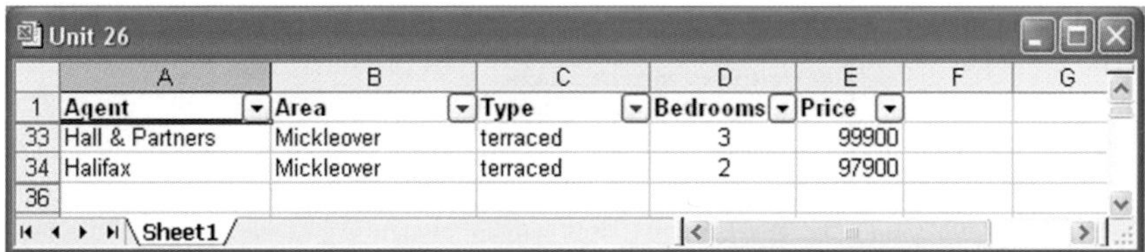

	A	B	C	D	E	F	G
1	Agent	Area	Type	Bedrooms	Price		
33	Hall & Partners	Mickleover	terraced	3	99900		
34	Halifax	Mickleover	terraced	2	97900		
36							

Excel hides the rows that do not meet the criteria and displays the row numbers in blue.

To restore your data click on ***Data > Filter > Show All***.

It is possible to do more advanced searching by choosing the custom option.

Filter 1

Suppose we wish to find properties in Mickleover or Littleover

1 Choose the **Area** drop-down and click on (Custom…).
2 The dialogue box in Figure 3.27 appears. Fill in as shown. Make sure that the **Or** button is chosen.

Figure 3. 27 ▶

The search produces 18 houses.

Filter 2

Suppose we wish to find properties with the price between £150 000 and £200 000.

1 Restore your data.
2 Click on the **Price** drop-down and click on **Custom**.
3 The dialogue box in Figure 3.28 appears. Fill it in as shown.

Figure 3. 28 ▶

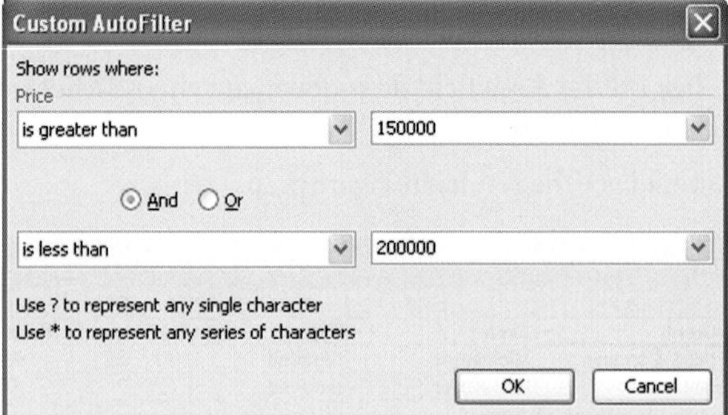

Four houses should be found as in Figure 3.29.

Figure 3. 29 ▶

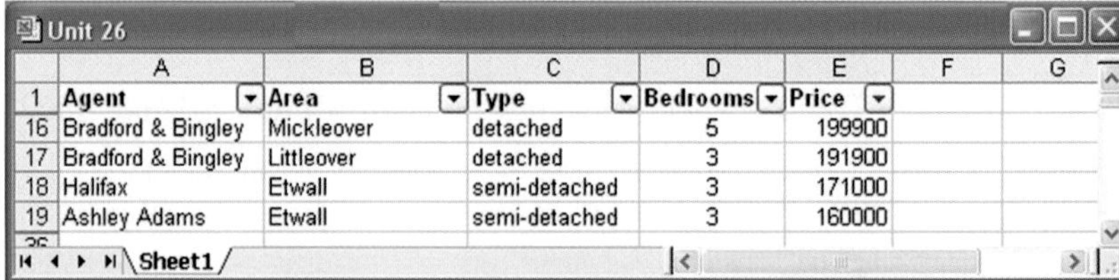

Unit 26

	A	B	C	D	E	F	G
1	Agent	Area	Type	Bedrooms	Price		
16	Bradford & Bingley	Mickleover	detached	5	199900		
17	Bradford & Bingley	Littleover	detached	3	191900		
18	Halifax	Etwall	semi-detached	3	171000		
19	Ashley Adams	Etwall	semi-detached	3	160000		

Sheet1

Some hints on using AutoFilter

- To remove AutoFilter for a particular column click on **(All)** from the drop-down list.
- To remove all AutoFilters, click on **Data** > **Filter > Show All**.
- You can use **AutoFilter** to find blank fields. If a column contains blanks you will see the entries (Blanks) and (NonBlanks) in the columns drop-down list.
- If you wish to remove rows with blank entries then choose **NonBlanks**.
- If you wish to find rows in which a column has no entry then choose **Blanks**.
- Auto filtered data can be copied and pasted to other areas of the worksheet in the usual way.

Data exercise 2

Use ***AutoFilter*** and the file ***Houses*** to answer the following:

1. A customer wants details of houses for sale in Etwall. How many are there?
2. A customer wants to purchase a house with four bedrooms. Search for details. How many are there?
3. A customer requires details of detached houses in Mickleover. Search for details.
4. A customer requires a three-bedroomed house in Littleover. Search for details.

The advanced filter option

The advanced filter command allows you to search on more than two fields and offers increased options. It can also be used to automate the moving of filtered data to another part of the worksheet.

A worked example

The first step is to define the cells that make up the database; this is called the ***list range***.

1. Using the same file, highlight the cells **A1** to **E35**.
2. From the ***Insert*** menu choose ***Name > Define*** and call the range ***Database*** and click **OK**.

The next stage is to set up and define the ***criteria range***. This is the range of cells which will store your search conditions.

3. Select the row headings in row 1 and copy and paste them to an area below your data list; we have chosen row 39.
4. In the rows below enter the search conditions as shown in Figure 3.30. We will produce a list of bungalows in Littleover.

Figure 3. 30 ▶

Unit 26

	A	B	C	D	E	F	G
34	Halifax	Mickleover	terraced	2	97900		
35	Hall & Partners	Littleover	terraced	2	95900		
36							
37							
38							
39	**Agent**	**Area**	**Type**	**Bedrooms**	**Price**		
40		Littleover	bungalow				
41							

Sheet1

5. Name the range A39 to E40 ***Criteria***.
6. Click on any cell in the database such as **A2**.
7. Click on ***Data > Filter > Advanced Filter***.
8. If you have named the ranges ***Database*** and ***Criteria***, they will be entered automatically as shown in Figure 3.31.

Figure 3. 31 ▶

Clicking on **OK** should produce the filtered list in Figure 3.32 which displays the one property in the database that meets the criteria.

Figure 3. 32 ▶

Unit 26

	A	B	C	D	E	F	G
1	**Agent**	**Area**	**Type**	**Bedrooms**	**Price**		
6	Raybould & Sons	Littleover	bungalow	3	364000		
36							
37							
38							
39	**Agent**	**Area**	**Type**	**Bedrooms**	**Price**		
40		Littleover	bungalow				
41							

Sheet1

Searches with **OR** can be built up in the same way.

The search criteria in Figure 3.33 will list three-bedroomed properties in Mickleover *or* Etwall as shown in Figure 3.34.

Figure 3. 33 ▶

Unit 26

	A	B	C	D	E	F	G
34	Halifax	Mickleover	terraced	2	97900		
35	Hall & Partners	Littleover	terraced	2	95900		
36							
37							
38							
39	**Agent**	**Area**	**Type**	**Bedrooms**	**Price**		
40		Mickleover		3			
41		Etwall		3			
42							
43							
44							
45							

Sheet1

The criteria range is now A39:A41, so change it in the Advanced Filter dialogue box. The named range ***Criteria*** will be amended automatically.

Figure 3. 34 ▶

Unit 26

	A	B	C	D	E	F	G
1	**Agent**	**Area**	**Type**	**Bedrooms**	**Price**		
5	Hall & Partners	Mickleover	detached	3	440000		
12	Ashley Adams	Mickleover	bungalow	3	233900		
13	Ashley Adams	Mickleover	bungalow	3	233900		
18	Halifax	Etwall	semi-detached	3	171000		
19	Ashley Adams	Etwall	semi-detached	3	160000		
24	Ashley Adams	Mickleover	semi-detached	3	149900		
26	Raybould & Sons	Mickleover	semi-detached	3	140000		
28	Bagshaws	Etwall	terraced	3	129000		
33	Hall & Partners	Mickleover	terraced	3	99900		
36							
37							

Sheet1

Data exercise 3

Use the advanced filter option to answer the following questions:

1 A customer requires a three-bedroomed house in Etwall or Mickleover. Search for details.

2 A customer requires a property in the Allestree, Darley Abbey area. Search for details.

3 A customer requires a three-bedroomed detached property in Mickleover. Search for details.

Copying data to another location

1 Set up the search as shown in Figure 3.35 to find three-bedroomed properties in Etwall or Mickleover.

Figure 3. 35 ▶

Unit 26

	A	B	C	D	E	F	G
34	Halifax	Mickleover	terraced	2	97900		
35	Hall & Partners	Littleover	terraced	2	95900		
36							
37							
38							
39	**Agent**	**Area**	**Type**	**Bedrooms**	**Price**		
40		Mickleover		3			
41		Etwall		3			
42							
43							
44							
45							

Sheet1

2 Make sure your named criteria range is A39 to E41.
3 Click in the database and go to ***Data > Filter > Advanced Filter***.
4 In the dialogue box check ***Copy to another location*** and enter **A44** in the ***Copy to*** box as shown in Figure 3.36.

Figure 3. 36 ▶

The search should produce the results in Figure 3.37.

Figure 3. 37 ▶

Unit 26

	A	B	C	D	E
34	Halifax	Mickleover	terraced	2	97900
35	Hall & Partners	Littleover	terraced	2	95900
36					
37					
38					
39	**Agent**	**Area**	**Type**	**Bedrooms**	**Price**
40		Mickleover		3	
41		Etwall		3	
42					
43					
44	**Agent**	**Area**	**Type**	**Bedrooms**	**Price**
45	Hall & Partners	Mickleover	detached	3	440000
46	Ashley Adams	Mickleover	bungalow	3	233900
47	Ashley Adams	Mickleover	bungalow	3	233900
48	Halifax	Etwall	semi-detached	3	171000
49	Ashley Adams	Etwall	semi-detached	3	160000
50	Ashley Adams	Mickleover	semi-detached	3	149900
51	Raybould & Sons	Mickleover	semi-detached	3	140000
52	Bagshaws	Etwall	terraced	3	129000
53	Hall & Partners	Mickleover	terraced	3	99900
54					

Sheet1

The output from the search is displayed in columns A to E in rows 44 to 53, which now becomes the named area ***Extract***. Check by clicking the name box drop-down.

Figure 3. 38 ▶

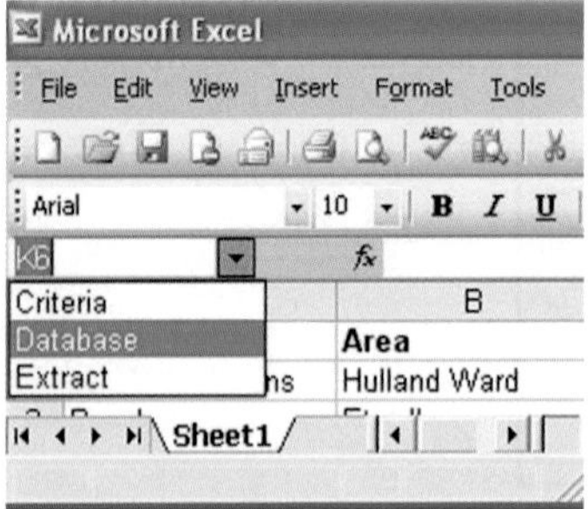

It is now possible to vary the criteria in the criteria range. Try changing the criteria to produce the output shown in Figure 3.39.

Figure 3. 39 ▶

Unit 26

	A	B	C	D	E
34	Halifax	Mickleover	terraced	2	97900
35	Hall & Partners	Littleover	terraced	2	95900
36					
37					
38					
39	**Agent**	**Area**	**Type**	**Bedrooms**	**Price**
40		Mickleover		2	
41		Etwall		2	
42					
43					
44	**Agent**	**Area**	**Type**	**Bedrooms**	**Price**
45	Halifax	Etwall	semi-detached	2	141000
46	Hall & Partners	Mickleover	semi-detached	2	135900
47	Bagshaws	Etwall	terraced	2	120000
48	Halifax	Mickleover	terraced	2	97900
49					

Sheet1

Using the database functions

Excel provides a number of **d** or **database** functions. Examples are **DCOUNT**, **DAVERAGE**, **DSUM**, **DMAX** and **DMIN**.

Database functions take the form **=Function(database,"field",criteria)** where:

- **Database** is the name of the database range you have defined.
- **Field** is the column you wish to operate on.
- **Criteria** is the criteria range you have defined.

Worked example

We are going to use the database functions to analyse house prices in the Mickleover area.

1 Set up the criteria and headings as shown in Figure 3.40.

Figure 3. 40 ▶

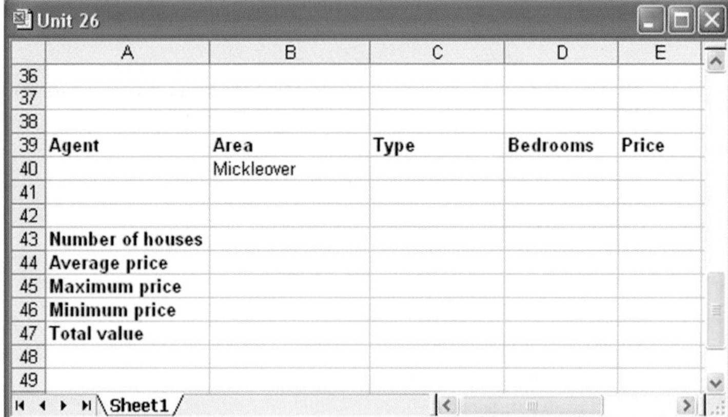

Unit 26

	A	B	C	D	E
36					
37					
38					
39	**Agent**	**Area**	**Type**	**Bedrooms**	**Price**
40		Mickleover			
41					
42					
43	**Number of houses**				
44	**Average price**				
45	**Maximum price**				
46	**Minimum price**				
47	**Total value**				
48					
49					

Sheet1

2 Make sure you have named the Database and Criteria ranges (A1:E35 and A39:E40).

3 Enter the formulas shown in Figure 3.41.

Figure 3. 41 ▶

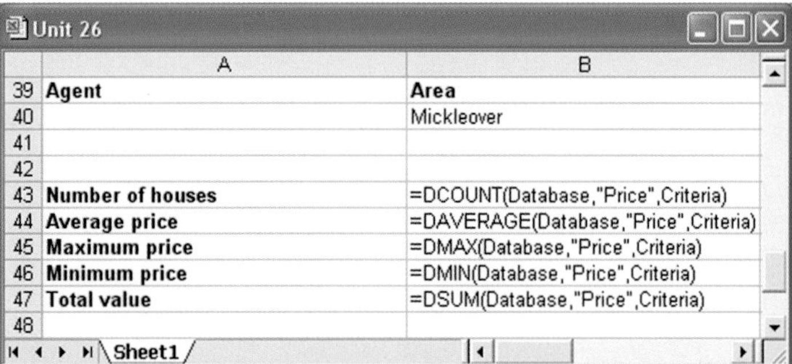

Unit 26

	A	B
39	**Agent**	**Area**
40		Mickleover
41		
42		
43	**Number of houses**	=DCOUNT(Database,"Price",Criteria)
44	**Average price**	=DAVERAGE(Database,"Price",Criteria)
45	**Maximum price**	=DMAX(Database,"Price",Criteria)
46	**Minimum price**	=DMIN(Database,"Price",Criteria)
47	**Total value**	=DSUM(Database,"Price",Criteria)
48		

Sheet1

4 The results should be as in Figure 3.42.

Figure 3. 42 ▶

Unit 26

	A	B	C	D	E
34	Halifax	Mickleover	terraced	2	97900
35	Hall & Partners	Littleover	terraced	2	95900
36					
37					
38					
39	**Agent**	**Area**	**Type**	**Bedrooms**	**Price**
40		Mickleover			
41					
42					
43	**Number of houses**	9			
44	**Average price**	£192,367.00			
45	**Maximum price**	£440,000.00			
46	**Minimum price**	£97,900.00			
47	**Total value**	£1,731,300.00			
48					
49					

Sheet1

When it works, try varying the search criteria, e.g. change the area to Littleover or narrow the search to houses with three bedrooms.

4 UserForm exercises

In this part you will learn how to run systems entirely from UserForms including entering data through the UserForm. It is recommended that you work through units 21 and 22 before doing these exercises.

1 The ideal weight exercise

Problem statement

Fitness, diet and healthy eating magazines often produce tables of ideal weights according to a person's sex and height as given in the file **weight.xls**. Load the file as shown in Figure 4.1

Figure 4. 1 ▶

weight

	A	B	C	D	E
1		Men		Women	
2		Min	Max	Min	Max
3	Height (cm)	Weight (kg)			
4	158	51	64	46	59
5	160	52	65	48	61
6	162	53	66	49	62
7	164	54	67	50	64
8	166	55	69	51	65
9	168	56	71	52	66
10	170	58	73	53	67
11	172	59	74	55	69
12	174	60	75	56	70
13	176	62	77	58	72
14	178	64	79	59	74
15	180	65	80	60	76
16	182	66	82	62	78
17	184	67	84	63	80

Sheet1 / Sheet2 / Sheet3

- A system will be produced to allow a user to enter their sex and height.
- The system will calculate from tables the user's ideal maximum and minimum weight range.
- The output will be to screen with an option to print.

Brief design overview

A spinner will be used to enter a person's height in centimetres. It will be linked to cell **J1**.

Option buttons will be used to enter the user's sex. This will be linked to cell **J2** which will store TRUE if male and FALSE if female.

J3 will be used to decide which columns to lookup based on whether the user is male or female. The minimum weight for a man is in column 2. The minimum weight for a woman is in column 4. So if the user is a man, this cell will read 2. If the user is a woman, the cell will display 4.

Cell **J4** will be used to lookup the minimum value from either column 2 or column 4.

Cell **J5** will be used to lookup the maximum value from either column 3 or column 5.

Setting up the worksheet

1. In cell **J2** of the worksheet enter **TRUE** (TRUE represents Male, FALSE represents Female.)
2. In J3 enter **=IF(J2=TRUE,2,4)** (This shows which column to look in for the minimum weight. Column 2 for male, column 4 for female.)
3. In **J4** enter **=VLOOKUP(J1,Table,J3)** (This looks up the minimum weight in either column 2 or column 4.)
4. In **J5** enter **=VLOOKUP(J1,Table,J3+1)** (This looks up the maximum weight in either column 3 or column 5.)

The formulas are shown in Figure 4.2.

Figure 4. 2 ▶

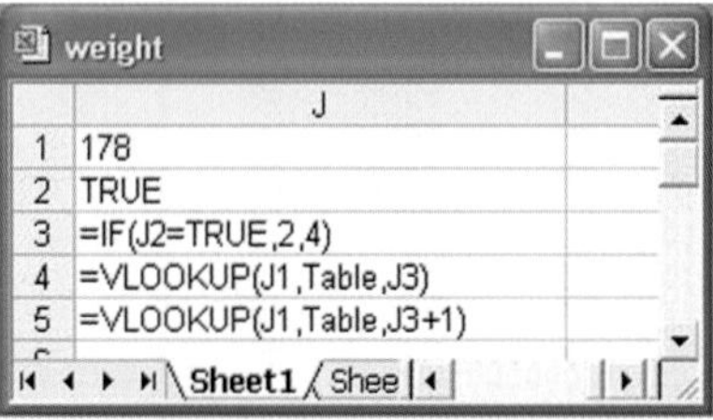

	J
1	178
2	TRUE
3	=IF(J2=TRUE,2,4)
4	=VLOOKUP(J1,Table,J3)
5	=VLOOKUP(J1,Table,J3+1)

The lookups in **J4** and **J5** look up the minimum and maximum weights for the height in **J1**. For a height of 178, they should read 64 and 79 if male.

Setting up the UserForm

1. Load the Visual Basic Editor Window by clicking on **Tools > Macro > Visual Basic Editor** or pressing ALT + **F11**.
2. Click on **Insert > UserForm** or click on the **Insert UserForm** icon.
3. In the Properties Window, set the Caption to **Your Ideal Weight**.
4. Also in the Properties Window, set the background colour to light grey.

Figure 4. 3 ▶

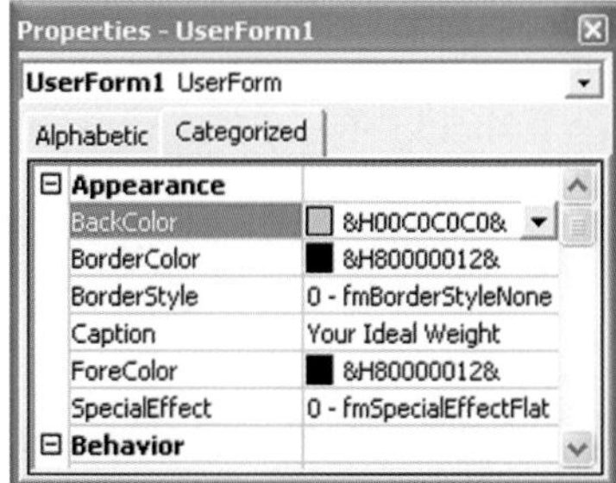

Note: Throughout this part you can use the Properties Window to format text and background colours as you wish.

5 Use a Label to put the title **What is your Ideal Weight?** at the top of your UserForm.

6 In the Properties Window, set the font size for the label to 16. You may wish to set the background colour of the label too. The UserForm will look like Figure 4.4.

Figure 4. 4 ▶

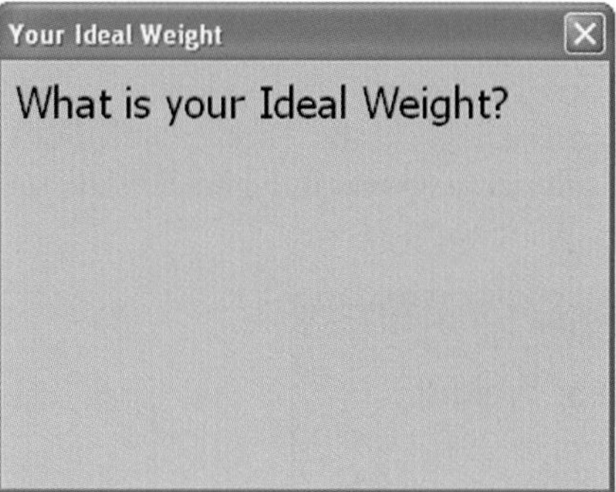

Setting up the Spinner to adjust the Height

1 Click on the Spin Button icon on the Toolbox and drag out a spinner near the top of the UserForm. If the spinner is pointing horizontally, hold down the ALT key and resize the spinner so that it points vertically.

2 With the spinner still selected, set Max in the Properties Window to **184**, Min to **158**, Small Change to **2** and then set the Control Source to **J1.**

3 Double click on the spinner and edit the text to read as follows:

```
Private Sub SpinButton1_Change()
Range("J1").Value = SpinButton1.Value
End Sub
```

This means that as you click the spinner, the value in cell **J1** updates immediately.

4 Click on the **Close** icon to return to the UserForm.

5 Click on the **Run Sub/UserForm** icon to load the UserForm as in Figure 4.5 and test the spinner. It should alter the numbers in J1, J4 and J5.

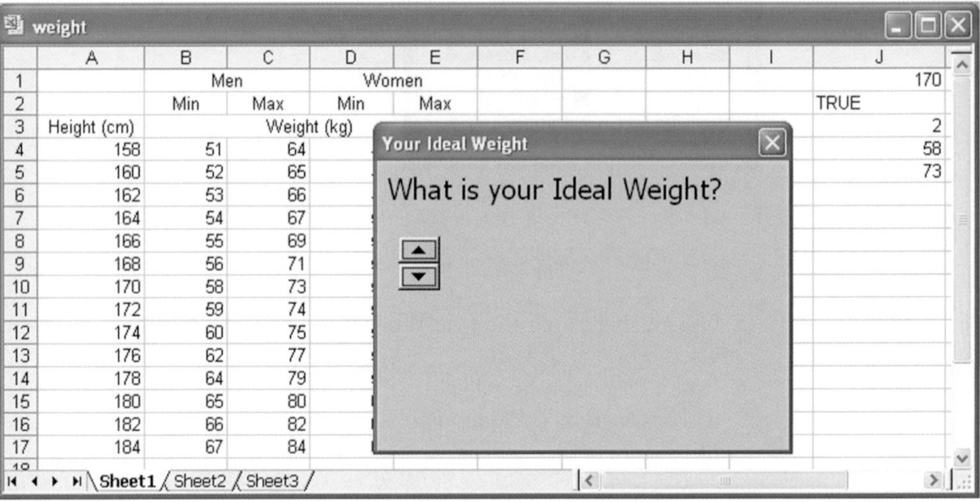

Figure 4. 5 ▲

Close the UserForm by clicking on the close icon. Save your file.

6 Click on the Text Box icon in the Toolbox and drag out a small text box underneath the spinner as shown in Figure 4.6 and set the Control Source in the Properties Window to **J1**.

Figure 4. 6 ▶

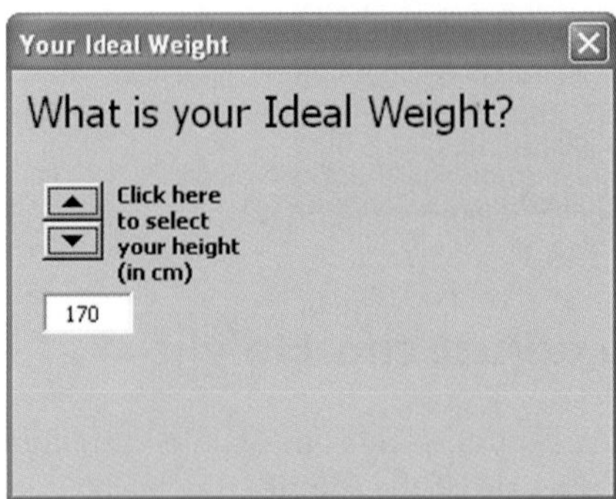

Add a label to your spinner as shown in Figure 4.6.

7 Click on the **Run Sub/UserForm** icon to test that the number in the text box goes up or down by 2 when the spinner is clicked. Save your file.

Adding option buttons for Male and Female

1 Click on the Option Button icon in the Toolbox and add an option button to your UserForm. Edit the label to **Male** as in Figure 4.7 and set the Control Source to **J2**.

Figure 4. 7 ▶

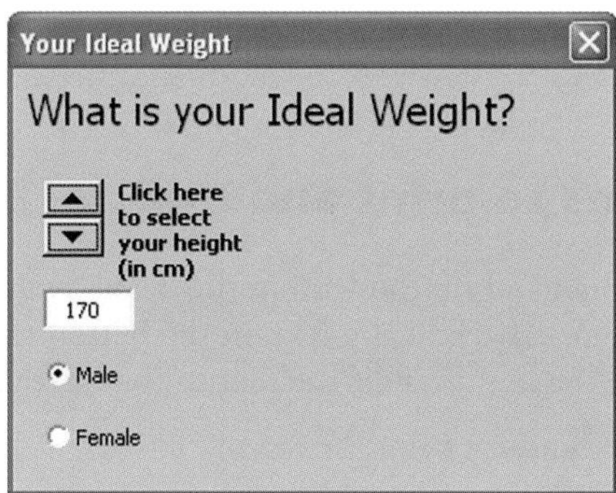

2 Add another option button labelled Female. You must not set the Control Source. Click on the **Run Sub/UserForm** icon to test that as you choose Female, the numbers change in J4 and J5. Save your file.

Adding List Boxes to look up the weight

1 Click on the List Box icon in the Toolbox and add a list box to your UserForm as shown in Figure 4.8. Set the **Row Source** to **J4**.

Figure 4. 8 ▶

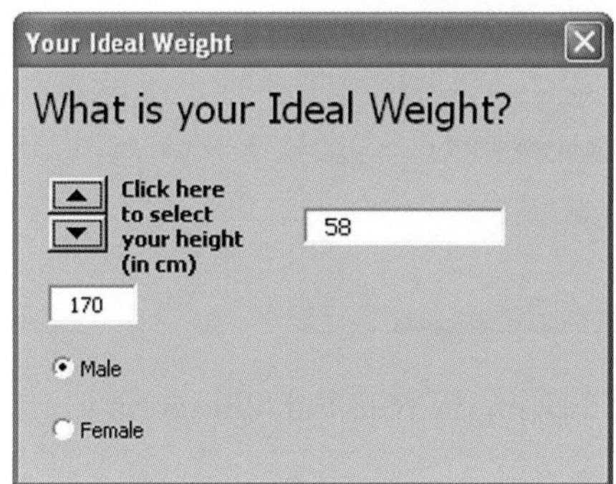

2 Add another list box with Row Source **J5** and add labels as shown in Figure 4.9.

Figure 4. 9 ▶

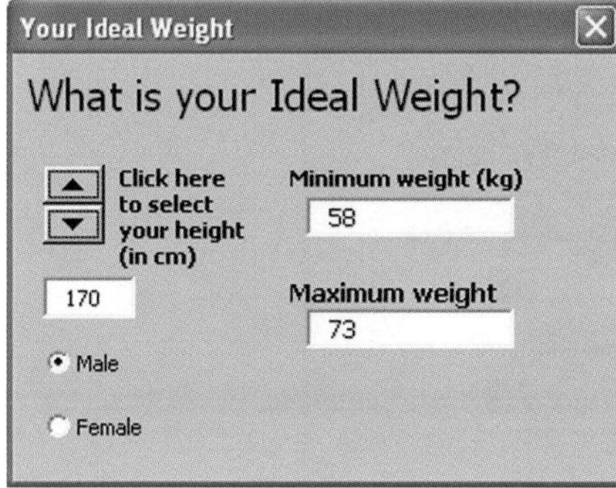

3 Click on the **Run Sub/UserForm** icon to test that as you click on the spinner, the maximum and minimum weights change. Save your file.

Note: When linking a UserForm box to a cell with a formula or a lookup, use a **list box**.

Adding Command Buttons to print and exit

1 Click on the Command Button icon in the Toolbox to add a command button as in Figure 4.10. Edit the text on the button to **Print**.

2 Double click on the button. Edit the text so that it reads as follows:

```
Private Sub CommandButton1_Click()
UserForm1.PrintForm
End Sub
```

3 Add another command button. Edit the text on the button to **Exit**.

4 Double click on the second button. Edit the text so that it reads as follows:

```
Private Sub CommandButton2_Click()
Application.Quit
End Sub
```

Figure 4. 10 ▶

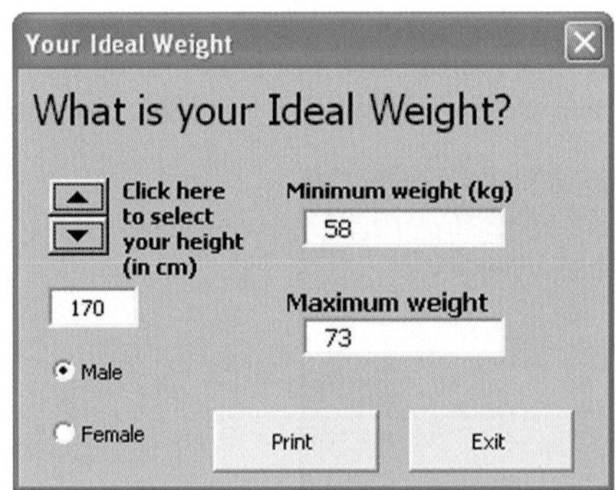

5 Save your file. Click on the **Run Sub/UserForm** icon and test the buttons.

Finishing the system

1 Enlarge the font size of the list boxes and centre the text as shown in Figure 4.11.

Figure 4. 11 ▶

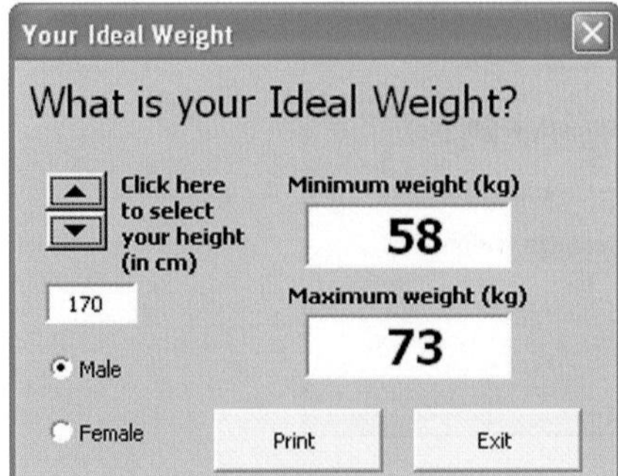

2 Click on **Insert > Module**. This opens a Visual Basic Editor window where macro coding is entered and stored.
3 Enter this macro in the Visual Basic Editor window:

```
Sub Auto_open()
Load UserForm1
UserForm1.Show
End Sub
```

4 Go back to Excel by clicking on the **View Microsoft Excel** icon.
5 Remove the gridlines by clicking on **Tools > Options** and unchecking **Gridlines**.
6 Highlight all the cells and set the text colour to white.
7 Save your file.
8 Close the file. Reload the file and test that the system works.

Ideas for further development

You can develop the system further by:

- removing row and column headings
- removing the toolbars
- removing the scrollbars
- removing the status bar, formula bar and tabs
- adding a second sheet storing the heights and weights in imperial units
- setting up a UserForm for the user to select either Imperial or metric units.

2a The invoice exercise: formulas

A common use of Excel is to set up and calculate invoices. In this section you will set up an invoice and use UserForms to enter data.

A sportswear shop supplies kits to football clubs.

We need to set up the spreadsheet to calculate and display the cost of kit and work out the total cost including VAT at 17.5 per cent.

1 Enter the data into a new spreadsheet as shown in Figure 4.12 or load the file **caseys.xls.** Don't forget to format the prices to Currency.

Figure 4. 12 ▶

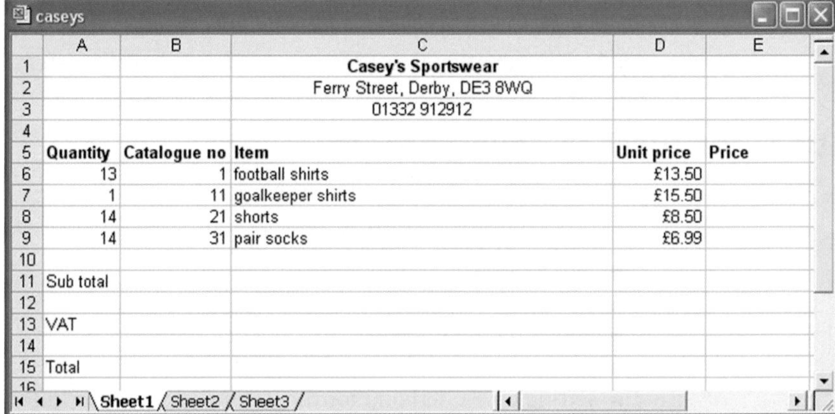

caseys

	A	B	C	D	E
1			**Casey's Sportswear**		
2			Ferry Street, Derby, DE3 8WQ		
3			01332 912912		
4					
5	**Quantity**	**Catalogue no**	**Item**	**Unit price**	**Price**
6	13	1	football shirts	£13.50	
7	1	11	goalkeeper shirts	£15.50	
8	14	21	shorts	£8.50	
9	14	31	pair socks	£6.99	
10					
11	Sub total				
12					
13	VAT				
14					
15	Total				

Sheet1 / Sheet2 / Sheet3

2 Enter the formula **=A6*D6** into cell **E6**. It should say £175.50
3 Replicate the formula in **E6** into cells **E7** to **E9**.

Note: As the formula is copied it changes. In row 7 it is =A7*D7, in row 8 =A8*D8 and so on.

4 Click on **E11** and use the **AutoSum** icon to add up the costs of the items.
5 Enter the formula for the VAT into **E13**.
6 Enter the formula for the Total into **E15**.
7 Format the totals in **E11** and **E15** to stand out.

Your spreadsheet should now look like Figure 4.13:

Figure 4. 13 ▶

caseys

	A	B	C	D	E
1			**Casey's Sportswear**		
2			Ferry Street, Derby, DE3 8WQ		
3			01332 912912		
4					
5	**Quantity**	**Catalogue no**	**Item**	**Unit price**	**Price**
6	13	1	football shirts	£13.50	£175.50
7	1	11	goalkeeper shirts	£15.50	£15.50
8	14	21	shorts	£8.50	£119.00
9	14	31	pair socks	£6.99	£97.86
10					
11	Sub total				**£407.86**
12					
13	VAT				£71.38
14					
15	Total				**£479.24**

Sheet1 / Sheet2 / Sheet3

Save your work as **caseys.xls**

2b The invoice exercise: lookups

Casey's Sportswear sell three different makes of football kit, all at different prices.

We want to set up the spreadsheet so that when the catalogue number is typed into column B, the item name and unit price automatically appear in columns C and D.

1 On Sheet2 enter the details of the items and prices as shown in Figure 4.14. If you loaded the file **caseys.xls**, this data will already be stored.
2 Define the area from A2 to C14 as **items** (**Insert > Name > Define**).

Figure 4. 14 ▶

caseys

	A	B	C	D
1	**Catalogue no**	**Item**	**Unit price**	
2	0	-	-	
3	1	football shirts (Jarvis & Co)	£13.50	
4	2	football shirts (Skinner Bros)	£14.00	
5	3	football shirts (BCW)	£16.00	
6	11	goalkeeper shirts (Jarvis & Co)	£15.50	
7	12	goalkeeper shirts (Skinner Bros)	£17.50	
8	13	goalkeeper shirts (BCW)	£20.00	
9	21	shorts (Jarvis & Co)	£8.99	
10	22	shorts (Skinner Bros)	£8.50	
11	23	shorts (BCW)	£10.00	
12	31	pair socks (Jarvis & Co)	£6.99	
13	32	pair socks (Skinner Bros)	£7.50	
14	33	pair socks (BCW)	£8.00	
15				

Sheet1 Sheet2 Sheet3

3 Switch back to Sheet1. In cell **C6** enter the formula **=VLOOKUP(B6,items,2)**.
This picks up the Catalogue Number in B6, finds that number in column A of the named area **items** and returns the description from the second column on that row.
4 In cell **D6** enter the formula **=VLOOKUP(B6,items,3)**.
This looks up the unit price for the catalogue number in B6.
5 **Copy** and **Paste** these two formulas down as far as cells **C9** and **D9**. Check that if you enter a catalogue number in column B, the right information appears in columns C and D.
6 Test that the lookups work. Investigate what happens if you type in a false product number in this workbook.
(a) Try one that is too big like 35
(b) Try one that is too small like −5
(c) Try one that doesn't exist like 7
7 To avoid such errors we can use validation. Click on **B6**. Use **Data Validation** so that only **1**, **2** or **3** can be entered into this cell as in Figure 4.15.

Figure 4. 15 ▶

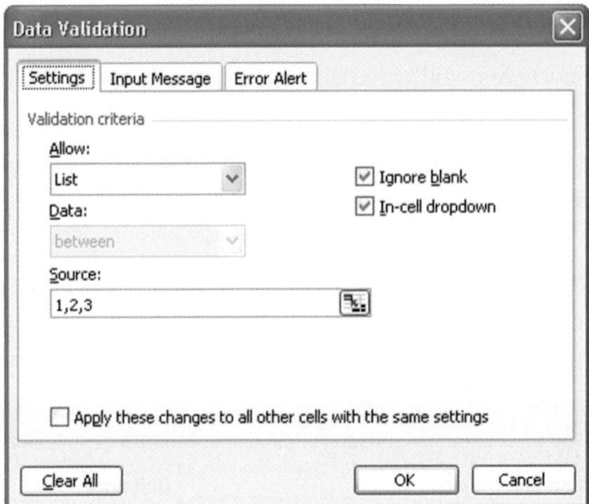

8 Similarly only 11, 12 or 13 can be entered into B7; 21, 22 or 23 into B8 and 31, 32 or 33 in B9.

9 To use the spreadsheet enter the catalogue number in column B and the quantity in column A. If a line is not being used, leave column B blank.

10 Check the lookups work for all possible values. Save your work.

2c The invoice exercise: option buttons

Football shirts are available in two types; plain or striped. Striped shirts cost an extra £1.00 per shirt.

1. Add option buttons to the bottom left of the spreadsheet. Link the buttons to cell **A17**.
2. Use the **IF** function in cell **E10**, so that if A17 is equal to 2, this cell is equal to A6. Else it is 0.
3. Make sure that the formula in **E11** is **=SUM(E6:E10)**.
4. Save the file.

Your spreadsheet should look like Figure 4.16.

Figure 4. 16 ▶

caseys

	A	B	C	D	E
1			**Casey's Sportswear**		
2			Ferry Street, Derby, DE3 8WQ		
3			01332 912912		
4					
5	**Quantity**	**Catalogue no**	**Item**	**Unit price**	**Price**
6	13	1	football shirts (Jarvis & Co)	£13.50	£175.50
7	1	11	goalkeeper shirts (Jarvis & Co)	£15.50	£15.50
8	14	21	shorts (Jarvis & Co)	£8.99	£125.86
9	14	31	pair socks (Jarvis & Co)	£6.99	£97.86
10					£0.00
11	Sub total				**£414.72**
12					
13	VAT				£72.58
14					
15	Total				**£487.30**
16					
17	1	◉ Plain shirts			
18					
19		○ Striped shirts			
20					

Sheet1 / Sheet2 / Sheet3

Hint: The formula required in E10 is **=IF(A17=2,A6,0)**.

2d The invoice exercise: using a macro to clear data

A very important use of a macro is to clear data from a sheet ready for new data entry. For example, the invoice may need to be cleared ready for a new customer. The steps are to clear all the data in cells A6 to B9 and A17. See Figure 4.16.

The data shown in Figure 4.16 will be cleared ready for another customer, as shown in Figure 4.17.

Figure 4. 17 ▶

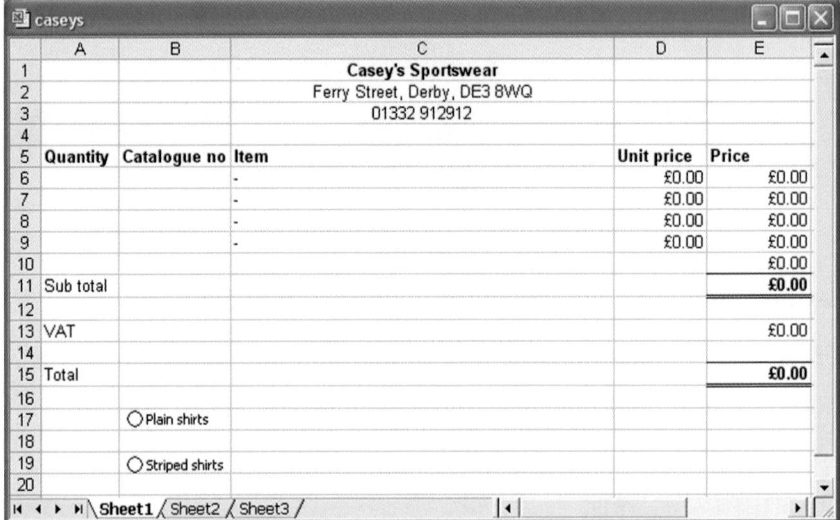

caseys

	A	B	C	D	E
1			**Casey's Sportswear**		
2			Ferry Street, Derby, DE3 8WQ		
3			01332 912912		
4					
5	**Quantity**	**Catalogue no**	**Item**	**Unit price**	**Price**
6			-	£0.00	£0.00
7			-	£0.00	£0.00
8			-	£0.00	£0.00
9			-	£0.00	£0.00
10					£0.00
11	Sub total				**£0.00**
12					
13	VAT				£0.00
14					
15	Total				**£0.00**
16					
17		○ Plain shirts			
18					
19		○ Striped shirts			
20					

Sheet1 / Sheet2 / Sheet3

1 Start recording a new macro called **Clear**.
2 Highlight cells **A6** to **B9**.
3 Select **Edit > Clear > All**.
4 Click on cell **A17**.
5 Select **Edit > Clear > All**. Click on cell **A1** and stop recording.
6 Make a button to run the Clear macro and test it.

2e The invoice exercise: setting up a message box

1 Click on **Tools > Macro > Visual Basic Editor** to load the Visual Basic Editor.
2 Double click on Module1 in the Project Explorer Window.
3 Scroll down to the bottom of the macro coding in the main Visual Basic Editor window.
4 Enter this text to set up a macro called Message1:

```
Sub Message1()
MsgBox "Our helpline is 01332 912912", vbOKOnly, "Casey's Sportswear"
End Sub
```

Note:

- As with recorded macros, the macro must begin with Sub and end with End Sub.
- You will not need to type in the **End Sub** part as when you enter a line beginning with Sub, the End Sub line is automatically inserted below.
- You can define the title (in this case Casey's Sportswear), the message (the helpline details) and the buttons.
- vbOKOnly means you get just an OK button.

5 Go back to Excel by clicking on the **View Microsoft Excel** icon.
6 Run the macro Message1: **Tools > Macro > Macros > Message1 > Run** and you will see the message box in Figure 4.18.

Figure 4. 18 ▶

7 Add a button to the worksheet to run this macro and label it **Help**.

2f The invoice exercise: UserForms

In this section you will use a UserForm as a user-friendly front end for an Excel solution.

A UserForm is a way of providing a customised user interface for your system. Sometimes it is called a dialogue box. A UserForm might look like the one in Figure 4.19 which we will set up in this exercise.

Figure 4. 19 ▶

1 Rename Sheet1 as **Invoice** and Sheet2 as **Data**.
2 Record a macro called **Data** to switch to the Data worksheet.
3 Record a macro called **Invoice** to switch to the Invoice worksheet.
4 Load the **Visual Basic Editor** by clicking on **Tools > Macro > Visual Basic Editor** or pressing ALT and F11.
5 Click on **Insert > UserForm** or click on the Insert UserForm icon. A blank UserForm will appear in the main Visual Basic Editor window as in Figure 4.20.

Figure 4. 20 ▶

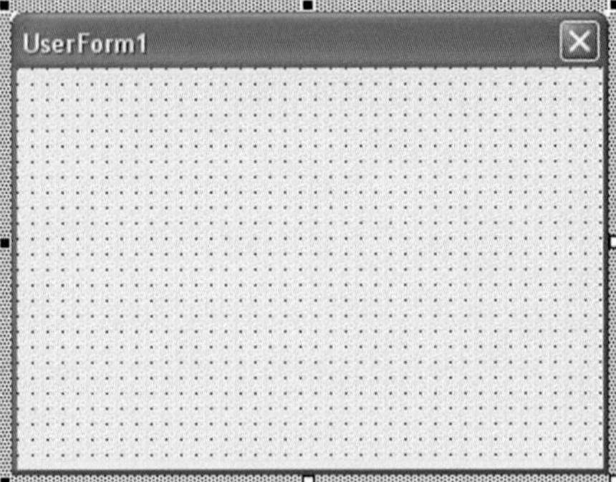

6 A set of icons called the Toolbox will also appear as shown in Figure 4.21. If it is not visible, click on the blank UserForm and click on **View > Toolbox**.

Figure 4. 21 ▶

7 On the Toolbox, click on the **CommandButton** icon and drag out a rectangle on the UserForm just below the middle on the left-hand side as in Figure 4.22.

8 The text on the button will say **CommandButton1**. Edit this by clicking once on the button. Delete and change to **View invoice**.

Figure 4. 22 ▶

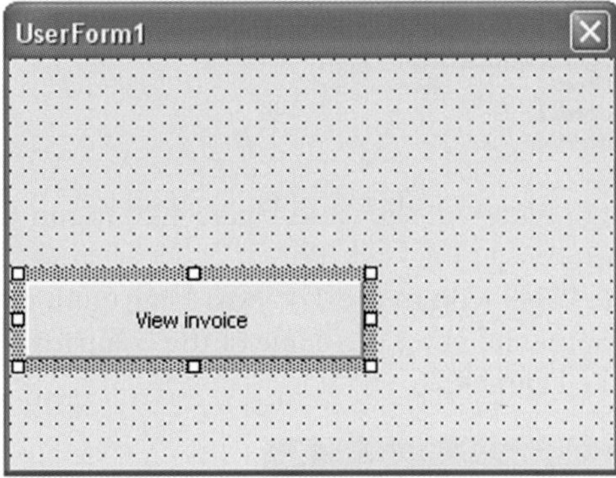

9 Double click on the button. You will see the code shown in Figure 4.23.

Figure 4. 23 ▶

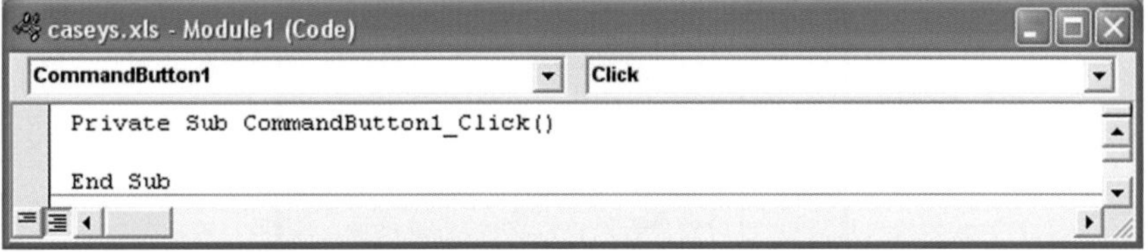

The cursor should be in the middle of these two lines. If not, click between the two lines.

10 Enter this text:

```
Invoice
UserForm1.Hide
```

It will now look like Figure 4.24.

Figure 4. 24 ▶

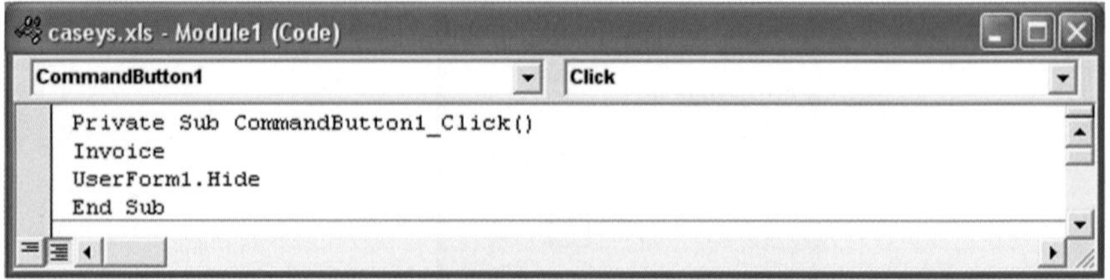

Invoice is the name of the macro that will run when you click on this button.

The command **UserForm1.Hide** removes the UserForm from the screen.

Note: The spelling and the punctuation must be exactly as above or it won't work.

11 Click on **View > Object** or click on the **View Object** icon in the Project Explorer Window (top left of screen) shown in Figure 4.25 to go back to the plan of the UserForm.

Figure 4. 25 ▶

12 Add one more button as shown in Figure 4.26 to run the other macro called **Data**.

13 Click on the **Label** icon in the Toolbox. Drag out a rectangle near the top of the UserForm and enter the name of the company. The UserForm will now look like Figure 4.26.

Figure 4. 26 ▶

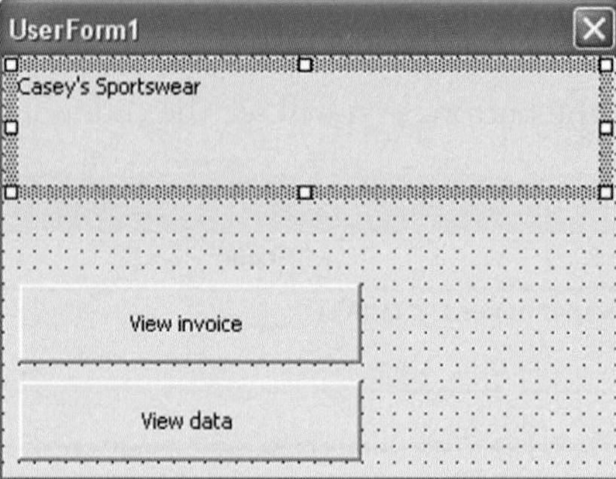

Using the Properties Window

The Properties Window at the bottom left-hand corner of the screen is used to set the properties of the UserForm and its controls. For example, it is used to set the caption, the size, the colour, the font and any links to cells in the spreadsheet.

1 Select the label **Casey's Sportswear**. In the **Properties Window** scroll down to **Font.** Click on the three dots icon and set the size to **18**.

2 Scroll down to the **Text Align** property and select **2-fm TextAlignCenter** to centre the text, as shown in Figure 4.27.

Figure 4. 27 ▶

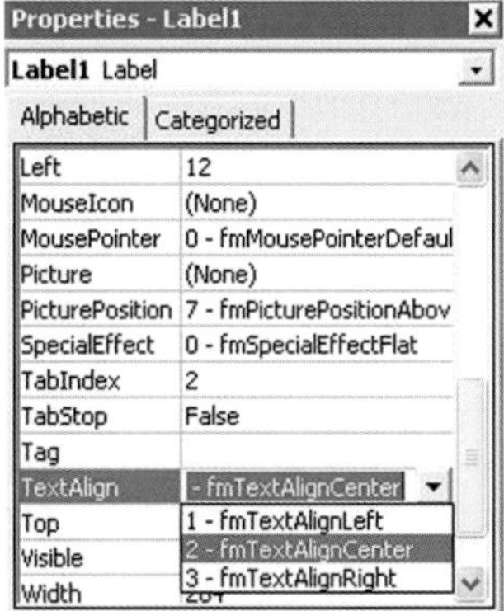

3 Click off the label and on the UserForm. Select the **Caption** property to set the Caption to **Casey's Sportswear**. The UserForm will now look like Figure 4.28.

Figure 4. 28 ▶

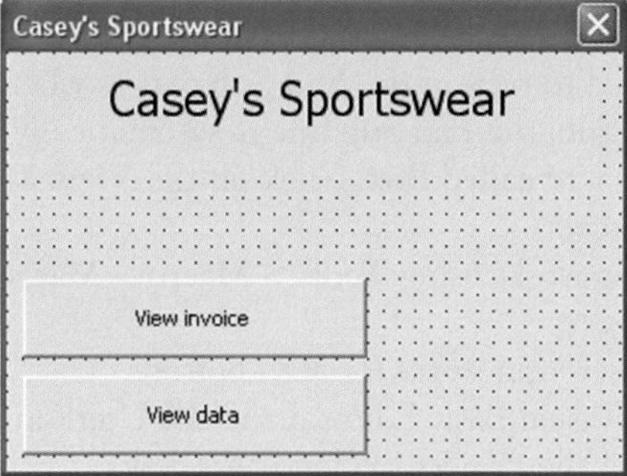

The UserForm is now set up but is not very attractive.

4 Save your file. Test the UserForm by clicking on the **Run Sub/UserForm** icon or by pressing **F5**. The UserForm will load. Click on the Close icon (the X in the top right-hand corner of the UserForm) to go back to the Visual Basic Editor.

Setting up a macro to display your UserForm

Once you have designed a UserForm, you will need to set up a macro to display it. The macro will be set up in Visual Basic and once again, exact syntax is vital.

1 In Excel, click on **Tools > Macro > Visual Basic Editor**.

2 Double click on Module1 in the Project Explorer Window, shown in Figure 4.29. (If Module1 is not visible click on the + sign next to **Modules** in the Project Explorer Window. Then double click on Module1.)

Figure 4. 29 ▶

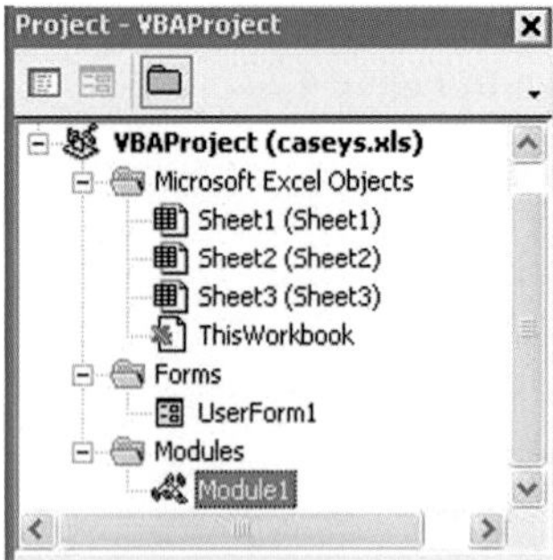

3 You should see the coding of the macros you have already set up. Scroll down to the bottom and underneath the last macro text, type in the following:

```
Sub Box()
Load UserForm1
UserForm1.Show
End Sub
```

The two middle lines of code load the UserForm and display it on the screen.
You will not need to type in the **End Sub** part as when you enter a line beginning with Sub, the End Sub line is automatically inserted below.

4 This sets up a macro called **Box**. Click on the **View Microsoft Excel** icon to go back to Excel.
5 Check the macro works using **Tools > Macro > Macros.** Click on **Box > Run.**
6 Test that the UserForm works for both buttons.
7 Go back to the Visual Basic Editor. Load the UserForm by double clicking on UserForm1 in the Project Explorer Window.
8 In the Properties Window set the **Height** of the UserForm to 220 or extend the UserForm just by dragging downwards. Add an extra button as in Figure 4.30. Edit the text on the button to read **Cancel**. Double click on the new button and make the text as follows:

```
Private Sub CommandButton3_Click()
End
End Sub
```

Figure 4. 30 ▶

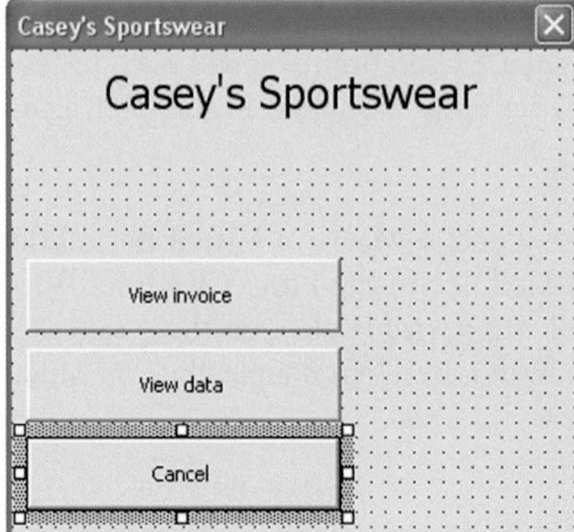

9 Save your file.

Each item on a UserForm such as a command button, a combo box or a text box is an object.

Each object has a unique name such as CommandButton1, TextBox6 or ComboBox4.

If you double click on the UserForm, you will see the code for each object. It will appear as in Figure 4.31.

Figure 4. 31 ▶

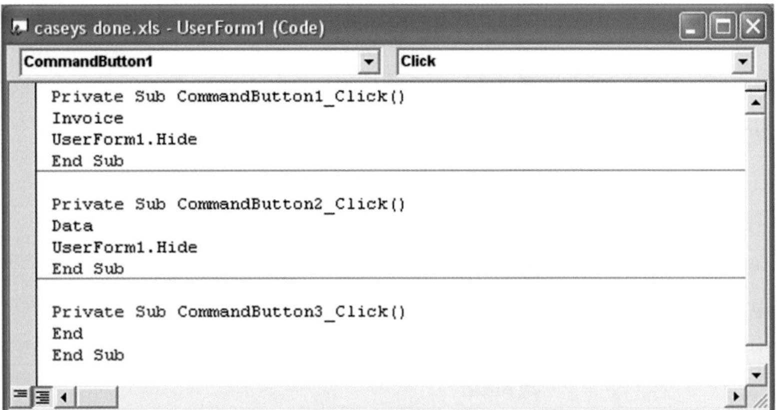

2g The invoice exercise: customising your UserForm

You can develop your UserForm in a number of ways for example by:

- editing background colours
- changing the font
- adding an image
- resizing the UserForm.

The properties of each object are set up in the Properties Window.

1 Go back to the **Visual Basic Editor** and load the UserForm by double clicking on UserForm1 in the Project Explorer Window as shown in Figure 4.32.

Figure 4. 32 ▶

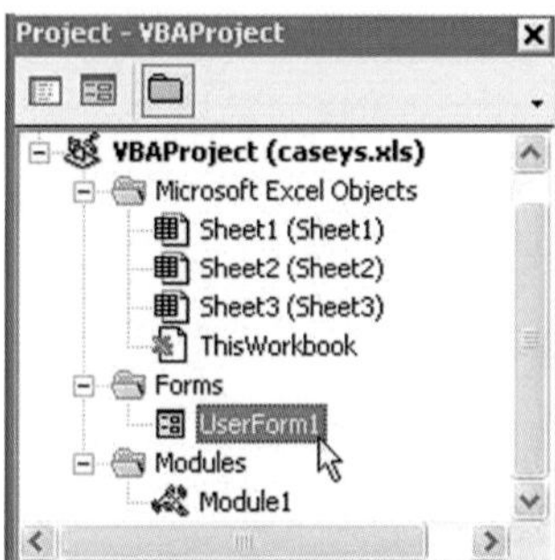

2 To edit the background colour, click on the UserForm. In the Properties Window, click on **BackColor**. Click on the drop-down arrow and choose Palette as in Figure 4.33. You have a variety of colours to choose from.

Figure 4. 33 ▶

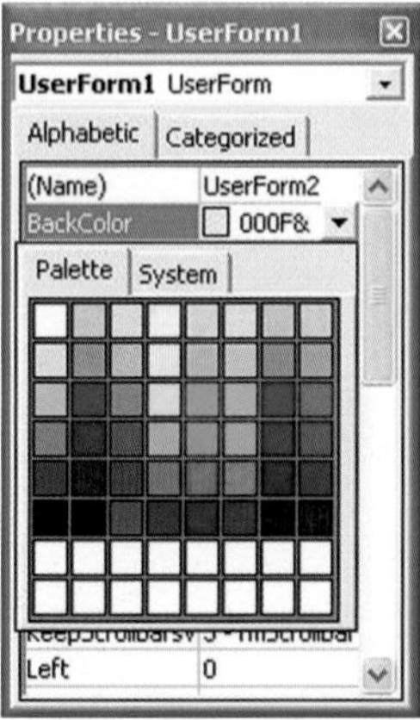

3 Click on one of the command buttons on the UserForm. Use the Properties Window to change the colour of the button, the colour of the text (**ForeColor**) and the font as required. Repeat this for the other buttons and the label.

4 To add a picture, click on the Image icon in the Toolbox and drag out a rectangle on the UserForm. Click on the row called **Picture** in the Properties Window. Double click on the icon with three dots to select a picture. Find the picture you require. Choose **3 – fmPictureSizeModeZoom,** so that the picture resizes to fit. Make the background colour transparent and the border style none.

5 Add a control tip text to your buttons using the Control Tip Text row of the Properties Window. Whatever you type in here appears on the screen as help text when you move the mouse over a control like a text box.
6 Resize the UserForm and the command buttons by dragging the controls in the normal way.
7 Save your file.

UserForms can be made to look eye-catching as shown in Figure 4.34.

Figure 4. 34 ▶

Hint: To add an extra line in your label, press CTRL and ENTER.

2h The invoice exercise: using UserForms to enter data

In this section you will learn about how UserForms can be used to enter data into an Excel workbook.

Text boxes on a UserForm can be linked to cells in a spreadsheet and can be used for entering data. List boxes can be used to display data from the spreadsheet in the UserForm.

Obviously you can just type the data straight into the cells, but using a UserForm can make it easier for the user and gives greater control.

You can include other controls in a UserForm such as command buttons, combo boxes and option buttons as shown by the example in Figure 4.35 which we will set up in this section.

Figure 4. 35 ▶

Setting up the UserForm

We need to set up the UserForm to enter the customer's name and address and details of purchases, i.e. catalogue number, quantity, whether VAT is payable and whether the shirts are plain or striped. The total price will be displayed.

1 Remove the option buttons from the spreadsheet and clear the linked cell A17.
2 Load the **Visual Basic Editor** by pressing ALT + **F11**. Insert a UserForm by clicking on **Insert > UserForm.** This will be called UserForm2.
3 Enlarge the UserForm so that it is 360 wide and 330 high. (These can be set using the **Width** and **Height** properties in the Properties Window.)
4 In the Properties Window, set the caption to **Casey's Sportswear**. Add a label with the company address (use font size 12) and a picture for a logo as shown in Figure 4.36.

5 Add a command button at the bottom right on the UserForm as in Figure 4.36. Edit its text to **OK**.

Figure 4. 36 ►

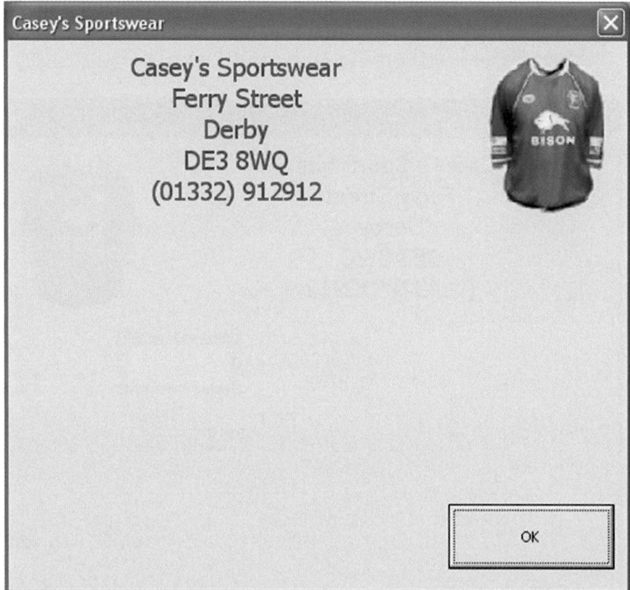

6 Double click on the button and add the text **UserForm2.Hide** as shown in Figure 4.37.

Figure 4. 37 ►

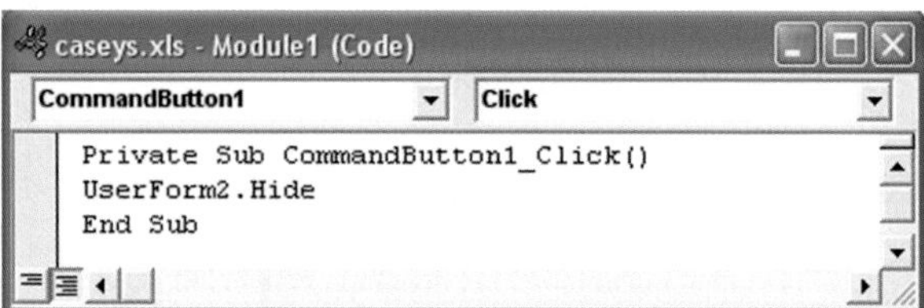

7 Double click on Module1 in the Project Explorer Window. Scroll down to the bottom and add this macro:

```
Sub Details()
Load Userform2
Userform2.Show
End Sub
```

This sets up a macro called **Details** to load the UserForm.

8 Switch back to Excel to test that running the macro displays the UserForm.

Adding text boxes

1 Switch back to the Visual Basic Editor. Double click on UserForm2. Click on the **TextBox** icon in the Toolbox. Drag out a box on the right-hand side of the UserForm as shown in Figure 4.38.

Figure 4. 38 ▶

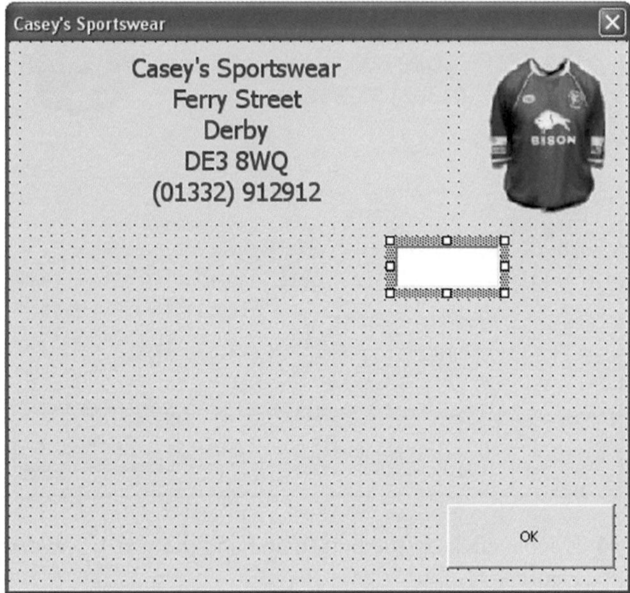

2 With the box selected, set the **Control Source** in the Properties Window to **A6** as in Figure 4.39.

Figure 4. 39 ▶

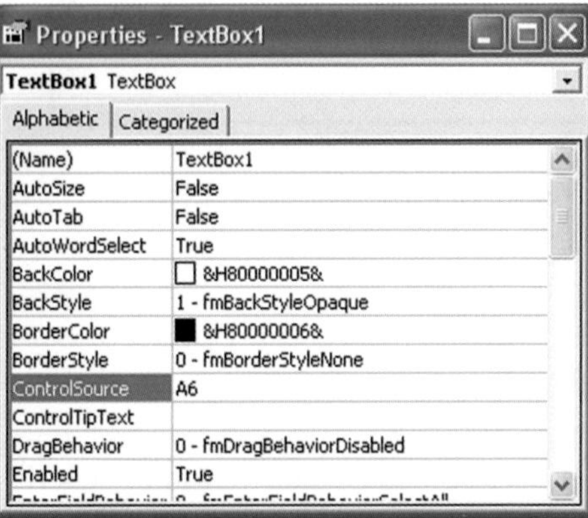

3 Click on the Label icon and drag out a box above the text box. Enter the text **Quantity** into the label as shown in Figure 4.40. Change the font, the colour of the text and the text alignment if required.

Figure 4. 40 ▶

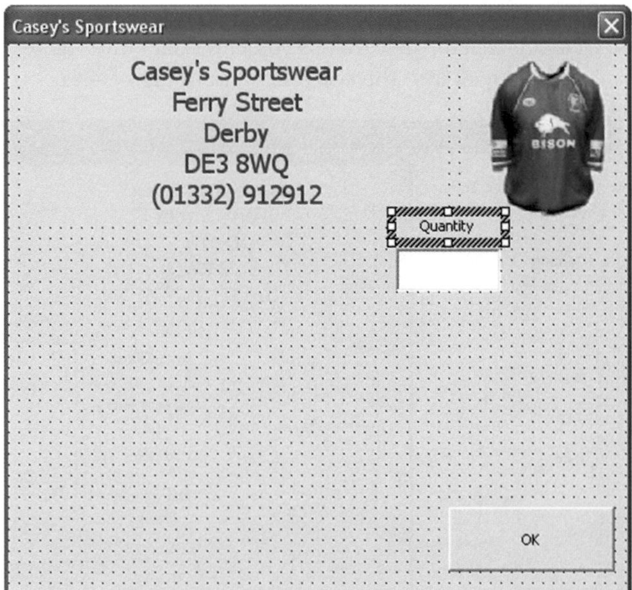

4 We now need to add extra text boxes and labels as shown in Figure 4.41.

Figure 4. 41 ▶

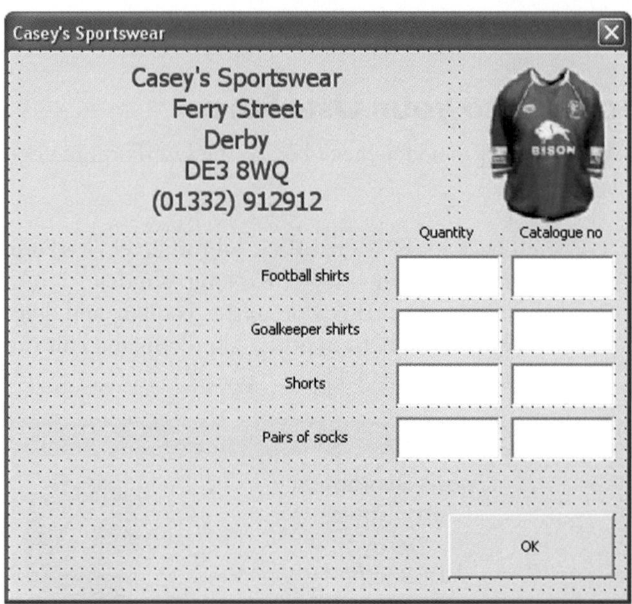

5 We need to set the control source for each text box as follows:
Football shirts catalogue number – **B6**
Goalkeeper shirts quantity – **A7**
Goalkeeper shirts catalogue number – **B7**
Shorts quantity – **A8**
Shorts catalogue number – **B8**
Pair of socks quantity – **A9**
Pair of socks catalogue number – **B9**

6 Switch back to Excel. Make sure that Sheet1 is showing and run the **Details** macro. Test that as you enter data into the text boxes the data entered goes into the correct cell as in Figure 4.42.

Figure 4. 42 ▶

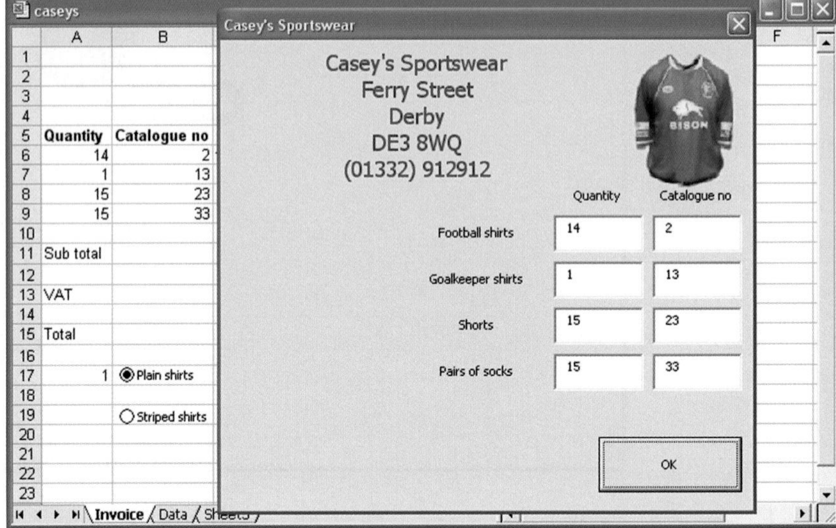

7 Save your file.

Adding a check box to your UserForm

We now want to add a check box to the UserForm to choose if VAT is payable.

1 Switch back to the Visual Basic Editor. Load UserForm2 by double clicking on UserForm2 in the Project Explorer Window.
2 Click on the **CheckBox** icon in the Toolbox and drag out a rectangle near the middle of the bottom of the UserForm and edit the text to read **VAT payable** as in Figure 4.43.

Figure 4. 43 ▶

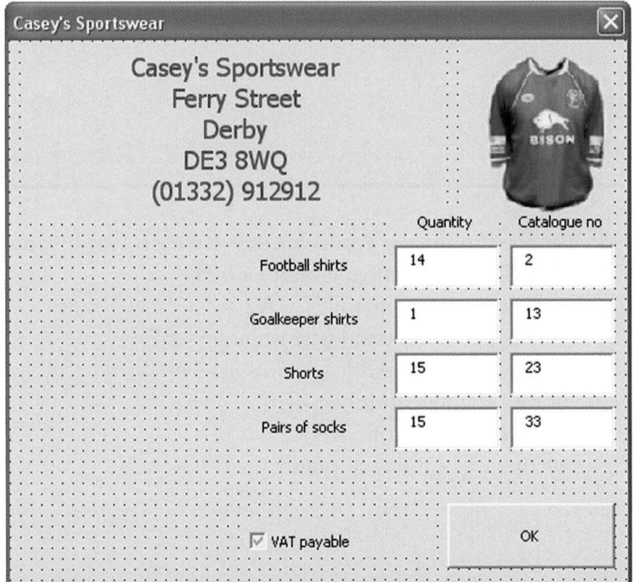

3 In the Properties Window set the control source to **A23**.
4 Switch to Excel and change the formula in cell **E13** to =IF(A23=FALSE,0,E11*17.5%)
5 Run the UserForm again. Test that the check box works by running the Details macro.

Adding option buttons

We now want to add option buttons to the UserForm to choose striped or plain shirts.

1 In the Visual Basic Editor, use the **OptionButton** icon in the Toolbox to add two option buttons as shown in Figure 4.44. Set the control source for Plain shirts to **A16**.

Figure 4. 44 ▶

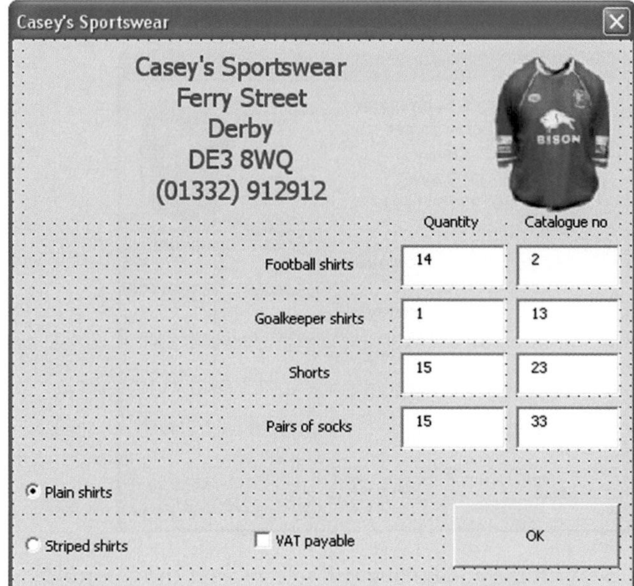

2 In Excel enter the formula **=IF(A16=TRUE,1,2)** into cell **A17**.
3 Run the Details macro and test that the option buttons work.

2i The invoice exercise: adding combo boxes to speed up data entry

As the catalogue number for football shirts can only be 1, 2 or 3, we can replace the top right text box on the UserForm with a combo box (drop-down box) giving a choice of 1, 2 or 3. This will speed up data entry and avoid mistakes. Set it up as follows:

1 In the Visual Basic Editor, load UserForm2 by double clicking on UserForm2 in the Project Explorer Window.
2 Click on the top right text box. (It is in the football shirts row and the catalogue number column.) Press **Delete** on the keyboard.
3 Click on the **ComboBox** icon in the Toolbox.
4 Drag out a box on the UserForm to replace the deleted text box as shown in Figure 4.45.

Figure 4. 45 ▶

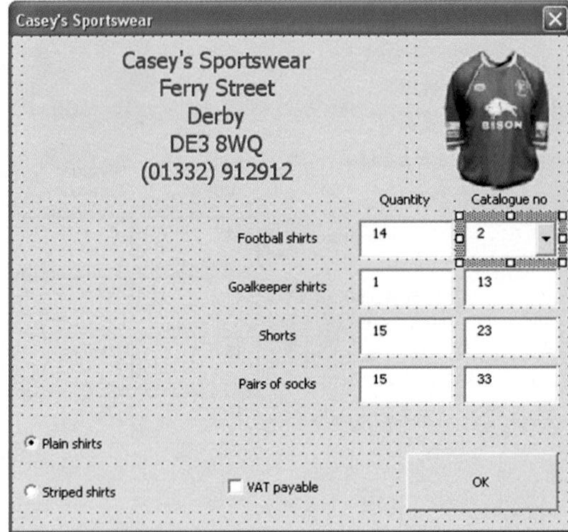

5 With the combo box still selected, set the Control Source in the Properties Window to cell **B6** and the Row Source to **Data!A3:A5**.
6 To test that it works, click on the UserForm and then press the **F5** key. The items in the drop-down list should be as shown in Figure 4.46.

Figure 4. 46 ▶

7 Develop the UserForm further by adding a combo box for the other three catalogue numbers as in Figure 4.47.

Figure 4. 47 ▶

Completing the design

1 Add five text boxes on the left of the UserForm as shown in Figure 4.48.
2 Add three labels as shown.

Figure 4. 48 ▶

3 In the Properties Window set the **Control Source** for these text boxes to **A24** to **A28** respectively. This enables the name and address of the customer to appear on the UserForm.
4 Still in the Visual Basic Editor, click on the **ListBox** icon in the Toolbox. Drag out a box above the OK button, as shown in Figure 4.49.
5 Add a label **Total Price** as shown.

Figure 4. 49 ▶

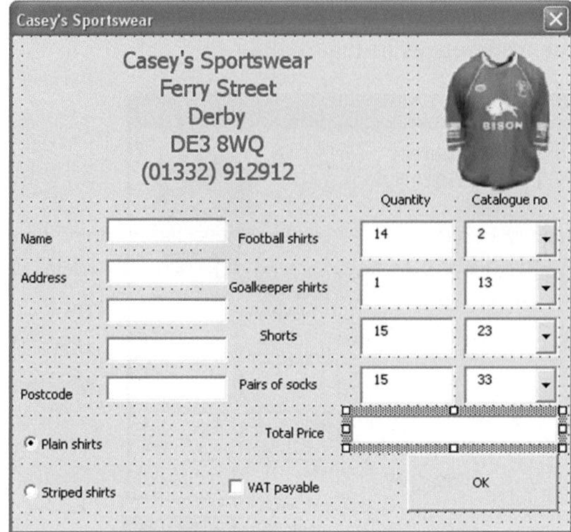

6 Select the list box. In the Properties Window, set the Row Source to **E15**, set the font to **bold** and align the text to the **right**.

7 Create a new macro called **Auto_open** as shown below so that UserForm2 is displayed when the file loads. Load Module1 and type in this coding.

```
Sub Auto_open()
Sheets("Invoice").Select
Load UserForm2
UserForm2.Show
End Sub
```

8 Save your file and test it thoroughly.

5 Project ideas

Here are some ideas for possible spreadsheet projects. You could adapt a problem or undertake a similar problem to meet the demands of a real user.

1 The stock controller

Client: Ron Wilson

Organisation: Wilson's Builders Merchants. A small builders' merchant specialising in selling small quantities of materials to the building trade.

Client's position: Owner

The problem:

Ron would like a system that will keep control of his stock, particularly to warn him when stocks get low. As an item is sold, he wants to create an invoice and automatically adjust the stock levels. Stock figures should also be updated as deliveries arrive.

The items sold, the prices and minimum stock levels are as follows.

Item	Quantity	Price	Minimum stock level
Building sand	1 tonne	£15.00	25
Grit sand	1 tonne	£10.00	10
Gravel	1 tonne	£40.00	10
Yorkshire flagstones	1 square metre	£50.00	10
Concrete paving blocks	1 square metre	£10.00	100
Yorkshire stone blocks	1 square metre	£65.00	25
Cement	25 Kg	£5.00	50
Concrete common bricks	Each	£0.25	1000
Red bricks	Each	£0.45	5000
Blue engineering bricks	Each	£0.80	1000

Ron wants to be able to set up a blank invoice for the next customer. He needs to be able to change the prices easily. He also wants the spreadsheet set up so that you cannot delete formulas and data by mistake.

The system must prevent anyone from ordering an item if it is not in stock.

(See Tips and tricks number 46 and 47.)

2 Print4U

Client: Harry Price

Organisation: Print4U – a printing company in Bradford

Client's position: Owner

The problem:

Print4U print leaflets, posters and flyers for customers, in all sizes from A0 to A7.

They can print in colour or in only one colour (usually black). This is called monochrome.

They print on various thickness of paper from 70 gram per square metre up to 250 gram per square metre. The thicker the paper, the more it costs.

At present Harry works out all quotes with a calculator and writes out quotations by hand. Harry has asked you to use spreadsheet software to set up an easy-to-use quotation system for them which will automatically work out the cost of printing and create a professional-looking quotation displaying the quote. He wants to be able to print this quote at the click of a button.

The prices per 1000 copies in monochrome are:

Paper size	70 gram	80 gram	100 gram	150 gram	200 gram	250 gram
A0	£756	£860	£1,121	£1,225	£1,616	£1,955
A1	£398	£453	£590	£645	£851	£1,029
A2	£209	£238	£310	£339	£448	£542
A3	£110	£125	£163	£179	£236	£285
A4	£58	£66	£86	£94	£124	£150
A5	£32	£37	£48	£52	£69	£83
A6	£18	£20	£27	£29	£38	£46
A7	£10	£11	£15	£16	£21	£26

Full colour is 50 per cent extra. Glossy paper is 20 per cent extra. The printed work can be folded once or twice at an extra cost of £10 per 1000 copies per fold.

Prices for more than 1000 copies are on a pro rata basis. This means that to find the price of 3000 multiply by 3 and so on. Print4U do not accept orders of less than 1000.

Harry also wants to be able to clear the quote at the click of a button and to be able to change the prices easily. He also wants the spreadsheet set up so that he cannot accidentally delete formulas and data or enter data which is unacceptable.

He also wants to store the invoices and the names of the customers in a table and for the system to have an automatic front end.

3 Carla's Salon

Client: Carla Jenkinson

Organisation: Carla's Beauty Salon

Client's position: Owner

The problem:

Carla Jenkinson runs a beauty salon in South Wales. The services that she offers and the prices are as follows:

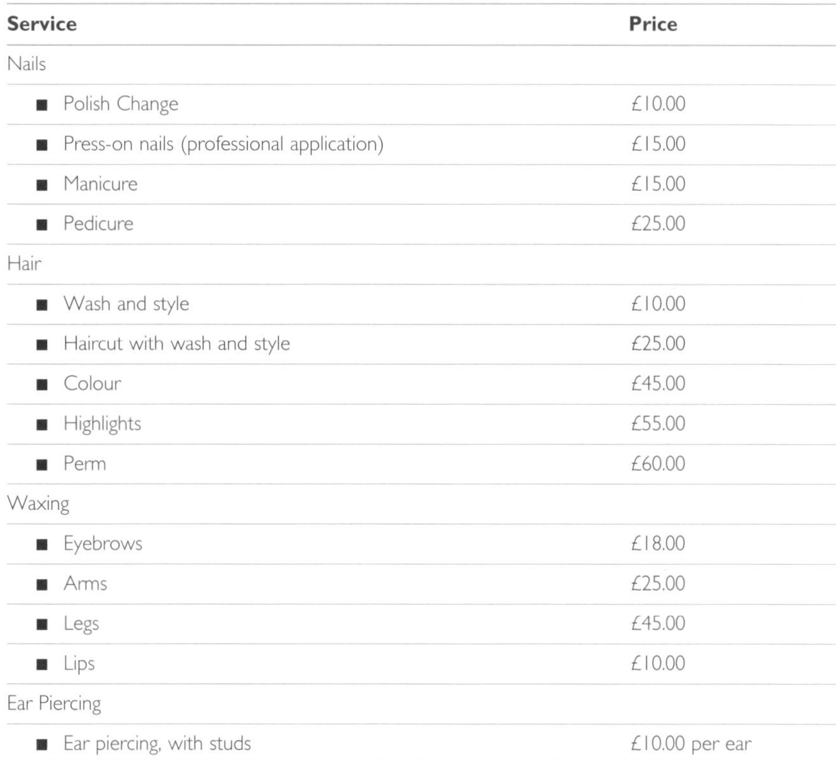

Service	Price
Nails	
■ Polish Change	£10.00
■ Press-on nails (professional application)	£15.00
■ Manicure	£15.00
■ Pedicure	£25.00
Hair	
■ Wash and style	£10.00
■ Haircut with wash and style	£25.00
■ Colour	£45.00
■ Highlights	£55.00
■ Perm	£60.00
Waxing	
■ Eyebrows	£18.00
■ Arms	£25.00
■ Legs	£45.00
■ Lips	£10.00
Ear Piercing	
■ Ear piercing, with studs	£10.00 per ear

Prices are reduced on some days of the week as follows: Monday and Tuesday 20 per cent off, Wednesday and Thursday 10 per cent off.

At present Carla works out all prices with a calculator and writes out receipts by hand.

Carla has asked you to use spreadsheet software to set up a pricing system for her which will automatically work out the cost of a beauty treatment and create a professional-looking receipt. She wants to be able to print this receipt at the click of a button.

Carla also wants to be able to clear the price calculations at the click of a button and to be able to change the prices easily. She also wants the spreadsheet set up so that you cannot delete formulas and data by mistake or enter data which is unacceptable.

She would like an automatic front end for the system.

4 Foreign exchange calculator

Client: Simon Smith

Organisation: Go Fast Travel

Client's position: Assistant

The problem:

Simon Smith works in a travel agency. Often customers want to be able to convert the local currency where they are going on holiday into UK pounds.

At present Simon carries out all calculations by hand but he realises that this is slow and may be inaccurate. He would like a computer system that will allow him to choose the country to be visited e.g. Italy from a list. It will display the currency in that country, e.g. Euros and also display the exchange rate for that currency. Simon can then enter a number of UK pounds and the system will convert this into the foreign currency. He will also be able to enter an amount of the foreign currency and then convert this into UK pounds.

All the details will be printed out at the touch of a button.

Simon also wants to be able to clear the calculations at the click of a button ready for the next customer and to be able to change the exchange rates easily. He also wants the spreadsheet set up so that he cannot accidentally delete formulas and data or enter data which is unacceptable, such as negative amounts.

Simon would like the system to operate so that the exchange rates are automatically updated from a website. (See Tips and tricks no. 43.)

5 Recording studio

Client: MC Slim Janie

Organisation: A recording studio called MC *Slim's* in Brighton. There are four different rooms that can be hired out by local musicians for up to four hours at a time.

Client's position: Owner

The problem:

MC Slim Janie owns a recording studio called MC *Slim's* in Brighton. She has four different rooms that she hires out to local musicians for up to four hours at a time.

At present MC Slim Janie works out all prices with a calculator and writes out invoices by hand.

MC Slim Janie wants you to use spreadsheet software to make an invoicing system which will work out the cost of using the studio and print an invoice at the click of a button.

MC Slim Janie also wants to be able to clear the invoice easily and to be able to change the prices. She also wants the spreadsheet set up so that you can't delete formulas and data by mistake and she also wants to prevent impossible data being entered.

MC Slim Janie wants to store all the invoices and the names of the customers in a table.

All details of rooms, prices and optional extras are given below:

Rooms are:

Studio 1	Eight track	£20 per hour
Studio 2	16 track	£50 per hour
Studio 3	32 track	£100 per hour
Studio 4	48 track	£150 per hour

Additional charges are as follows:

■ use of session musicians	£50 per musician per hour
■ video sessions	£30 per hour
■ use of grand piano	£60
■ either 24HD system	£25 per hour
■ or RADAR IZ 24	£35 per hour
■ UREI graphic equaliser	£30 per hour
■ sound technician	£20 per hour
■ instrument hire	from £10 per hour

6 Golf scoreboard

Client: Debbie Green

Organisation: North Dunbar Golf Club

Client's position: Secretary

The problem:

A number of tournaments are held every year at the club. Most tournaments are for one round of 18 holes.

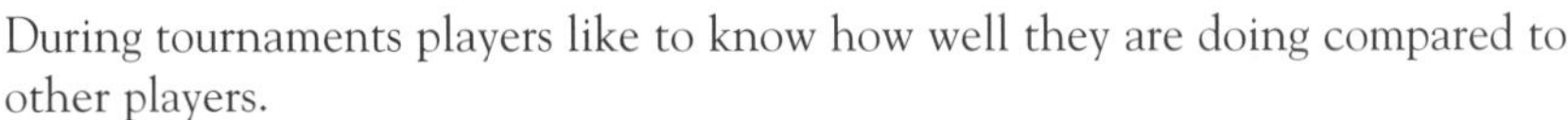

During tournaments players like to know how well they are doing compared to other players.

Debbie would like to use a spreadsheet system to record the scores. The system would need to:

- store the names of the players and their handicap
- allow the score for each player to be entered for each hole
- store the par score for each hole
- calculate each player's total score so far, e.g. 63 after 14 holes
- calculate each player's total score compared with par, e.g. 3 over par
- sort the scores compared with par into order
- display the leaderboard for current leading players
- calculate the final score for the round and take off any handicap.

Debbie wants a template that can be used for each tournament. She also wants the spreadsheet set up so that she can't delete formulas and data by mistake or enter any impossible data.

7 Green Valley Car Hire

Client: Lisa McClure

Organisation: Green Valley Car Hire

Client's position: Owner

The problem:

Green Valley Car Hire rent cars to local businesses for periods from one day to two weeks. They have around 15 different cars on their books and hire to 12 different businesses. The prices are:

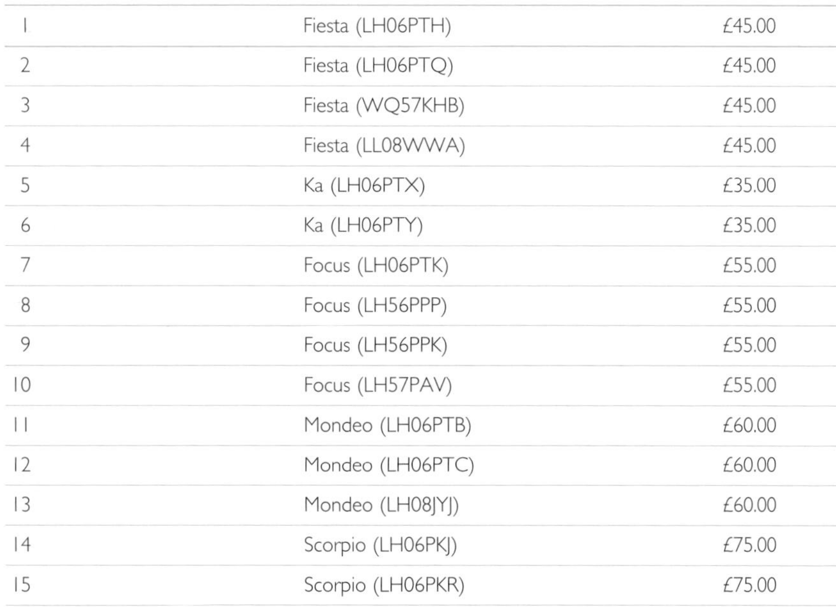

1	Fiesta (LH06PTH)	£45.00
2	Fiesta (LH06PTQ)	£45.00
3	Fiesta (WQ57KHB)	£45.00
4	Fiesta (LL08WWA)	£45.00
5	Ka (LH06PTX)	£35.00
6	Ka (LH06PTY)	£35.00
7	Focus (LH06PTK)	£55.00
8	Focus (LH56PPP)	£55.00
9	Focus (LH56PPK)	£55.00
10	Focus (LH57PAV)	£55.00
11	Mondeo (LH06PTB)	£60.00
12	Mondeo (LH06PTC)	£60.00
13	Mondeo (LH08JYJ)	£60.00
14	Scorpio (LH06PKJ)	£75.00
15	Scorpio (LH06PKR)	£75.00

Charge is per day – any 24 hour period

- Cars can be hired for up to 14 days
- 25 per cent discount for more than 3 days

Additional charges are as follows:

■ Insurance. No excess	£7 per day
■ Additional driver	£10 per day
■ Bring back with fuel empty	£35
■ International insurance	£12 per day
■ AA cover or	£5 per day
■ RAC cover or	£4.50 per day
■ Green Flag cover	£4.65 per day

The owner, Lisa McClure, calculates the price with a calculator. Now she wants a computer system to work out the charges. She has asked you to help.

Lisa wants you to use spreadsheet software to make an invoicing system which will work out the cost of hiring a car and print an invoice at the click of a button. She also wants to be able to clear the quote at the click of a button and to be able to change the prices easily. She also wants the spreadsheet set up so that you can't delete formulas and data by mistake.

She would like the system to have an automatic front end.

8 Shed orders

Client: Alan Rivers

Organisation: Alan Rivers Sheds

Client's position: Owner

The problem:

Alan makes garden sheds and sells them through eBay. He makes eight different sheds.

He works out the cost of a shed on scraps of paper in his workshop. He knows this is not good enough and wants a computer system to calculate the costs and store all the orders. He has asked you to help.

The prices are given below:

1	Warwick	£ 99.00
2	Stafford	£115.00
3	Leicester	£125.00
4	Derby	£145.00
5	Nottingham	£165.00
6	Lancaster	£175.00
7	Lincoln	£199.00
8	York	£225.00

Additional charges are as follows:	
■ Yale door lock or	£10
■ Three lever lock or	£30
■ Five lever lock	£50
■ Shed insurance	£32 for twelve months
■ Shed fire extinguisher	£24.99
■ Sooper-dooper roof felt	£43.99
■ Maxi-Guttering	£48.99

Alan Rivers wants you to use spreadsheet software to make an invoicing system which will work out the cost of a shed and print an invoice at the click of a button.

He also wants to be able to clear the quote at the press of a button and to be able to change the prices easily. He also wants the spreadsheet set up so that you can't delete formulas and data by mistake.

He also would like to store details of the invoices and customers in a table.

9 Departmental stationery account

Client: Marian Wilkins

Organisation: Snetterton High

Client's position: Head of English Department

The problem:

The English department has a stationery budget to be spent on items such as A4 lined paper, white board pens, document wallets.

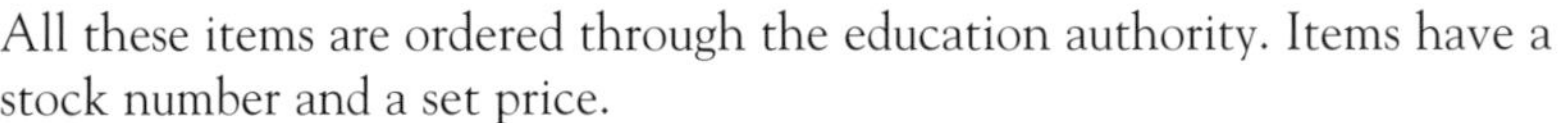

All these items are ordered through the education authority. Items have a stock number and a set price.

Marian would like a spreadsheet where she can put in the stock number and the quantity of the order and the computer system will calculate the cost and the remaining balance.

Details of items ordered would be stored along with the starting balance. Marian would like to predict likely year-end figures.

She wants the system to look professional and to be able to produce meaningful graphs of budget.

She also wants the spreadsheet set up so that she cannot accidentally delete formulas and data or enter data which is unacceptable.

10 Orders for a joke shop

Client: James McKay

Organisation: Jim's Jokes is a joke shop in Nottingham that sells items by mail order, mainly to smaller joke shops around England.

Client's position: Owner

The problem:

The work of the shop has expanded in recent months and they can no longer cope with storing sales on paper. They have asked you to help.
Jim's Jokes sells twenty different items.

1	Big squeaky spider	£1.50
2	Cockroach	£0.75
3	Exploding lighter	£6.99
4	Exploding pen	£9.50
5	Fake fried egg	£2.50
6	Fake parking ticket	£1.25
7	False teeth	£2.50
8	Fake sick	£5.00
9	Fang caps glow in dark	£1.99
10	Fly in ice cube	£2.00
11	Fun blood	£3.99
12	Glow in the dark spider	£3.50
13	Loaded dice	£3.00
14	Long fangs	£10.00
15	Monster teeth	£1.25
16	Rubber snake	£4.29
17	Stink bombs (5)	£9.99
18	Tarantula	£1.50
19	Vampire teeth	£2.25
20	Vicar's teeth	£1.45

Jim's Jokes want you to use spreadsheet software to make a professional invoicing system which will work out the cost of an order and print an invoice.

James also wants to be able to clear the quote at the press of a button and to be able to change the prices easily. He also wants the spreadsheet set up so that you can't delete formulas and data by mistake.

He would like to store the invoices and the names of the customers in a table and have an automatic front end for the system.

11 Carpets R Us

Client: Richie Fitzsimons

Organisation: Carpets R Us who sell carpets throughout the country

Client's position: Store manager

The problem:

At present Carpets R Us work out all prices with a calculator and write out invoices by hand. The cost of a carpet depends on its area in square metres, although all carpets start as a rectangular shape. As a result the area is the length (in metres) times the breadth (in metres).

The types of carpet available are:

Type	**Price per square metre**
Berber	£12.99
Wool	£19.99
Nylon	£11.99
Olefin	£9.99
Polyester	£10.99
Acrylics	£12.99
Sisal	£7.99

Optional extras include:	
■ Underlay	£3.99 per square metre
■ Fitting	£50.00 per room
■ Carpet gripper	£17.99 per door in the room
■ Stainmaster treatment	£60.00
■ Extended 5 year warranty	£119

Carpets R Us have asked you to use spreadsheet software to set up an invoicing system for them which will automatically work out the cost of the carpet and create a professional-looking invoice. They want to be able to print the invoice at the click of a button.

Carpets R Us also want to be able to clear the quote at the press of a button and to be able to change the prices easily. They also want the spreadsheet set up so that you can't delete formulas and data by mistake.

All carpets are subject to 17.5 per cent VAT. You must show the VAT on the invoice.

12 Rugby scoreboard

Client: Reg Winter

Organisation: Netherton Rugby Club

Client's position: Club secretary

The problem:

Reg Winter is responsible for the scoreboard that keeps the score during matches. He employs a young student to operate the scoreboard, putting up the numbers when a try or goal is scored.

Reg thinks that an electronic scoreboard linked to a scoring system on his laptop would make it much easier. Essentially he wants the solution to be automatic and remove the need for paying a youngster.

Reg has suggested that there are different buttons on the screen to represent, for example, a try for Netherton (5 points) and a try for visitors (5 points) etc.

The solution must display the name of the visiting team, must be able to reset back to 0–0 at the end of the game and prevent the accidental deletion of any data. There should be a way of undoing an error in case a try has been disallowed. Also it must store the final result and the date of the match in a table.

More project ideas can be found on the website that supports this book.

Practice assignments

1 Happy Days

Mr and Mrs Steven Robins
request the honour of your presence
at the marriage of their daughter
Megan Elizabeth
to
Mr Charles Henderson
at St Mary's Church, Netherfield
on Saturday 28 September 2008
at 2 p.m.

Client: Sandra Welsh

Organisation: Happy Days is a specialist company that designs and produces invitations to events such as weddings, christenings, house warming parties, 40th birthday parties, etc. Prices are not cheap but this reflects the high quality of the invitations.

Client's position: Accounts clerk

The problem:

Sandra wants a reliable way of calculating the costs of printing the invitations and printing an invoice.

Invitations are normally A6 size. The company uses three different thicknesses of card: standard, luxury and superior. Happy Days will produce any number from 20 to 1000.

The prices per invitation are:

Quality	Price each
Standard	£0.57
Luxury	£0.95
Superior	£1.35

Happy Days will produce any number from 20 to 1000.

At present Happy Days works out all quotes with a calculator and writes out quotations by hand. Happy Days has asked you to set up a system for them, which will automatically work out the cost of the invitations and create a professional-looking invoice displaying the number of cards to be printed, the choices made, the type of party and the amount of the quote.

They want to be able to print this quote at the click of a button.

Optional extras	
Gold leaf print	£0.25 extra
Gold leaf edging	£0.30 extra
Crinkle edge	£0.10 extra
Embossed	£0.35 extra

Happy Days also wants to be able to clear the quote at the click of a button and to be able to change the prices easily. They also want the system set up so that they cannot delete formulas and data by mistake or enter data that is unacceptable.

They would like an automatic front end for the system.

2 Planet Fireplace

Client: Sally McLeish

Organisation: Planet Fireplace is a shop that sells fireplaces. The shop is at 67 High Street, Wilmington, WN3 8KW. The phone number is (0119) 451 1122.

Client's position: Proprietor

The problem:

When customers buy a fireplace, they have to buy a fire, a surround and a fret (the decorative front of the fire).

Sally would like a computer system that will allow her to enter customers' choices easily, automatically calculate the total cost including the VAT, easily produce and print a delivery note, easily produce and print a professional invoice for the customer and allow her to edit the prices of all the products.

The prices are given below. Some frets are free. Other frets cost as much as £30.

The surround can be 42, 48 or 54 inches wide but this makes no difference to the cost. For an extra £100, the customer can have a remote control for their fire. The customer can collect the fireplace themselves or get it delivered for £25. Planet Fireplace will install the fireplace for a customer if required for £100. All costs, (price, delivery and installation) are subject to VAT at 17.5 per cent.

Fires

Name	Manufacturer	Price	Type
Airflame Convector 16	Wonder Fires	£324.00	coal effect
Airflame Convector 18	Wonder Fires	£345.00	coal effect
Atlanta chimney glass front	Flavel Leisure	£349.99	pebble
Belvedere Gas Brass	Robinson Willey	£270.00	coal effect
Blenheim C1 hotbox	Valor	£189.99	log effect
Blenheim slimline	Valor	£199.99	coal effect
Ceram 60	Matchless	£350.00	coal effect
Class I/II Hot Box	Real Cozy Fires	£189.99	pebble
Crystal Sunrise	Crystal fires	£528.00	pebble
Designer Elegance Black	Focal Point	£320.00	log effect

Frets

Name	Manufacturer	Price
Blenheim Black Front	Sirocco	£0.00
Blenheim Brass Front	Sirocco	£0.00
Blenheim Silver Front	Sirocco	£0.00
Royal Black	Sirocco	£10.00
Royal Chrome	Sirocco	£10.00
Style Front	Sirocco	£30.00

Surrounds

Name	Manufacturer	Price
Adelaide	Antique Pine	£219.99
Barcelona	Marble	£615.00
Belmont	Light oak	£327.00
Celtic	Cast iron	£328.00
Cranborme	Limestone	£599.00

6 Documenting your project

An ICT project is much more than just setting up the system using Microsoft Excel. You must also include additional documentation such as:

- Specification requirements
- Design
- Implementation
- Testing
- A user guide
- Technical documentation
- Evaluation

The following pages show you how to document your system by looking at some of the documentation provided with the Denton Gazette system.

Note:
1 This documentation is not complete but each section offers examples, pointers and hints to what is considered good practice.
2 Specifications for different qualifications have different requirements. Always check the specification.

1 Contents section

A contents page is very useful; it will help you check that every part of your documentation is present and also help the person who will mark your project to find the various sections.

Denton Gazette

Contents

2 Introduction

In this section you need to give some of the background to your proposed system and its requirements. You will need to answer questions like:

- Who is the client?
- Who is the user?
- What is the problem?
- Why do they want a spreadsheet solution?

Who is the client?

The *Denton Gazette* is a weekly newspaper in the small town of Denton. The client is the owner of the *Denton Gazette*, Janice Peters.

What is the problem?

Dozens of local businesses advertise in the *Gazette*. Advertisements can be in colour or black and white, they can be a full page, a half page, a quarter page, an eighth of a page or a twelfth of a page.

The cost of an advertisement depends on:

- the size of the advertisement; a table of prices is given below
- whether the advertisement is in black and white or in colour
- the page on which the advertisement will be printed

SIZE	COST
Full page	£560.00
Half page	£300.00
Quarter page	£160.00
Eighth page	£85.00
Twelfth page	£60.00

This is the cost of a black and white advertisement on an inside page. A colour advertisement costs 30 per cent more.

If an advertisement is on the front page, it costs an extra 50 per cent. If the advertisement is on the back page it costs an extra 40 per cent. Advertisements on either the front page or the back page cannot be bigger than a quarter of the page.

Advertisers can book for up to 26 weeks. If they book for between four and nine consecutive weeks they get a discount of 10 per cent. If they book for ten or more consecutive weeks they get a discount of 20 per cent.

At present when someone places an order for an advertisement in the newspaper, the cost of the advertisement is calculated manually.

The owner of the *Denton Gazette,* Janice Peters, is worried about errors in the calculations and would like an easy-to-use computer system that will calculate the price of placing advertisements in the newspaper. The system must use the company's colour scheme of green and light green, use Verdana for their house font and use the company logo of a dove.

Who is the user?

The system will be used by Katie Walker, the accounts clerk at the *Gazette* who currently deals with all advertisements, calculates the costs, sends the invoices, and files details in the filing cabinet.

Katie is highly IT-literate and has a computer on her desk that she uses for word-processing. However she will need a comprehensive user guide to show her how to use the new system.

Such a system would be faster and more reliable than the present manual system.

3 User requirements

In this section you need to make a list of all of the requirements of the user. What exactly do they need?

You will probably need to interview your user/client to find out these requirements. The user and the client may be the same person but in this example, they are not. Everything that they require must be listed. When you have set up the system, you will need to test that you have met every requirement.

It is a good idea to number the requirements.

What are the user requirements?

Examples of user requirements for the *Denton Gazette* system are as follows:

1 A system is required to be able to give a quick quotation accurately and efficiently.

2 The system should enable phone enquiries to be dealt with far more quickly than at present.

3 Issued quotes need to be stored with the facility to view them at a later date.

4 The system must be user-friendly, yet have a professional look and feel.

5 The system should be easy to transfer easily between the laptop and office-based PC.

6 It must be easy to access the price details and amend them when necessary.

4 Inputs, processing and outputs

Once you have made a list of the user requirements, you will need to work out the inputs, processes and outputs for your solution.

You may find it easiest to start with the outputs – what information must the solution provide? From here work backwards to find out what data must be entered to get these outputs. Then specify what processes must take place to turn the inputs into outputs.

Give as much detail as possible about the outputs. What format are they in? Give some examples.

Defining the inputs

Some solutions may require that the user enters data like a name, a date of birth and a price.

Don't just say that the input data will be the name, date of birth and price. State exactly what format the data will be in and give an example.

Input examples

Title (one of Mr, Mrs, Miss, Ms), e.g. Ms

Surname maximum 20 characters, e.g. Brown

Forename maximum 15 characters, e.g. Kathryn

Date of birth in form dd/mm/yyyy, e.g. 17/06/1992

Price: in pounds to 2 decimal places, e.g. £5.99

If the input data is chosen from a list (such as the Title above) give all the possible choices.

Inputs

The user needs to input:

- customer name (this is the company name so is only one field)
- customer address in four fields; the last field is the post code
- the date from the computer's clock (format dd/mm/yyyy)
- size of the advertisement (full page, half page, quarter page, eighth page or twelfth page)
- the colour of the advertisement (colour or black and white)
- the position of the advertisement (front, back or inside page)
- the number of weeks (1 to 26)
- the standard prices for advertisements particularly if there is any change (see page 163).

Defining the processing

Examples of processing that you might use in other solutions include:

- calculating
- looking up data in a table
- making decisions such as in IF statements
- sorting (into a specified order)
- searching
- grouping information.

Again make sure that you say exactly what the processing involves, no matter how obvious it may seem.

Processes

The system needs to be able to:

- look up the cost of each size of advertisement from a table of costs (see page 163)
- calculate the additional cost of colour or black and white
- calculate the additional cost of the advert position
- calculate the basic price without discount by adding the above components
- calculate the discount based on number of weeks
- subtract discount to work out final cost
- clear the calculations for the next customer through clicking just one button
- automatically store the information on a separate sheet.

Defining the outputs

If the output is an invoice, don't just say that the output is an invoice. Describe what information must be on the invoice. This is likely to include:

- company details – name, address, post code, phone number, fax number, email address
- customer details – name, address, post code
- the date
- the invoice number
- the word 'invoice'
- a list of all the items purchased

- the quantity of each item
- the total cost of each item
- the sum of these total costs
- the VAT at 17.5 per cent
- the grand total
- payment details.

You should specify the format of the date. For example, is it 15/11/08 or 15 November 2008? You should specify the format of other data. For example, will the customer name be one field or more than one field? What fields are necessary to store the address?

It is a good idea to give examples of output.

Outputs

The system should produce:

- on-screen quotation that is clear and easy to understand, including the final total and the discount in Verdana font to include the date, the customer details, colour scheme and the options chosen
- an on-screen file of the quotations supplied to customers including the customer name and address, the date the quotation was issued in format dd/mm/yyyy, the choices made and the total costs, e.g.

15/04/2008	Gibbs and Gibbs	7 High Street	Denton	Cheshire	DN6 9AB	Full page	Colour	Inside pages	14 weeks	£8,153.60

- a printed version of this quotation to include details of header and footer, position of logo, orientation of print, size of paper.

5 Design

The project should be broken down into clear sub-tasks or modules, which should relate to the user requirements. Present these tasks in an order of build. Produce design plans for each sub-task.

It usually takes much longer to produce designs on computer than by hand so it is best to hand draw your design plans. Use one side of A4 for each worksheet and use a ruler.

It is a good idea to draw your designs on a blank grid from an Excel spreadsheet.

Good spreadsheet designs will include details of:

- sheet naming, named cells and cell ranges
- validation and cell protection
- labels and formulas used
- links between sheets
- general sheet layouts
- interfaces and screen designs
- macros and macro buttons
- any customised outputs.

The designs for the sub-tasks highlighted in bold are shown below.

Sub-tasks

I will break the *Denton Gazette* problem down into the following sub-tasks:

1. Creating the Prices worksheet with details of prices of advertisements.
2. **Creating the Quotation worksheet with the input controls to enter the details of the advertisement.**
3. Creating a LOOKUP function on the Quotation worksheet to bring in the price data.
4. Creating the Quotation worksheet by entering formulas used in calculating the quotation.
5. Creating formulas to calculate the final price of the quotation.
6. **Creating the QuoteFile worksheet to store details of quotations issued.**
7. **Automating the filing of quotations using a macro.**
8. **Automating clearing the current screen.**
9. Automating navigation of the system using macros and buttons.
10. Preventing impossible combinations.
11. Protecting the sheet from accidental deletion.
12. Customising the interface and added finishing touches.
13. **Adding the Front End.**

The designs for the sub-tasks highlighted in bold are shown below.

Hints

- Do present your plans in a format such that a reasonably competent person could take them and make a start on setting up your system.
- Do make them legible and neat. This person must be able to read them.
- Don't use screenshots from the actual system as part of your design plans.

Sub-task 2

The Quotation worksheet

Figure 6. 1 ▼

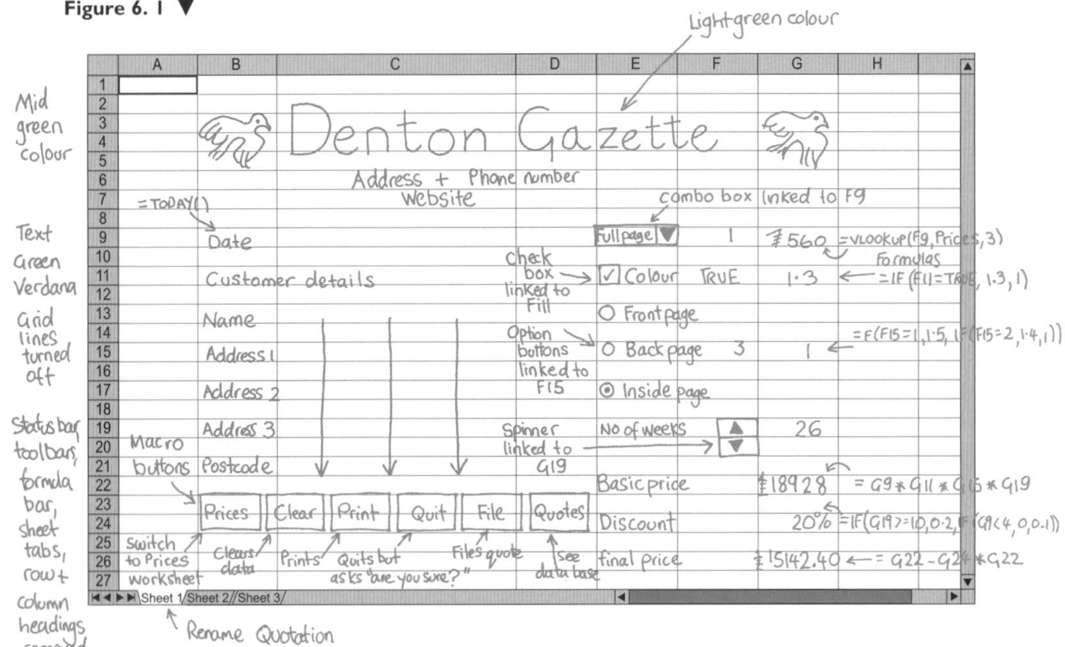

Sub-task 6

The QuoteFile worksheet

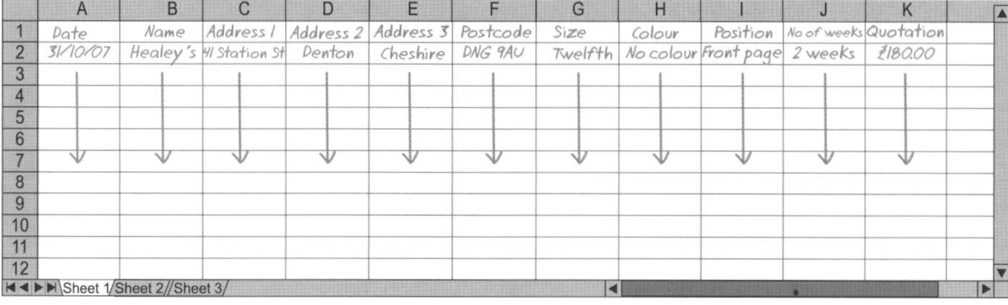

	A	B	C	D	E	F	G	H	I	J	K
1	Date	Name	Address 1	Address 2	Address 3	Postcode	Size	Colour	Position	No of weeks	Quotation
2	31/10/07	Healey's	41 Station St	Denton	Cheshire	DNG 9AU	Twelfth	No colour	Front page	2 weeks	£180.00
3											
4											
5											
6											
7											
8											
9											
10											
11											
12											

Figure 6. 2 ▲

Sub-task 7

Macro to file the quotations

The macro must:

1 Go to the QuoteFile worksheet
2 Select row 2
3 Insert a row
4 Go back to Quotation worksheet
5 Select cells A31 to G31
6 Copy
7 Go back to Quotation worksheet
8 Paste Special > Paste Values
9 Click on cell C13
10 Press the Escape key
11 End

Sub-task 8

Macro to clear the screen

The macro must:

1 Select the Quotation worksheet
2 Select cells C13, C15, C17, C19, C21, F9, F11, F15 and G19
3 Clear the contents
4 Select cell C13
5 Display a message box to say 'Quotation cleared for next customer'
6 End

Sub-task 13

The Start-up screen and options

Figure 6. 3 ▶

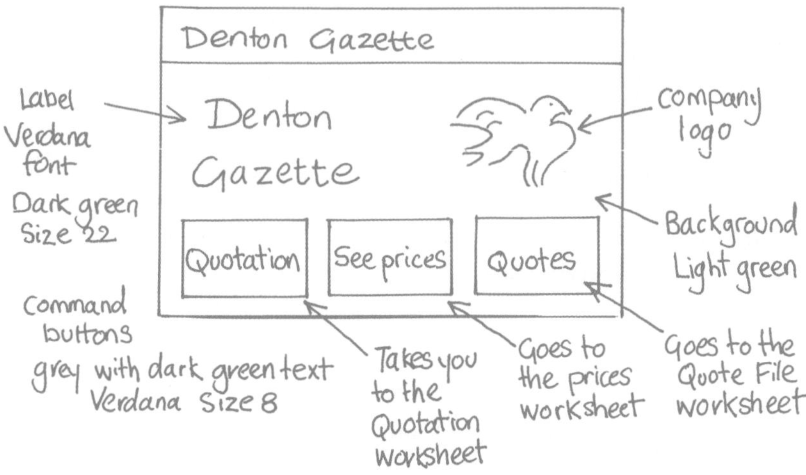

6 Implementation report

This section should contain clear evidence that you have implemented each part of your system.

This is likely to include the following as evidence of work done:

- an annotated screenshot of every worksheet
- printouts from the system
- a screenshot in formula view of any worksheet containing formulas
- annotated coding of any macros used
- screenshots of any UserForms, message boxes used
- commentary on the work you have done.

In setting up the system, I have performed the following tasks:

1. **Set up the Prices worksheet with details of prices of advertisements**
2. **Set up the Quotation worksheet with the input controls to enter the details of the advertisement**
3. Set up a LOOKUP function on the Quotation worksheet to bring in the price data
4. Set up the Quotation worksheet by entering formulas used in calculating the quotation
5. **Set up formulas to calculate the final price of the quotation**
6. Set up the QuoteFile worksheet to store details of quotations issued
7. Automated the filing of quotations using a macro
8. **Automated clearing the current screen to enter a new quotation using a macro**
9. Added navigation buttons for the system
10. **Prevented impossible combinations**
11. Protected the sheet from accidental deletion
12. Customised the interface and added finishing touches
13. **Added the Front End**

Six of the steps are documented in this section as examples of documentation. The tasks documented are shown above in bold. The implementation section would go on to explain and illustrate how each of the other sub-tasks was implemented.

1. Setting up the Prices worksheet with details of prices of advertisements

I named this worksheet **Prices**. I entered the sizes and prices. Each size has a number attached in column A which will later be used to lookup the price.

I named the area A2 to C6 **Prices**.

Figure 6. 4 ▶

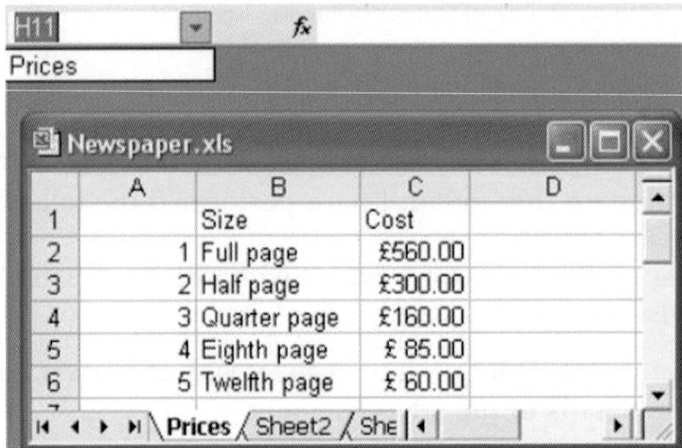

2. Setting up the Quotation worksheet with the input controls to enter the details of the advertisement

This part of the system deals with the part of the worksheet where the advertisement options are entered as in Figure 6.5. I named this worksheet **Quotation**.

Figure 6. 5 ▶

I dragged a combo box over cell E9 and linked it to cell F9. I set the input range to Prices!B2:B6. This will make the drop-down display the sizes listed in column B on the Prices worksheet.

In cell E11 I placed a checkbox linked to cell F11. It returns TRUE when checked and FALSE when not.

Three option buttons were placed over cells E13 to F17 and linked to cell F15. The number returned in F15 gives the position of the advertisement, 1 for front page, 2 for back page and 3 for inside pages.

I set a spinner control over cells F19 and F20 linked to cell G19, setting the minimum value to 1 and maximum to 26 to allow for up to 26 weeks.

5. Calculating the final price of the quotation

The basic price of the quotation is calculated by multiplying the numbers in G9, G11, G15 and G19 of the Quotation worksheet.

The discount is calculated using the formula

=IF(G19>=10,0.2,IF(G19<4,0,0.1))

The final price is then the basic price minus the discount. The formulas are shown in Figure 6.6.

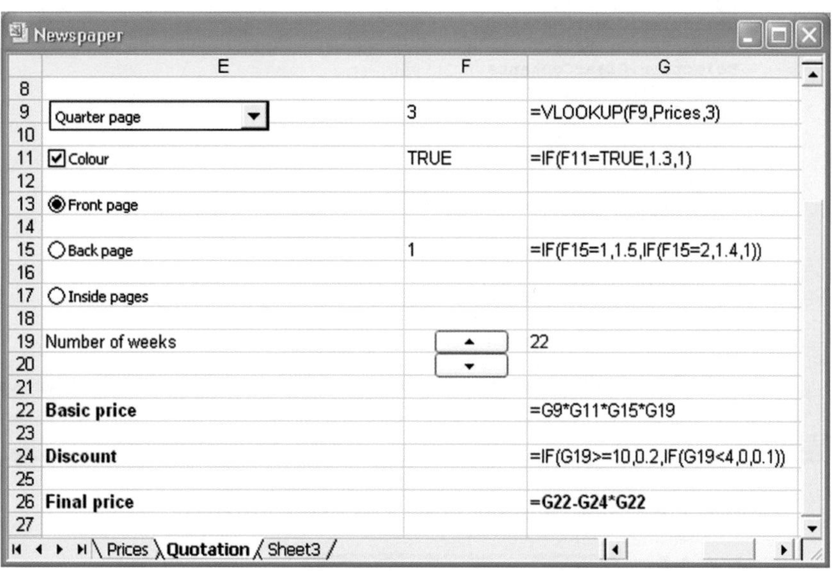
Newspaper

	E	F	G
8			
9	Quarter page	3	=VLOOKUP(F9,Prices,3)
10			
11	Colour	TRUE	=IF(F11=TRUE,1.3,1)
12			
13	Front page		
14			
15	Back page	1	=IF(F15=1,1.5,IF(F15=2,1.4,1))
16			
17	Inside pages		
18			
19	Number of weeks		22
20			
21			
22	**Basic price**		=G9*G11*G15*G19
23			
24	**Discount**		=IF(G19>=10,0.2,IF(G19<4,0,0.1))
25			
26	**Final price**		**=G22-G24*G22**
27			

Prices / Quotation / Sheet3

Figure 6. 6 ▶

8. Automatically clearing the current screen to enter a new quotation

I need to clear the screen for a new quotation.

The cells on the screen that need clearing are cells C13, C15, C17, C19, C21, F9, F11, F15 and G19 of the Quotation worksheet.

I recorded a macro called **Clear**. I highlighted in turn the cells C13, C15, C17, C19, C21, F9, F11, F15 and G19 using CTRL and click. I then clicked **Edit > Clear > Contents.**

I finished the macro by adding a message box to say that the data had been cleared for the next customer.

The macro code generated is shown below.

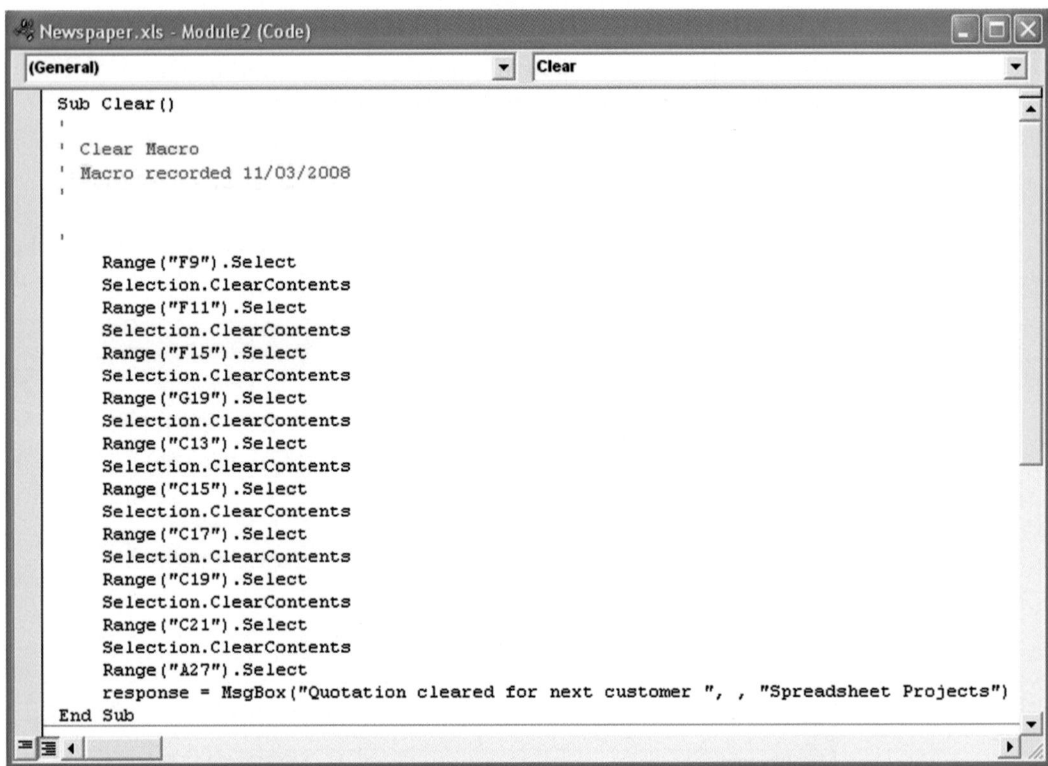

Newspaper.xls - Module2 (Code)
(General)
Clear
Sub Clear()
'
' Clear Macro
' Macro recorded 11/03/2008
'

'
Range("F9").Select
Selection.ClearContents
Range("F11").Select
Selection.ClearContents
Range("F15").Select
Selection.ClearContents
Range("G19").Select
Selection.ClearContents
Range("C13").Select
Selection.ClearContents
Range("C15").Select
Selection.ClearContents
Range("C17").Select
Selection.ClearContents
Range("C19").Select
Selection.ClearContents
Range("C21").Select
Selection.ClearContents
Range("A27").Select
response = MsgBox("Quotation cleared for next customer ", , "Spreadsheet Projects")
End Sub

Figure 6. 7 ▲ The message box looks like Figure 6.8.

Figure 6. 8 ▶

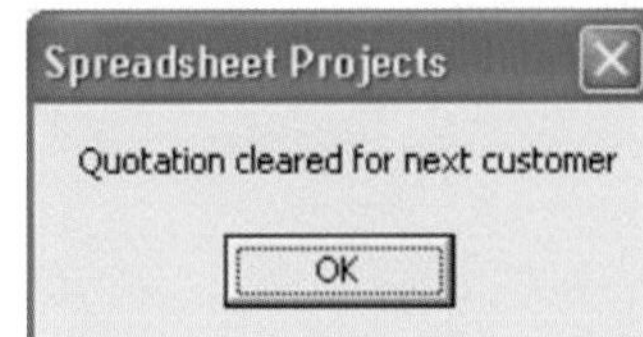

10. Preventing impossible combinations

It is not possible to have a full page or half page advertisement on the back or front pages. So I have written the following macro code to prevent this from happening.

Figure 6. 9 ▶

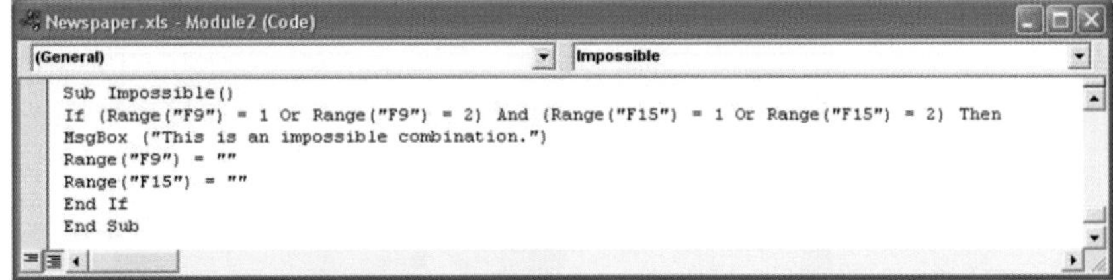

Newspaper.xls - Module2 (Code)

(General) | Impossible

```
Sub Impossible()
If (Range("F9") = 1 Or Range("F9") = 2) And (Range("F15") = 1 Or Range("F15") = 2) Then
MsgBox ("This is an impossible combination.")
Range("F9") = ""
Range("F15") = ""
End If
End Sub
```

The macro is called **Impossible** and is run whenever a user clicks on the first or the second option button. I have done this by assigning it to the option buttons using **Assign Macro**.

Figure 6. 10 ▶

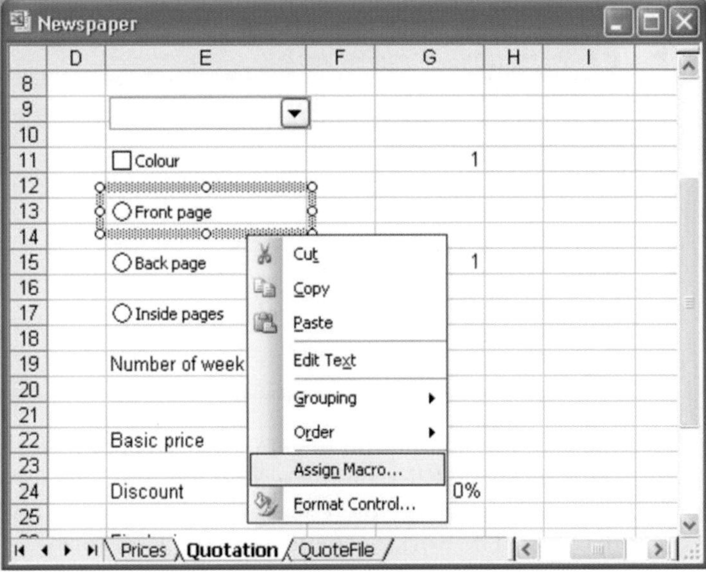

The second line of the macro checks if the value of F9 is 1 or 2 and the value of F15 is 1 or 2. These are the impossible combinations.

If an impossible combination has been chosen, the message box in Figure 6.11 appears and F9 and F15 are cleared. Acceptable combinations are allowed of course.

Figure 6. 11 ▶

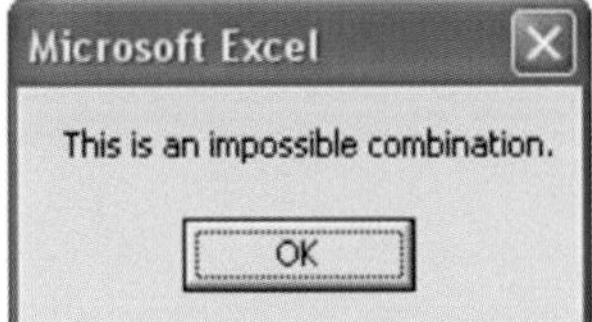

13. Adding the Front End

I have set up a UserForm using the Visual Basic Editor.

Figure 6. 12 ▶

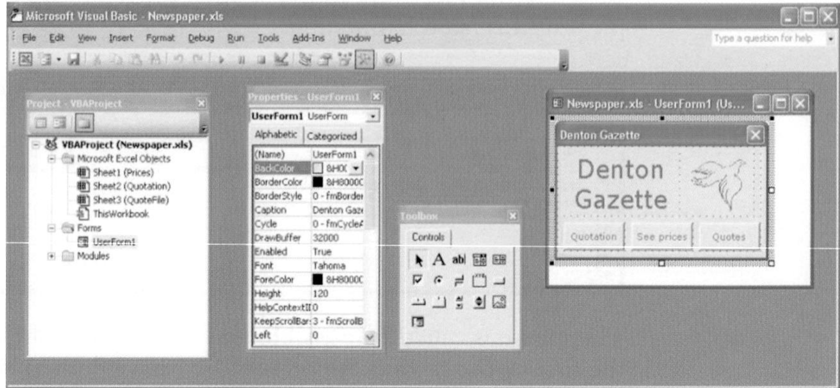

I have added commands to the three buttons as follows:

Figure 6. 13 ▶

Newspaper.xls - UserForm1 (Code)

CommandButton1 | Click

```
Private Sub CommandButton1_Click()
Sheets("Quotation").Select
UserForm1.Hide
End Sub

Private Sub CommandButton2_Click()
Sheets("Prices").Select
UserForm1.Hide
End Sub

Private Sub CommandButton3_Click()
Sheets("QuoteFile").Select
UserForm1.Hide
End Sub
```

Click on the first button to get to the Quotation worksheet and close the UserForm. Click on the second button to get to the Prices worksheet and close the UserForm. Click on the third button to get to the QuoteFile worksheet and close the UserForm.

I then wrote a macro called Box to load this UserForm.

Figure 6. 14 ▶

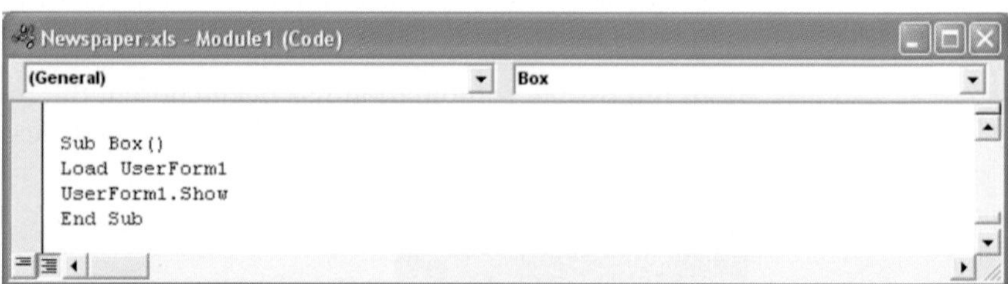

Newspaper.xls - Module1 (Code)

(General) | Box

```
Sub Box()
Load UserForm1
UserForm1.Show
End Sub
```

I then recorded a macro called **Auto_open** to remove the toolbars, sheet tabs, row and column headings, scroll bars, etc. This macro will run automatically when the file loads. I added a line at the end with the command Box to run the Box macro when the file loads.

Figure 6. 15 ▶

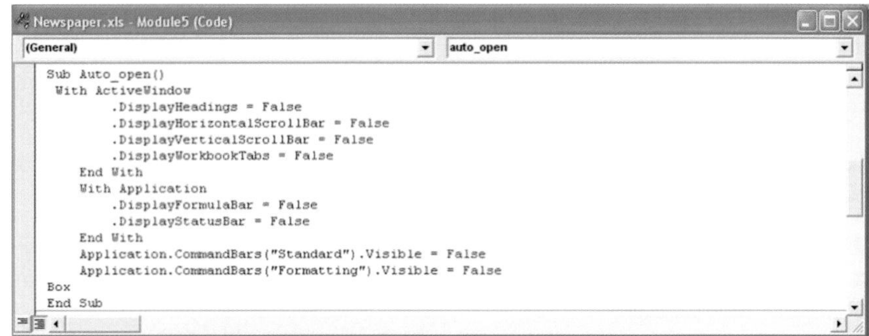

```
Sub Auto_open()
 With ActiveWindow
        .DisplayHeadings = False
        .DisplayHorizontalScrollBar = False
        .DisplayVerticalScrollBar = False
        .DisplayWorkbookTabs = False
    End With
    With Application
        .DisplayFormulaBar = False
        .DisplayStatusBar = False
    End With
    Application.CommandBars("Standard").Visible = False
    Application.CommandBars("Formatting").Visible = False
Box
End Sub
```

When you load the file the UserForm appears.

Figure 6. 16 ▶

I also recorded an **Auto_close** macro that replaces the toolbars, etc when the file is closed.

Implementation Hints

- Do be clear and concise.
- Do use screenshots to support your explanation.
- Describe clearly the features of the software you have used.
- Describe any validation you have included.
- Don't undersell the work you have done. Remember the person marking the project can only give credit for what they can see.
- Don't submit self-generating code and claim it as work done by you.
- Don't reproduce large tracts of Excel manuals.

7 Test plan

Testing is an integral part of developing an IT system. You should create a test plan and follow it.

The test plan should cover every aspect of your solution, saying exactly what will be tested, what the test (input) data will be and what the expected output data should be. Particular attention should be given to checking that the output from the system (in this case the advertisement price quotation) is correct.

Test plans should include a range of suitable test data together with expected outcomes. Your test plan should include tests that will ensure:

- output is 100 per cent accurate
- output is clear
- data input is validated
- printed output is as expected, e.g. all fitting on one side of A4
- that the solution meets the requirements of the user/client.

The test plan might say that the process of calculating the quotations will be tested for several different customers. The actual amount will also be calculated by the old method and the results compared.

Extreme data, for example, high but acceptable numbers or long double-barrelled surnames should be used to test that they fit. For example, work out the cost of the most expensive quotation. Does it fit in the column?

Erroneous test data such as impossible combinations will also be used in the tests and should be rejected. The system will also be tested by one of the staff of the *Denton Gazette* (user testing).

Tests in the test plan should:

- be numbered
- state the purpose of the test
- specify the test data to be used
- outline the expected result.

You may want to set the tests out in a table.

Include sets of test data – combinations of data that you will enter and check that the outputs are as expected.

It is not necessary to perform dozens of similar tests. For example, if data validation has been applied to many cells, it is not necessary to repeat the same test on each cell.

The test plan below gives examples of the sort of tests that will be required.

Test plan

Setting up the Quotation worksheet – testing the input controls for entering the details of the advertisement

Test Number	Purpose of Test	Test Data Used	Expected Outcome	Actual Outcome and Comments
1	Contents of Combo box	-	Should be full page, half page, quarter page, eighth page, twelfth page	
2	Combo box	Eighth page	Returns 4 in F9	
3	Test Check box returns TRUE/FALSE	Check the check box and uncheck it	Returns TRUE/FALSE in F11	
4	Test Option buttons	Back page	Returns 2 in F15	
5	Test the Spinner control	Increment spinner	Number in G19 should vary from 1 to 26	

Preparing the Quotations – testing the options

Test Number	Purpose of Test	Test Data Used	Expected Outcome	Actual Outcome and Comments
6	Test VLOOKUP in G9 returns correct price	Twelfth page	Price should be £60	
7	Test VLOOKUP in G9 returns correct price	Full page	Price should be £560	
8	Test IF function in G11 returns correct value	Check colour	1.3 is returned in G11	
9	Test nested IF function in G15 returns correct value	Check front page	1.5 is returned in G15	
10	Test discount – boundary test	Spinner set at 10 weeks	Discount is 20%	
11	Test discount – boundary test	Spinner set at 9 weeks	Discount is 10%	
12	Test discount – boundary test	Spinner set at 4 weeks	Discount is 10%	
13	Test discount – boundary test	Spinner set at 3 weeks	Discount is 0%	

Calculating the total cost of the quotation

Test Number	Purpose of Test	Test Data Used	Expected Outcome	Actual Outcome and Comments
14	Test the formulas in G22 and G26 calculate bill correctly	Data set 1 (see below)	Bill worked out on calculator Total cost = £1123.20	
...				

Data set 1

Quarter page, front page, colour, 4 weeks

McKenzie and McKenzie Ltd, 6 High Street, Denton, Cheshire, DN6 9BB

Data set 2

Full page, inside page, no colour, 3 weeks

Shelley and Reeves, 7 Station St, Denton, Cheshire, DN6 7YH

Data set 3

Twelfth page, back page, colour, 20 weeks

FW Reynolds and Son, 41 New Street, Denton, Cheshire, DN6 8GH

Data set 4

Full page, inside pages, colour, 26 weeks
Denton Opticians, 35 New Street, Denton, Cheshire, DN6 8GH

Automating the filing of quotations

Test Number	Purpose of Test	Test Data Used	Expected Outcome	Actual Outcome and Comments
17	Test the macro 'Filequote' to see if data is transferred correctly to the QuoteFile worksheet	Normal data, data set 2	On running the macro, details should appear in the QuoteFile sheet	
18	Test the macro 'Filequote' to see if data is transferred correctly to the QuoteFile worksheet and within the column widths set	Normal data BUT the longest name, data set 1	On running the macro, details should appear in the QuoteFile sheet	
19	Test the macro 'Filequote' when no data is entered	No data entered	A blank row should appear in the QuoteFile sheet	

Clearing the current screen to enter a new quotation

Test Number	Purpose of Test	Test Data Used	Expected Outcome	Actual Outcome and Comments
20	Test Clear macro	N/A	Screen should be clear of data	
21	Test Clear macro after it has been run once	No data	Screen should be clear of data	

Testing the Quit macro

Test Number	Purpose of Test	Test Data Used	Expected Outcome	Actual Outcome and Comments
22.	Test the Are you sure? message of the Quit macro		Message box appears. Choose yes – exits program. Choose no – returns to program	
...				

Testing impossible combinations

Test Number	Purpose of Test	Test Data Used	Expected Outcome	Actual Outcome and Comments
26	Checks impossible combinations are rejected	Front page, full page	Rejected. Error message appears and data is cleared	
27		Back page, full page	Rejected. Error message appears and data is cleared	
28		Front page, half page	Rejected. Error message appears and data is cleared	
29		Back page, half page	Rejected. Error message appears and data is cleared	
30		Inside pages, half page	Accepted	
31		Front page, quarter page	Accepted	
...				

Testing the display

Test Number Comments	Purpose of Test	Test Data Used	Expected Outcome	Actual Outcome and
36	To test that columns are wide enough to display the information	The highest possible priced quotation, data set 4	£15,142.40	

Customising the interface and finishing touches

Test Number Comments	Purpose of Test	Test Data Used	Expected Outcome	Actual Outcome and
37	Test the Auto_open macro starts the system correctly	N/A	System loads, removes Excel standard features and displays UserForm	
38	Test the Auto_close macro closes down the system properly	N/A	System closes and restores Excel standard features	

Testing the front end

Test Number	Purpose of Test	Test Data Used	Expected Outcome	Actual Outcome and Comments
39	Test the Quotation button	None, test button	Quotation worksheet loads. UserForm closes	
40	Test the See prices button	None, test button	Prices worksheet loads. UserForm closes	
41	Test the Quotes button	None, test button	QuoteFile worksheet loads UserForm closes.	

Hint: Many exam boards encourage the grouping of similar tests.

Printed output testing

Test Number	Purpose of Test	Test Data Used	Expected Outcome	Actual Outcome and Comments
42	Test that the printed output is as expected	The highest possible priced quotation, data set 4	Printed output fits onto a sheet of A4 paper. Details are clear. Final price = £15142.40.	

User test plan

Test Number	Purpose of Test	Test Data Used	Expected Outcome	Actual Outcome and Comments
43	Provide data sets 1, 2, 3 and 4 to the user and ask her to enter the data for each quotation, print the quotation, file the quotation	The highest possible priced quotation, data sets 1, 2, 3 and 4	Printed output fits onto a sheet of A4 paper. Details are clear. Totals are: £1123.20 £1680.00 £2184.00 £15142.40	
44	Install the system in the office of the *Denton Gazette* for a week for the staff to see if it meets their requirements			

Remember: Include your name and candidate number in the footer of your printed output.

8 Testing

You now need to follow your test plan to test that your spreadsheet is fully working.

The purpose of the testing is to try and provoke failure. Better to find the mistakes now than when installed at your user's office. Try to make your system go wrong!

Remember that you are testing whether the data is processed correctly, not just whether a button works or not.

You must provide evidence, in the form of screenshots and printouts. Number any output and cross-reference it to the number of the test that it refers to. Try to present the evidence next to the test plan as it is much easier for the marker. Try to avoid appendices at the back which make it harder to mark. Examples are shown below.

Check that the actual results match the expected results. Provide screenshots and outline any corrective action needed or taken.

The user should also be involved in testing or if there is not a real user get a friend to go through your system.

You could use a questionnaire and analyse the results.

They may comment on:

- its ease of use
- consistencies of layout, fonts, buttons, colours used
- look and feel of the interface
- simple vocabulary, spelling and grammar used.

Here is a selection of test results for the *Denton Gazette* system.

Test results

Setting up the Quotation worksheet

Test Number	Purpose of Test	Test Data Used	Expected Outcome	Actual Outcome and Comments
1	Contents of Combo box	-	Should be full page, half page, quarter page, eighth page, twelfth page	Full page, half page, quarter page, eighth page, twelfth page

Figure 6. 17 ▶

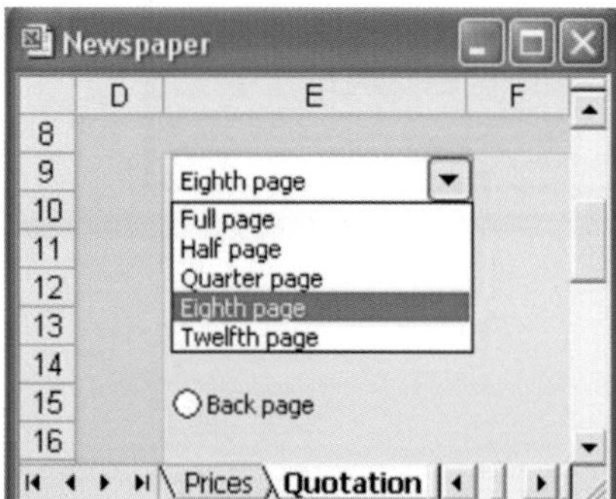

2	Combo box	Eighth page	Returns 4 in F9	Returns 4 in F9

Figure 6. 18 ▶

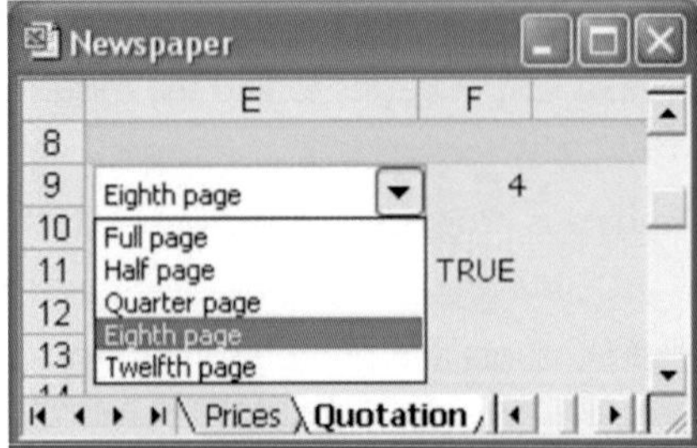

Preparing the Quotations – testing the options

Test Number	Purpose of Test	Test Data Used	Expected Outcome	Actual Outcome and Comments
6	Test VLOOKUP in G9 returns correct price	Twelfth page	Price should be £60	The price is £60

Figure 6. 19 ▶

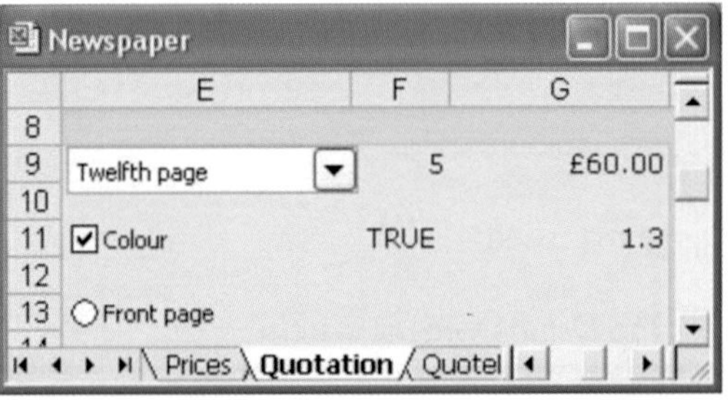

10	Test discount – boundary test	Spinner set at 10 weeks	Discount is 20%	Discount is 20%

Figure 6. 20 ▶

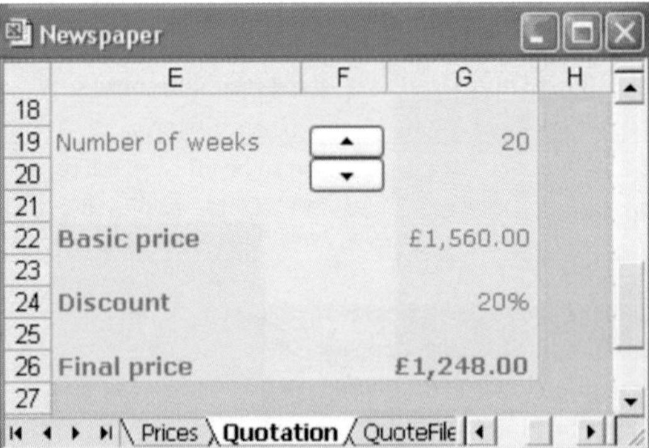

Calculating the total cost of the quotation

Test Number	Purpose of Test	Test Data Used	Expected Outcome	Actual Outcome and Comments
14	Test the formulas in G22 and G26 calculate bill correctly	Data set 1 (see below)	Bill worked out on calculator. Total cost = £1123.20	Total cost is £1123.20

Data set 1

Quarter page, front page, colour, 4 weeks

Figure 6.21 ▶

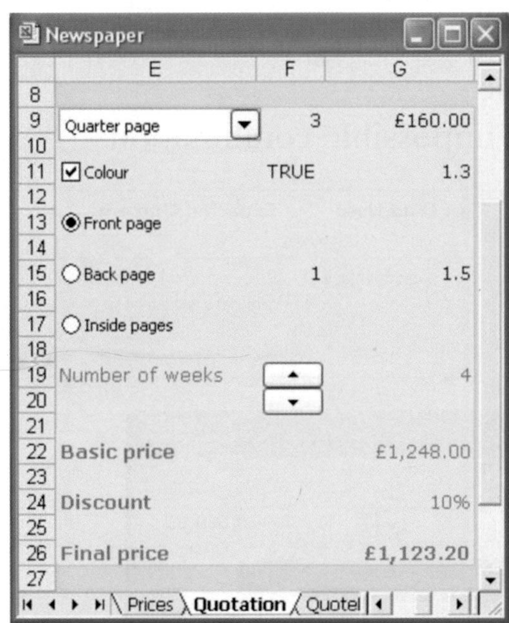

Testing the Quit macro

Test Number	Purpose of Test	Test Data Used	Expected Outcome	Actual Outcome and Comments
22	Test the Are you sure? message of the Quit macro		Message box appears. Choose yes – exits program. Choose no – returns to program	Message box appears. Choose yes – exits program. Choose no – returns to program

Figure 6. 22 ▶

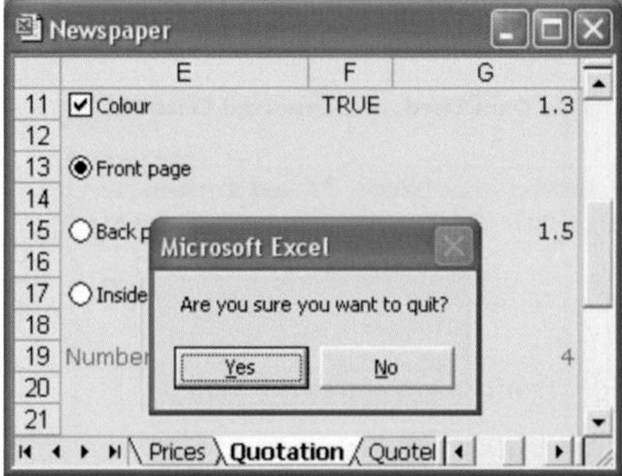

Testing impossible combinations

Test Number	Purpose of Test	Test Data Used	Expected Outcome	Actual Outcome and Comments
26	Checks impossible combinations are rejected	Front page, full page	Rejected. Error message appears and data is cleared	Error message appears (Figure 6.23) and data is cleared when OK is clicked. (Figure 6.24)

Figure 6. 23 ▶

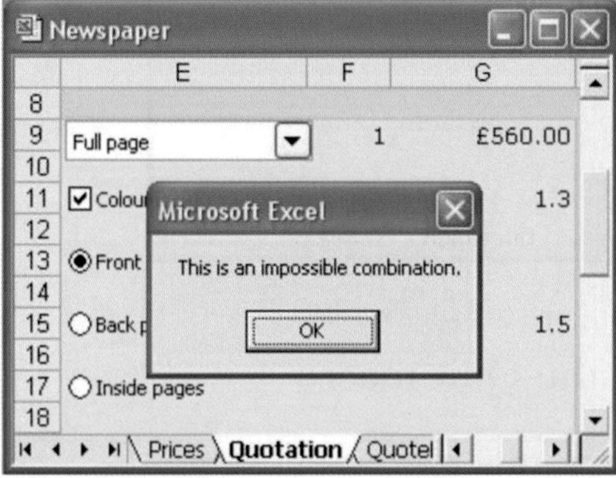

Figure 6. 24 ▶

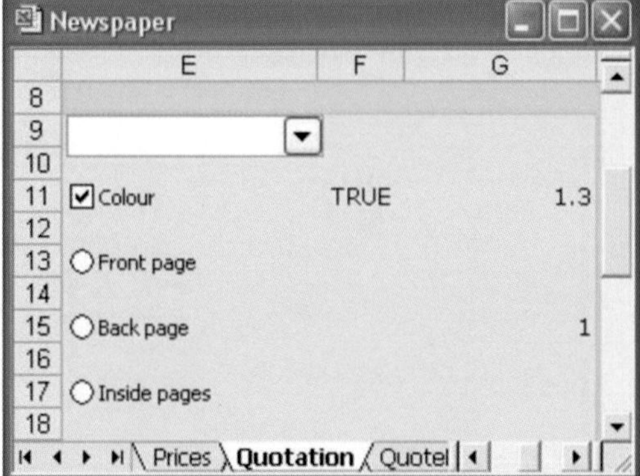

Testing the display

Test Number	Purpose of Test	Test Data Used	Expected Outcome	Actual Outcome and Comments
36	To test that columns are wide enough to display the information	The highest possible priced quotation, data set 4	£15,142.40	# # # # # # displayed in cell G26. Column not wide enough. Action needed.

Figure 6. 25 ▶

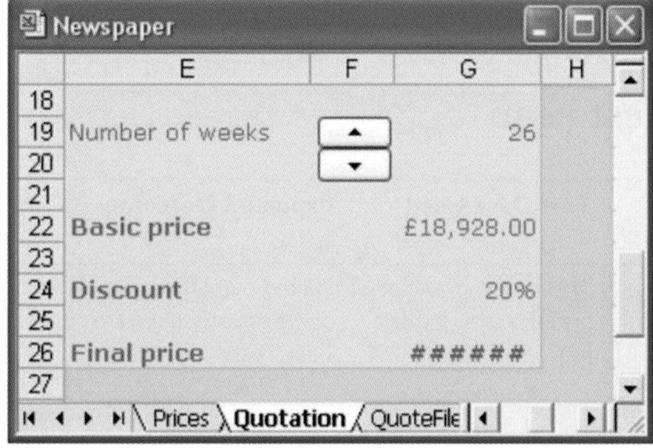

Corrective action (if any)

Test Number	Problem	Action taken	Expected Outcome	Actual Outcome and Comments
36	Width of column G was too narrow - 11.	Width reformatted to 14	£15,142.40	£15,142.40

Figure 6. 26 ▶

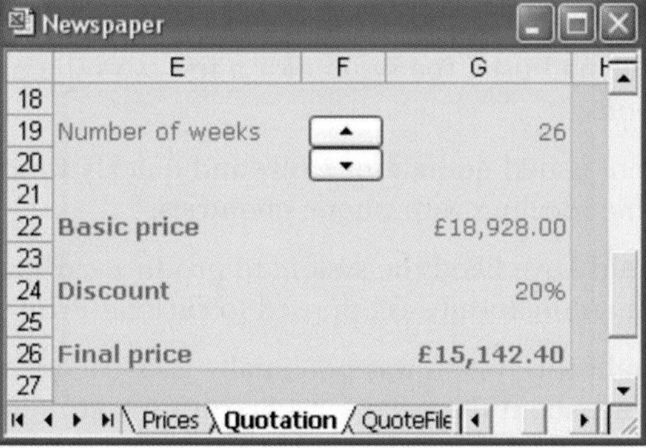

Printed output testing

Test Number	Purpose of Test	Test Data Used	Expected Outcome	Actual Outcome and Comments
42	Test that the printed output is as expected	The highest possible priced quotation, data set 4	Printed output fits onto a sheet of A4 paper. Details are clear. Final price = £15142.40.	Printed in colour on a sheet of A4. Totals clear. Colour scheme was easy to read. Details in the header as expected Total = £15142.40

User test plan

Test Number	Purpose of Test	Test Data Used	Expected Outcome	Actual Outcome and Comments
43	Provide data sets 1, 2, 3 and 4 to the user and ask her to enter the data for each quotation, print the quotation, file the quotation	The highest possible priced quotation, data sets 1, 2, 3 and 4	Printed output fits onto a sheet of A4 paper. Details are clear. Totals are: £1123.20 £1680.00 £2184.00 £15142.40	Katie had no problems with using the system. Her comments are below. Totals were exactly as expected.
44	Install the system in the office of the *Denton Gazette* for a week for the staff to see if it meets their requirements			

User comments

The system was tested by Katie Walker, a clerk at the *Denton Gazette*. After Katie had used the system for a few days she made the following observations:

The system issued quotations easily and quickly which was particularly useful when dealing with phone enquiries.

Katie would have liked the system to produce carbon copies of the quotation automatically as opposed to clicking Print a number of times.

She thought the system was potentially user-friendly but had reservations about the need for a Startup screen. All she wanted to do was get started and that slowed her down and eventually became irritating during the course of the day.

She found it a little confusing that when the Quotation worksheet loaded if you clicked on cells like A1, nothing happened as these cells were locked. I will need to make it clear in the user guide that you start in cell C13.

Katie also suggested that it would be easier for the user if the cells in which data is entered such as C13, C15, etc were a different colour to make them stand out.

She also commented that if the same customer had two quotations, she had to type in their address twice. She suggested that I have some way of finding previous customers' details and inserting the address automatically.

As she used the system the file of customer quotations built up very quickly, eventually going off the screen. She found she needed advice as to how to search for a particular quotation or sort them into alphabetical order.

Katie was worried about how to back up the system and what would happen in case of computer breakdown. She also forgot to save the file regularly and wondered if this could be built into the system.

9 User guide

A user guide is just that – a guide for the user or users of your system.

It should include details of:

1 The purpose of the system
2 The minimum hardware and software requirements needed to run your system – you can find these at the Microsoft website
3 How to install the system
4 Getting started
5 Using the system
6 Common problems or error messages and possible solutions
7 Security measures, backup procedures and passwords needed

Part of a user guide is given below.

User Guide to the Denton Gazette Quotation system

4. Getting started

4.1. To start the system double click the file icon called Newspaper.xls.
You will see this menu:

Figure 6. 27 ▶

4.2. To make a quotation click on the first button.

4.3. To see and edit prices, click on the second button.

4.4. To see past quotations, click on the third button.

5. Using the system

5.1. Making a quotation.

5.1.1 You will see this screen.

Figure 6. 28 ▶

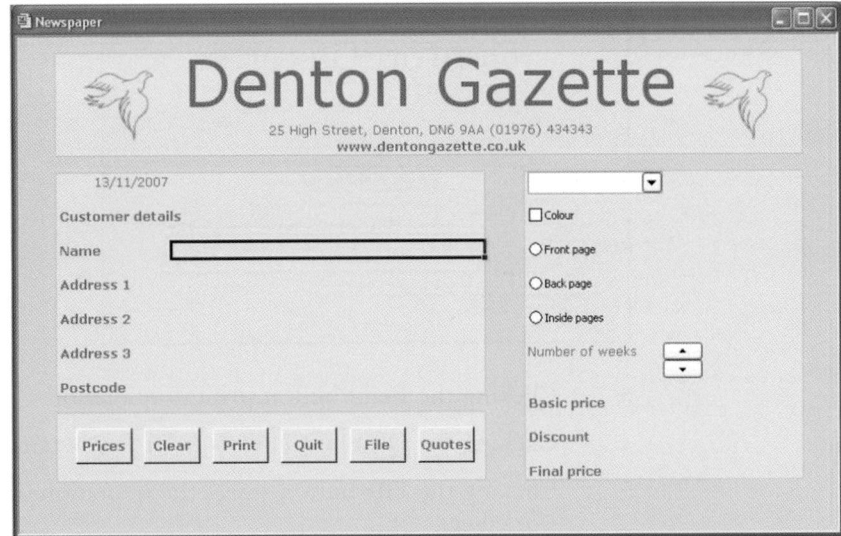

5.2 To make a quotation, firstly click on the cell to the right of **Name**. Enter the customer name. Enter the address in the cells below.

5.2.1 Click on the drop-down box to select the advertisement size.

5.2.2 If you want a colour advertisement, click on the check box.

5.2.3 Use the buttons to choose the page where you want the advertisement placed.

5.2.4 Use the spinner to adjust the number of weeks that you require. The price will automatically be displayed as in Figure 6.29.

Figure 6. 29 ▶

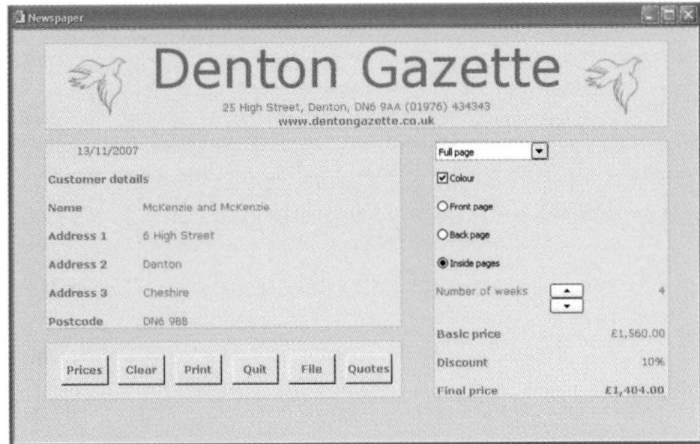

5.2.5 You have a variety of other options.

1 Clicking the **Prices** button allows you to see and edit prices.

2 Clicking the **Clear** button deletes this customer's data.

This button clears the old data (but not the date), switches to the cell to enter the customer name and displays a message box to say that the data has been deleted. (See figure 6.30.)

Figure 6. 30 ▶

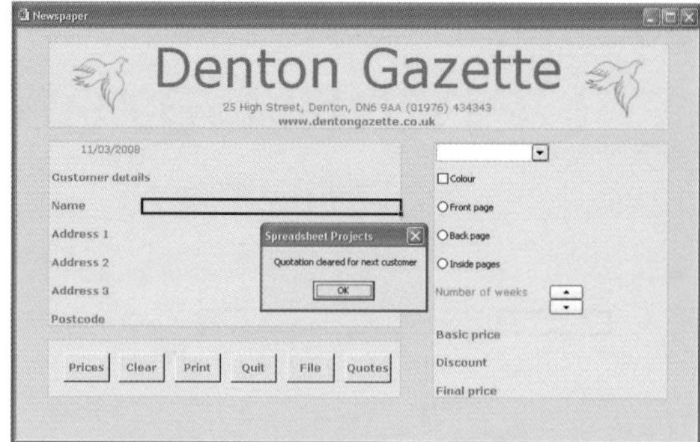

3 Clicking the **Print** button prints a quotation.

4 Clicking the **Quit** button exits from the system.

5 Clicking the **File** button stores the quotation on the QuoteFile worksheet.

6 Clicking the **Quotes** button loads all the old quotes in an on-screen form.

This section of the user guide would go on to describe:

- How to edit prices
- How to file quotations
- How to review quotations
- Sorting quotations into order
- Error messages
- Adding a customer

User Guide Hints

- Do use simple, clear, step by step instructions to using your system.
- Don't use jargon.
- Do provide helpful screenshots.
- Don't produce a guide to using Excel; it should be a guide to your system.
- Don't include large tracts of text from user manuals.

10 Technical documentation

You may also need to produce technical documentation for your solution. This is documentation for the people who will maintain the system, rather than those who use it.

Technical documentation should include:

- the original specification
- hardware, software and other resource requirements
- instructions for installing and opening the spreadsheet
- instructions for regular maintenance of the system such as archiving records when a file is too big or adding additional customers to the system
- details of all calculations, formulas and functions used
- macro coding
- details of verification and validation procedures
- passwords and security information.

11 Evaluation report

An evaluation report is an important part of a project at this level.

You will need to ask yourself:

- What was I supposed to do?
- Have I met the end-user requirements?
- Have I provided evidence of meeting the end-user requirements?
- What limitations are there that might affect the user?
- What improvements could I make to my system?

You must refer to the original user requirements.

Evaluation Report

To evaluate my system I will look at the initial end-user requirements and also take on board comments made by the users when testing the system. There were originally six end-user requirements and I will refer to each one to see if I have met the requirement, giving evidence if appropriate.

1 **A system is required to be able to give a quick quotation accurately and efficiently.**
The system produced does issue quotes accurately. The system was tested thoroughly and no errors found during the trial period with Katie Walker. It enabled her to deal with on-line phone enquiries far more quickly.

2 **The system should enable phone enquiries to be dealt with far more quickly than at present.**
A test comparison was held between the old manual system and the new system. The old system took 1 minute 44 seconds. The new system took 21 seconds to enter the details and file the quote.

3 **Issued quotes need to be stored with the facility to view them at a later date.**
Quotes can be stored effectively but there is still room for improvement. The file soon gets very big and it is not easy to find an old quotation. However it is possible to use a Data Form or the Excel filter. I need to add instructions to the User Guide on how to tackle this.

4 **The system must be user-friendly, yet have a professional look and feel.**
My client, Janice Peters, feels the system is user-friendly and she was impressed by the interface. I may need to customise the other worksheet to match the quotation sheet and give a common feel to the system.

Katie found that it was not always easy to click in the right place when entering customers' details. She suggested that the cells in which the customer name and address are entered should be in a different colour.

5 **The system should be easy to transfer easily between the laptop and office-based PC.**
The initial system uses 111 Kb of disc space. Using copy and paste I added 1000 customers, which increased the file size to 347 Kb. The system can be easily transferred using a memory stick.

6 **It must be easy to access the price details and amend them when necessary.**
The price details are stored on a different worksheet. There is a macro to switch to this worksheet and the user can easily run this macro by clicking on the appropriate button. Prices can be amended.

Limitations and possible enhancements

1 I might in a future version of the system remove the start up screen by adjusting the auto_open macro so that it is quicker for the users to start work.

2 I could customise the user interface further by running the whole system from a UserForm.

3 It might be easier to handle if every quotation was issued with a quotation reference number and a date of issue to aid searching in the future.

4 Over a period of time this file will get very large and the user needs to establish procedures for clearing out quotations that are not needed. This could be manually done in Excel but I might try to automate this feature in the future.

5 Adding a customer is not easy at present and I would like to add a macro to do this.

6 My user was concerned about saving data and backups. I need to edit the FileQuote macro so that it saves the file whenever a quotation is filed. I can easily edit the VBA coding to do this. It is only one additional line:

ActiveWorkbook.Save

7 I will need to discuss back-up options with my user and provide advice in the User Guide.

8 I could create an additional worksheet that takes the data from the Quotation worksheet but sets it out as an A4 portrait document. When printed this would produce a professional black and white quotation.

9 I could extend the system to produce an invoice for customers who decide to place an advertisement and a receipt when they have paid.

10 A limitation is that the combo box and spinner have a white background and this can't be changed. Therefore to be consistent, I could make all the data entry cells have a white background. That would mean that they stand out for the user as suggested by Katie.

11 Another limitation is that the text for the option buttons and the check box has to be in black. I could put the text in the underlying cell and format it to the dark green colour, Verdana font.

12 I could introduce a way of automatically inserting the name and address of returning customers. I could give each customer a number. Typing the number into a particular cell would automatically insert this customer data in the spreadsheet.

Evaluation Hints

- You must look at your original end-user requirements and report on whether you have achieved what you wanted to including successes, problems and possible solutions.
- No system is perfect. There will always be room for improvement. Outline any limitations and possible further developments.
- Don't moan about the lack of time. Time management is your responsibility.
- Don't pretend it is all working when some parts are incomplete. Do not be afraid to tell the truth.
- Don't report on how well you did but focus on how well your system achieved its aims.

12 Getting your project ready to hand in

When your project is finished you should:

- Produce a front cover. Your name, centre and candidate number should be clear. Make it look good. You will have spent a lot of time on this project, so don't hand in something that looks as if you don't care.
- Get your project in order. It should be in the order in which it will be marked. Page numbering and the use of headers and footers are to be encouraged.
- Produce a contents page which clearly cross-references to each section in the project.
- Bind your project securely. Often coursework has to be sent away for checking. It needs to be firmly attached but ring binders are not encouraged.

7 Tips and tricks

Here are fifty tips and tricks that have been found to be more than useful in implementing Excel projects. Many of them have been discovered by students themselves.

1 Getting more than one line of text in a cell
2 A quick way of displaying formulas
3 Putting a tick into a cell
4 Formatting non-adjacent areas
5 Using the fill handle
6 Using AutoFill to quickly enter data
7 What is a circular reference?
8 What is the difference between Paste and Paste Link?
9 Inserting multiple rows and columns
10 Quickly copying cell formats to other cells or cell ranges
11 Switching rows of cells to columns or columns to rows
12 Keys to use for running macros
13 Displaying the Date and Time
14 Fixing problems with dates
15 Entering numbers as text
16 Calculating with dates
17 What day of the week is a date?
18 The Visual Basic toolbar
19 Hiding columns
20 Hiding the contents of a cell
21 Creating an automatic backup of your work
22 A quick way of closing all those open files
23 Adding Comments to your work
24 Automatically correcting common typing errors (AutoCorrect)
25 Stopping a header row disappearing off the screen (Freeze Panes)
26 Combining the contents of two columns
27 A table stores names as John Smith. How do I split this into John and Smith?
28 A quick way of entering the name of a range of cells (Paste name)
29 Using Go To Special
30 Highlighting changed cells
31 Splitting panes
32 Adding up a column of figures
33 Switching between relative and absolute references
34 Changing the status bar and caption text
35 Clicking on a cell so it automatically changes 0 to 1 and 1 to 0
36 MsgBox Carriage Return
37 Running different macros depending on the value of a cell
38 Selecting an image when you run a macro
39 A splashscreen in Excel
40 Synchronising one combo box with another

1. Getting more than one line of text in a cell

Press ALT + ENTER to start a new line in the same cell.

Or if your text is too long to fit in a cell, highlight the cells, and click on **Format > Cells.** Click on the **Alignment** tab and click on **Wrap text**. The text will be displayed on multiple lines.

Figure 7. 1 ▶

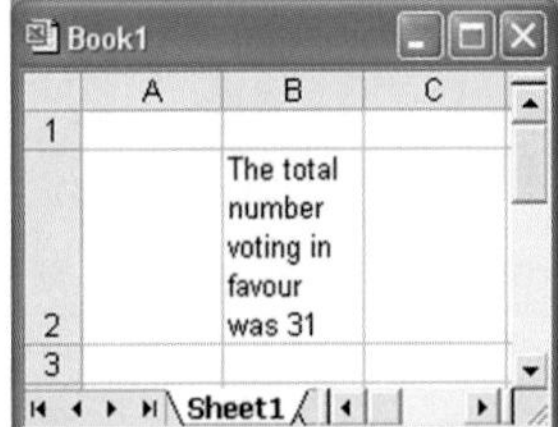

2. A quick way of displaying formulas

Hold down the CTRL + ` (next to 1 on the keyboard). This will switch to showing formulas. Press these keys again to return to normal mode.

Figure 7. 2 ▶

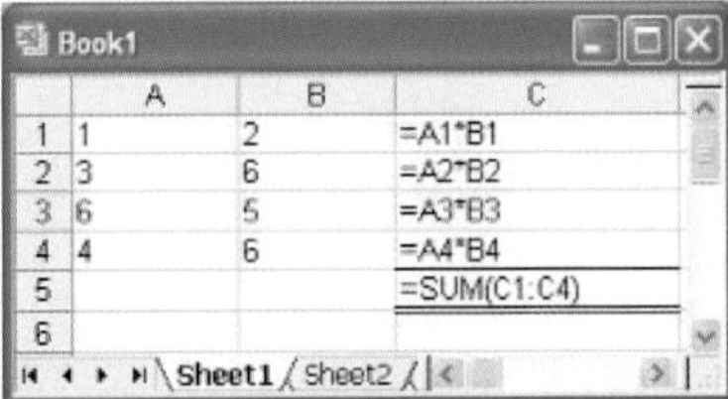

3. Putting a tick into a cell

Type **=CHAR(252)** in the cell and then set the font to **Wingdings**.

=CHAR(251) will give you a cross.

Figure 7. 3 ▶

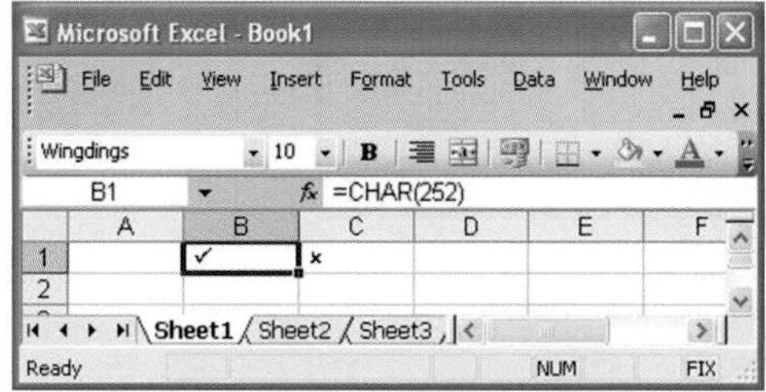

You can now copy the tick to other cells.

4. Formatting non-adjacent areas

If you want to format groups of cells on a worksheet that are not next to each other, you need to select them. Do this by:

(a) Dragging to select the first group of cells.
(b) Holding CTRL down and dragging across any other groups of cells.

Use this method if you want to draw a graph of data in non-adjacent cells.

5. Using the Fill Handle

When a cell is selected there is a small black square in the bottom right-hand corner. This is called the fill handle. If you move the cursor over this square, it changes from the usual white cross to a hairline black cross.

Figure 7. 4 ▶

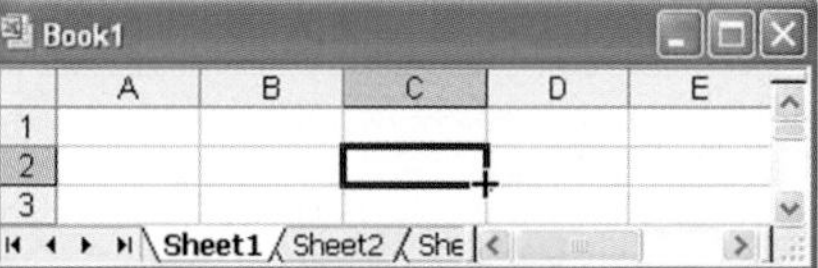

If you now drag this cross down to other cells it will copy the contents of the first cell to all the others; it will also make an intelligent guess at a sequence.

Try the operation on a word, a formula, Product 1, a day, a month in a cell.

Figure 7. 5 ▶

Book1

	A	B	C	D	E
1	Good	=G1*H1	Product 1	Monday	January
2	Good	=G2*H2	Product 2	Tuesday	February
3	Good	=G3*H3	Product 3	Wednesday	March
4	Good	=G4*H4	Product 4	Thursday	April
5	Good	=G5*H5	Product 5	Friday	May

Sheet1 / Sheet2 / Sheet3

If you enter the first two numbers of a number sequence or a date sequence, highlight both cells and drag down, the sequence continues.

Figure 7. 6 ▶

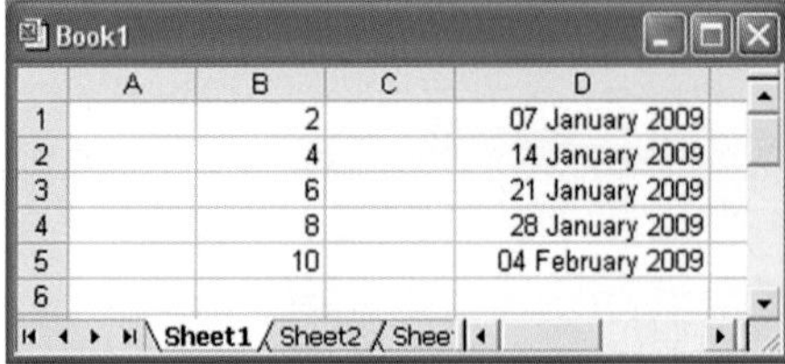

If the fill handles are not visible:

(a) Click on **Tools > Options**
(b) Click on the **Edit** tab
(c) Click the **Allow cell drag and drop** check box.

6. Using AutoFill to enter data quickly

Another way of performing the same operation is to:

(a) Enter the first piece of data in the series.
(b) Highlight the cells you wish to fill including the cell with the first piece of data.
(c) Click on **Edit > Fill > Series.**
(d) Click on **AutoFill,** enter the **Step value** and then click on **OK**.

7. What is a circular reference?

Type = **A6 + A7** into A7.

You will see this error message.

Figure 7. 7 ▶

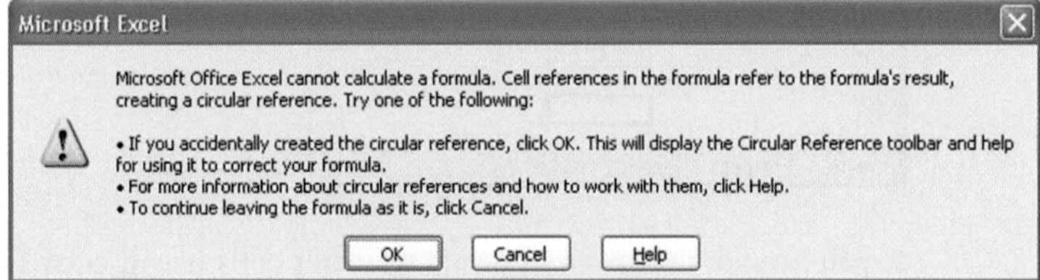

This is because the formula in A7 refers to A7. This error is called a circular reference.

8. What is the difference between Paste and Paste Link?

When you copy data from one cell and paste it into another cell, if the first cell changes the second cell does not change.

By using **Paste Link** you can link the two cells, so that if the first cell is updated, so is the second.

(a) Click on the source cell and click on the **Copy** icon.
(b) Click on the second cell and click on **Edit > Paste Special.**
(c) Click on the **Paste Link** button.

9. Inserting multiple rows and columns

If you need to insert one row, select a row by clicking on the row number, right click and click on **Insert**.

To insert multiples (for example, three rows), select three rows, right click and click on **Insert**. Three rows will be inserted. This also works for columns.

10. Quickly copying cell formats to other cells or cell ranges

(a) Click on the cell whose formatting you wish to copy.
(b) Click on **Format Painter** icon (a paintbrush picture on the **Standard** toolbar).
(c) Click on the cell or cell range you want to copy the formatting to.

Note: To continue formatting to a number of locations double click **Format Painter** and click the button again when you have finished.

11. Switching rows of cells to columns or columns to rows

How can we change this:

Figure 7. 8 ▶

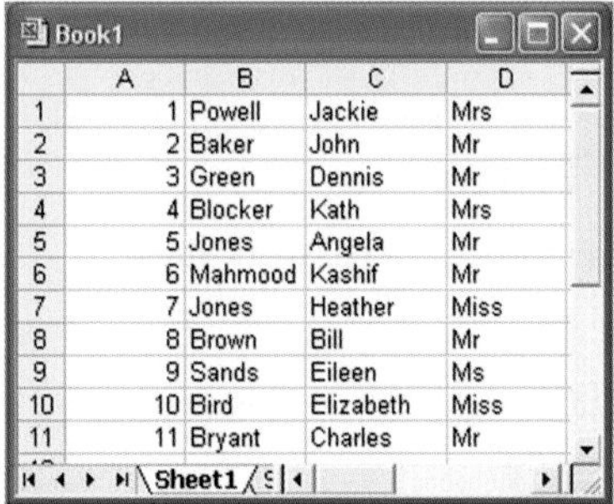

	A	B	C	D
1	1	Powell	Jackie	Mrs
2	2	Baker	John	Mr
3	3	Green	Dennis	Mr
4	4	Blocker	Kath	Mrs
5	5	Jones	Angela	Mr
6	6	Mahmood	Kashif	Mr
7	7	Jones	Heather	Miss
8	8	Brown	Bill	Mr
9	9	Sands	Eileen	Ms
10	10	Bird	Elizabeth	Miss
11	11	Bryant	Charles	Mr

into this:

Figure 7. 9 ▶

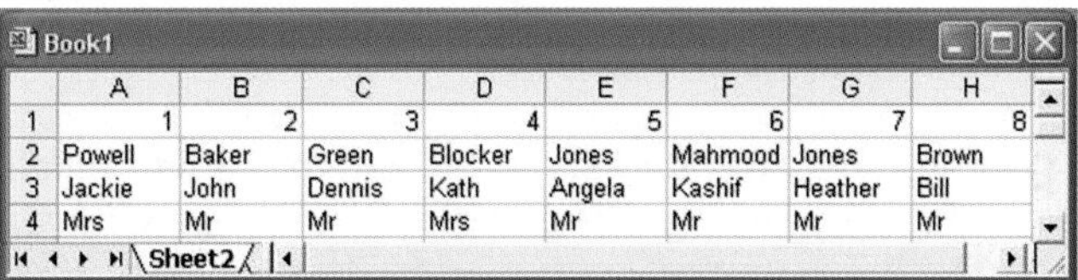

	A	B	C	D	E	F	G	H
1	1	2	3	4	5	6	7	8
2	Powell	Baker	Green	Blocker	Jones	Mahmood	Jones	Brown
3	Jackie	John	Dennis	Kath	Angela	Kashif	Heather	Bill
4	Mrs	Mr	Mr	Mrs	Mr	Mr	Mr	Mr

without retyping or a lot of cut and paste?

(a) Select the cells that you want to switch.
(b) Click on **Edit > Copy**.
(c) Click on the top-left cell of the paste area. The paste area must be outside the copy area. In the example shown in Figure 7.9, a new worksheet has been used.
(d) Click on **Edit > Paste Special**.
(e) Select the **Transpose** check box. Click on **OK**.

12. Keys to use for running macros

When you record a macro, you can set up a keyboard short cut such as CTRL E to run the macro. Some of these shortcut keys already have a meaning in Excel.

Figure 7. 10 ▶

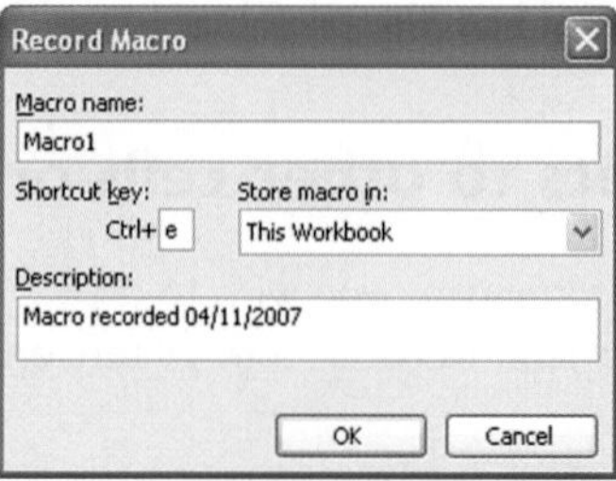

The following keys are not used and are therefore suitable for macros:

(a) CTRL + E
(b) CTRL + J
(c) CTRL + L
(d) CTRL + M
(e) CTRL + Q
(f) CTRL + T
(g) CTRL + + SHIFT + any letter except O

13. Displaying the Date and Time

To enter the date and time into an Excel worksheet:

(a) Click on the required cell.
(b) Enter **=TODAY()** for today's date.

Figure 7. 11 ▶

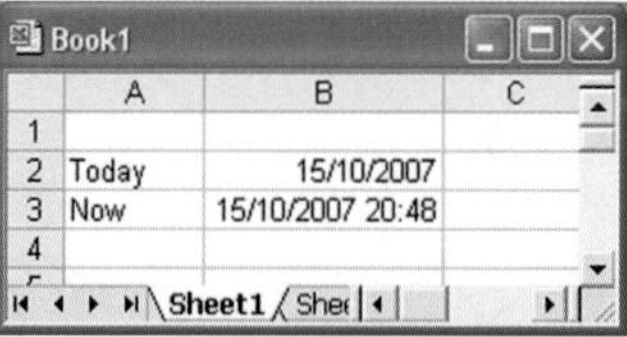

(c) Enter **=NOW()** for today's date and the current time.
The format may not be exactly how you require the date.
(d) Use **Format > Cells** to format the date or time as required using the options shown in Figure 7.12.

Figure 7. 12 ▶

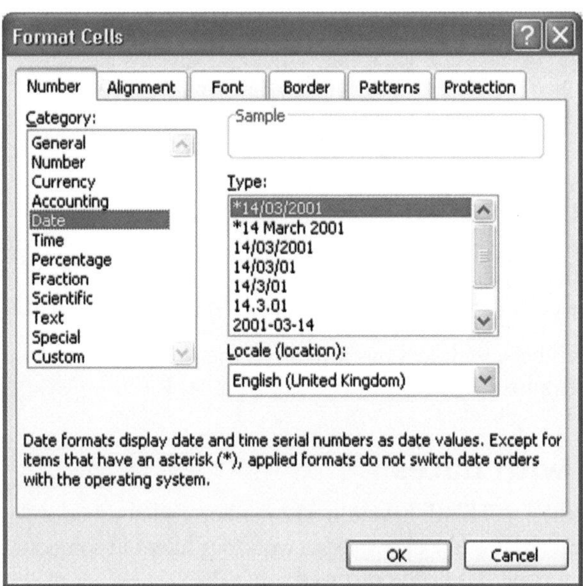

Dates and times entered using **=TODAY()** or **=NOW()** will be updated when you next open the file.

Note: You can enter the current date or time quickly:

- To enter the current date in a cell, press CTRL + **;** (semi-colon).
- To enter the current time in a cell, press CTRL + **:** (colon).

Dates and times entered using this method will **NOT** be updated when you next open the file.

14. Fixing problems with dates

Sometimes the date appears as a number such as 36680. This is because Excel stores dates as numbers in order starting on 1 January 1900 which is stored as 1.

For example, 3 June 2000 is stored as 36680. To change the number back to a date, click on **Format, Cells** and select **Date**.

To change a date back to a number, click on the **Comma Style** icon on the Formatting toolbar.

15. Entering numbers as text

If you wish to enter a number as a code, e.g. 000262, Excel will store it as a number and only display 262.

To enter 000262, type in an apostrophe first **'000262**. The apostrophe formats the cell to text format. 000262 is displayed and not the apostrophe.

However, the apostrophe is displayed in the formula bar as shown in Figure 7.17.

Figure 7. 13 ▶

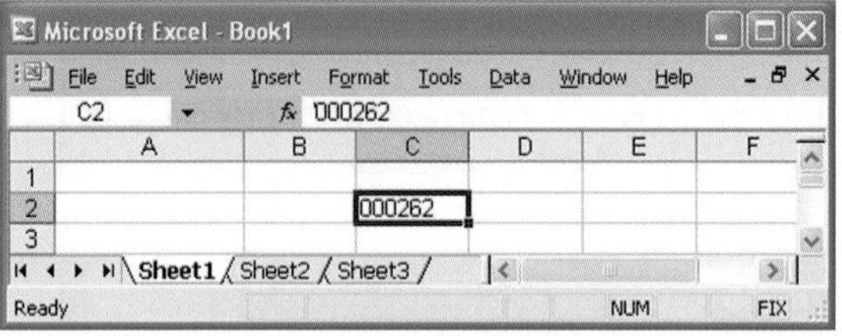

Similarly, you might have conducted a survey and typed 1-4, 5-8 and 9-12 into three cells. Excel changes them to 1 April, 5 August and 9 December.

This is because Excel has formatted the cells as dates. To prevent this, type an apostrophe at the start of the data, e.g. **'1-4**.

16. Calculating with dates

Use the DATEDIF function to calculate the number of days, months or years between dates, for example, to work out how old someone is or for how many days a book has been borrowed.

(a) Put the first date in A1.
(b) Type **=NOW()** in A2.
(c) Type **=DATEDIF(A1,A2,"y")** in A3.

You will see the difference between the two dates in full years.

Figure 7. 14 ▶

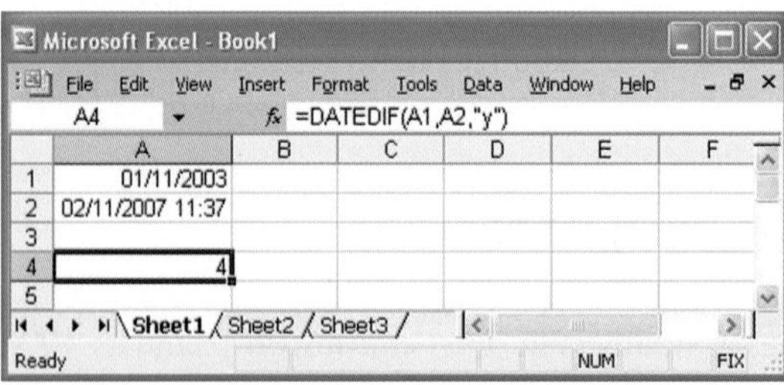

Use **'m'** instead of **'y'** for the number of full months in the period and **'d'** for the number of days.

17. What day of the week is a date?

(a) Type a date in A2.
(b) Click on **Format > Cells**.
(c) Click on the **Number tab** and choose **Custom** in the Category list.
(d) In the type box, type in **dddd**.

This gives the day of the week in full, e.g. Sunday. For the abbreviation such as Sun, type in **ddd**.

Figure 7. 15 ▶

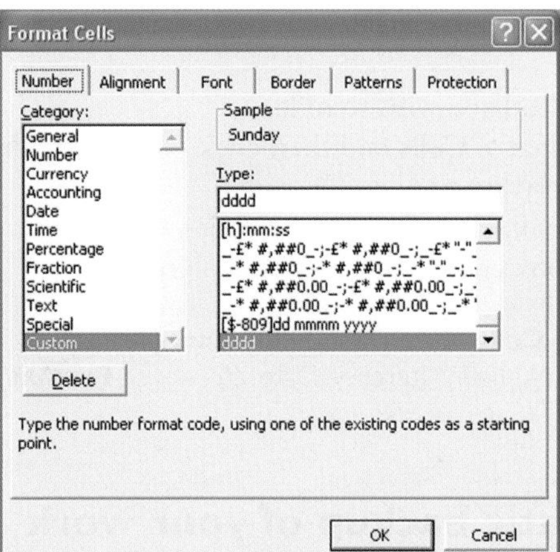

Figure 7. 16 ▶

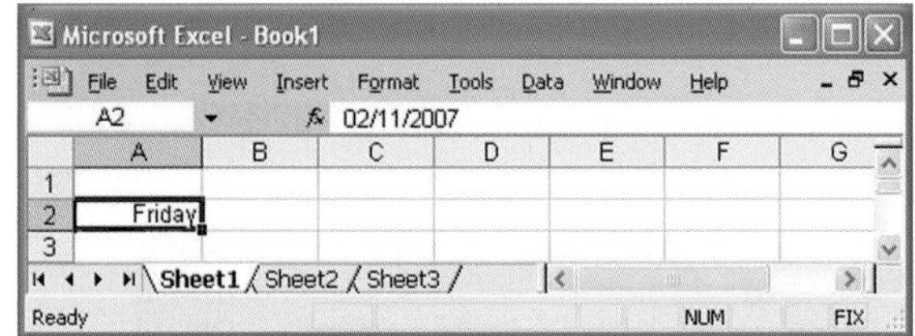

18. The Visual Basic toolbar

Figure 7. 17 ▶

This toolbar can speed things up when you are working with macros.

- Display it by clicking on **View > Toolbars** and choosing the Visual Basic toolbar.
- The arrow button is the same as **Tools > Macro > Macros** and is used to run or edit a macro.
- The circle is a shortcut for **Tools > Macro > Record New Macro,** and while you are recording a macro it changes to the **Stop Recording** icon.

19. Hiding columns

Suppose you want to hide all of column C from the user.

(a) Select column C by clicking on the C in the column heading.
(b) Right click anywhere on the column.
(c) Click on **Hide**.

To show the column again:

(a) Highlight the two columns on either side of the hidden column (B and D).
(b) Right click anywhere on one of these columns.
(c) Click on **Unhide**.

20. Hiding the contents of a cell

(a) Select the cell(s) you wish to hide.
(b) Click on **Format** > **Cells** and then click on the **Number tab**.
(c) In the Category list click on **Custom**.
(d) In the Type box select the existing codes and delete.
(e) In the Type box enter **;;;** (three semicolons).

Note: To undo this click on **Format > Cells > Number**. In the **Category** list click on whatever category the cell was before, e.g. General, Number, Currency, Date, etc. or use **Format Painter**.

21. Creating an automatic backup of your work

Excel allows you to create an automatic backup of a file as you work, so that you cannot lose all your work if the system crashes.

(a) Click on **Tools** > **Options** and click on the **Save** tab.
(b) Set the AutoRecover settings to the appropriate time.

Figure 7. 18 ▶

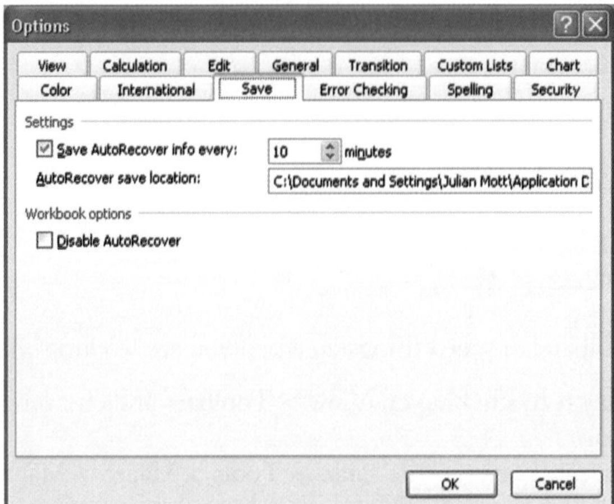

22. A quick way of closing all those open files

Clicking on **File** > **Close** only closes the active Excel file.

Figure 7. 19 ▶

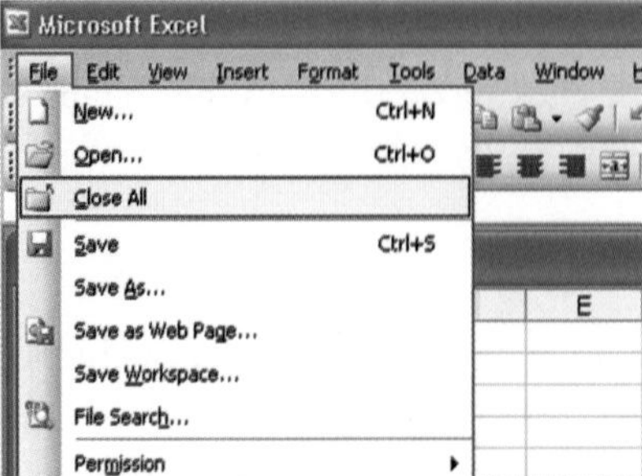

Close all open Excel files by holding down the SHIFT key and clicking on **File** > **Close All**.

23. Adding Comments to your work

A comment is a small on-screen 'Post-It' note that you can attach to a cell to tell the user some more information.

If a cell has a comment attached, there is a red triangle in the top right-hand corner of the cell.

As you move the cursor over the cell, the comment appears.

Figure 7. 20 ▶

Book1

	A	B	C	D	E
5	School Play Ticket Sales				
6	Day	Time	Adult	Ch	
7	Wednesday	evening	45		121
8	Thursday	evening	54		135
9	Friday	evening	52		172
10	Saturday	matinee	92	46	138
11	Saturday	evening	66	106	172

First night.
Tickets
£2.50 adult
£3.50 adult

Sheet1 / Sheet2

To enter a comment:

(a) Click on the cell.
(b) Click on **Insert > Comment**.
(c) Enter the comment.

To delete a comment, right click on the cell and click on **Delete Comment.**

24. Automatically correcting common typing errors (AutoCorrect)

Microsoft Excel has a useful feature called AutoCorrect. Common spelling mistakes are automatically corrected as you type. For example *recieve* would automatically be corrected to *receive*. The word *I* is automatically capitalised.

You can customise it to add your own words using **Tools > AutoCorrect Options...**

Figure 7. 21 ▶

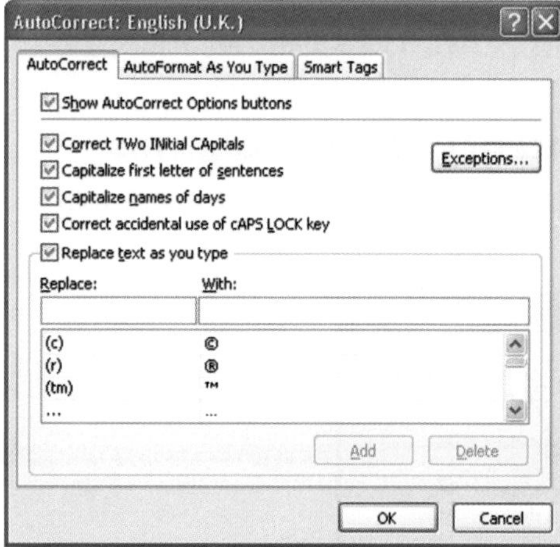

Enter the incorrect word and the correct word into the boxes.

Another useful feature of AutoCorrect is if you accidentally leave the Caps Lock turned on and type in a name like *sMITH* it automatically changes the word to *Smith* and turns off the Caps Lock.

The AutoCorrect feature also exists in Microsoft Word.

25. Stopping a header row disappearing off the screen (Freeze Panes)

A company has details of customers stored in an Excel worksheet. As they scroll down the page the top line (the heading row) disappears.

Figure 7. 22 ▶

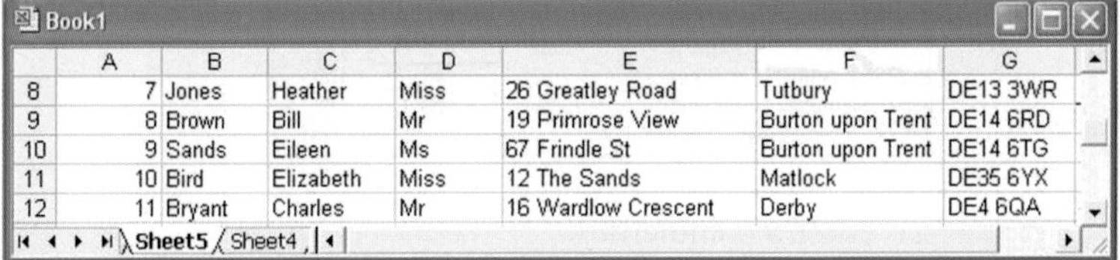

Book1

	A	B	C	D	E	F	G
8	7	Jones	Heather	Miss	26 Greatley Road	Tutbury	DE13 3WR
9	8	Brown	Bill	Mr	19 Primrose View	Burton upon Trent	DE14 6RD
10	9	Sands	Eileen	Ms	67 Frindle St	Burton upon Trent	DE14 6TG
11	10	Bird	Elizabeth	Miss	12 The Sands	Matlock	DE35 6YX
12	11	Bryant	Charles	Mr	16 Wardlow Crescent	Derby	DE4 6QA

Sheet5 / Sheet4

They want to keep the column headings on the screen. They can do this using **Freeze Panes.**

(a) Click on row header 2 to highlight row 2.
(b) Click on **Window > Freeze Panes**.

Figure 7. 23 ▶

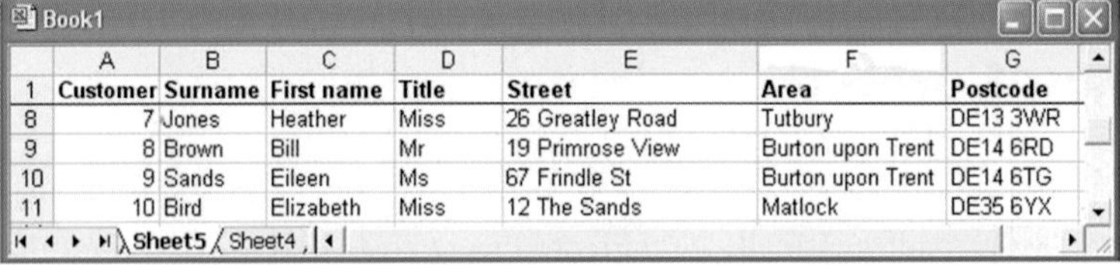

Book1

	A	B	C	D	E	F	G
1	**Customer**	**Surname**	**First name**	**Title**	**Street**	**Area**	**Postcode**
8	7	Jones	Heather	Miss	26 Greatley Road	Tutbury	DE13 3WR
9	8	Brown	Bill	Mr	19 Primrose View	Burton upon Trent	DE14 6RD
10	9	Sands	Eileen	Ms	67 Frindle St	Burton upon Trent	DE14 6TG
11	10	Bird	Elizabeth	Miss	12 The Sands	Matlock	DE35 6YX

Sheet5 / Sheet4

The top line is now locked.

(c) Test it works.

To turn it off click on **Window > Unfreeze Panes.**

26. Combining the contents of two columns

When storing details of customers' names, it is usual to store the data in three different fields: surname, first name and title.

Figure 7. 24 ▶

Book1

	A	B	C	D
1	1	Powell	Jackie	Mrs
2	2	Baker	John	Mr
3	3	Green	Dennis	Mr
4	4	Blocker	Kath	Mrs
5	5	Jones	Angela	Mr
6	6	Mahmood	Kashif	Mr
7	7	Jones	Heather	Miss
8	8	Brown	Bill	Mr

Sheet1 / Sheet2

This means that we can not only sort into alphabetical order but can also send out personalised letters. The name on the invoice will be either Mrs Jackie Powell or Mrs J. Powell.

Joining two or more words together into one word is called **CONCATENATION**.

To do this in Excel use the CONCATENATE function using the ampersand key (&) as follows:

(a) Enter the data in Figure 7.25.
(b) In E1 enter the function **= D1&C1&B1.**
(c) Copy and paste the function down the column.

Figure 7. 25 ▶

Book1

	A	B	C	D	E
1	1	Powell	Jackie	Mrs	MrsJackiePowell
2	2	Baker	John	Mr	MrJohnBaker
3	3	Green	Dennis	Mr	MrDennisGreen
4	4	Blocker	Kath	Mrs	MrsKathBlocker
5	5	Jones	Angela	Mr	MrAngelaJones

Sheet1 / Sheet2 / Sheet3

The function joins the text together. You then need to force spaces between the words.

(a) In E1 change the function to **= D1&" "&C1&" "&B1** (there is a space between the quotation marks).

Figure 7. 26 ▶

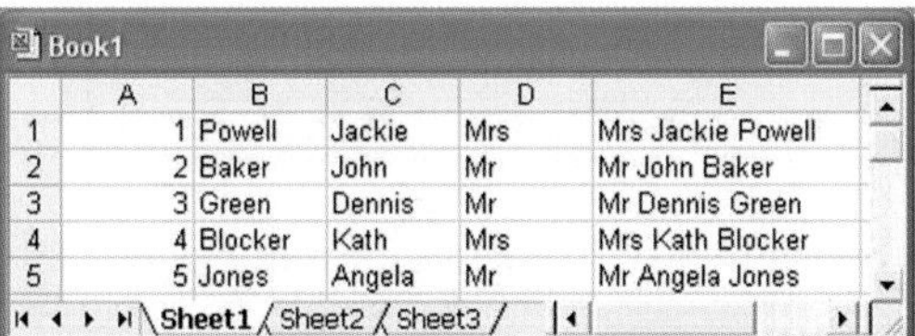

Book1

	A	B	C	D	E
1	1	Powell	Jackie	Mrs	Mrs Jackie Powell
2	2	Baker	John	Mr	Mr John Baker
3	3	Green	Dennis	Mr	Mr Dennis Green
4	4	Blocker	Kath	Mrs	Mrs Kath Blocker
5	5	Jones	Angela	Mr	Mr Angela Jones

Sheet1 / Sheet2 / Sheet3

(b) If we want the name Mrs J. Powell to appear on the invoice, we need to use the LEFT function.
=LEFT(C1,1)

This is the first letter of the word in C1.

Join the two functions together as follows:
= D1&" "&LEFT(C1,1)&" "&B1

Note: There are **RIGHT** and **MID** functions as well.
For example:
RIGHT(D5,3) will take the three characters at the end of the word(s) in D5.
MID(E40,5,8) will take 8 characters from the middle of the text in E40, starting at the 5th character.

27. A table stores names as John Smith. How do I split this into John and Smith?

Suppose you have names in cells A1 to A3 as shown in Figure 7.27.

Figure 7. 27 ▶

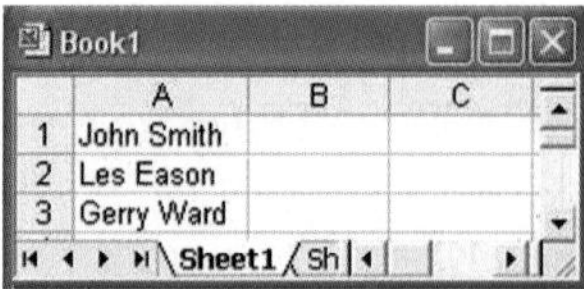

	A	B	C
1	John Smith		
2	Les Eason		
3	Gerry Ward		

(a) Highlight the cells and click on **Data > Text to Columns...**
(b) A wizard will start. Click on **Delimited** and click on **Next.**
(c) Check the **Space** box as shown in Figure 7.28.

Figure 7. 28 ▶

Convert Text to Columns Wizard - Step 2 of 3

This screen lets you set the delimiters your data contains. You can see how your text is affected in the preview below.

Delimiters: ☐ Tab ☐ Semicolon ☐ Comma ☑ Space ☐ Other:

☑ Treat consecutive delimiters as one

Text qualifier: "

Data preview

John	Smith
Les	Eason
Gerry	Ward

Cancel | < Back | Next > | Finish

(d) Click on **Finish** to give the data shown in Figure 7.29.

Figure 7. 29 ▶

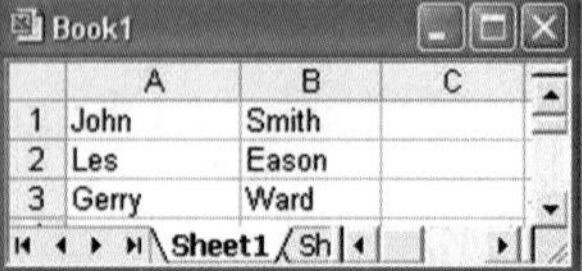

	A	B	C
1	John	Smith	
2	Les	Eason	
3	Gerry	Ward	

28. A quick way of entering the name of a range of cells (Paste name)

If you are using a named range of cells in a function such as SUM or VLOOKUP, you do not need to type in the name. Just press F3 to get a list of names available.

29. Using Go To Special

You can use **Go To Special** to highlight special cells on your workbook, e.g. cells with formulas, cells with validation, cells with comments or cells with conditional formatting.

(a) Click on **Edit > Go To.**
(b) Click on the **Special** button.
(c) Select the type of cell required.

30. Highlighting changed cells

Click on **Tools > Track Changes > Highlight Changes** and check **Track changes while editing.**

Cells that are changed have a blue triangle in the top left-hand corner.

Figure 7. 30 ▶

You can choose whether to accept or reject these changes by clicking on **Tools > Track Changes > Accept or Reject Changes.**

31. Splitting panes

Click on **Window > Split** to split your window into four sections. You can scroll on each section separately.

This is very useful if you want to work on two or more parts of the same worksheet that are not close to each other.

Click on **Window > Remove Split** to return to the conventional screen.

32. Adding up a column of figures

Suppose I want to add up amounts of money in a column. In this case they are in cells C2 to C9. But if I add another row to the table, the data will be in C2 to C10. In which case the formula will be different. How can I still add them up?

The simplest way to do this is to put the total in another column, say D6 and use the formula **=SUM(C:C)**

This will add up all the amounts in column C. It will work no matter how many records you have in column C.

Figure 7. 31 ▶

Book2

	A	B	C	D
1	Item no	Item	Price	
2	1	apples	£ 1.12	
3	2	pears	£ 0.95	
4	3	oranges	£ 1.30	
5	4	bananas	£ 0.90	
6	5	carrots	£ 0.65	£ 7.27
7	6	onions	£ 0.55	
8	7	potatoes	£ 0.25	
9	8	leeks	£ 0.70	
10	9	cabbage	£ 0.85	
11	End of table			

Sheet1 / Sheet2

33. Switching between relative and absolute references

A relative reference is something like:
=SUM(C6:C10)

An absolute reference (which doesn't change when cells are copied) is something like:
=SUM($C$6:$C$9)

To switch between the two automatically and so avoid having to enter the $ signs:

(a) Enter the formula with relative references.
(b) Highlight the cell or range in the formula bar.
(c) Press the **F4** key.

If you press F4 again, only the rows are set as absolute references:
=SUM(C$6:C$9)

Press F4 again for the columns to be set as absolute references:
=SUM($C6:$C9)

Press F4 again to return to relative references.

34. Changing the status bar and caption text

Try this macro.

```
Sub display()
Application.Caption = "St Mary's School Play"
Application.DisplayStatusBar = True
Application.StatusBar = "Project by L.J.Smith ©2008"
End Sub
```

Figure 7. 32 ▶

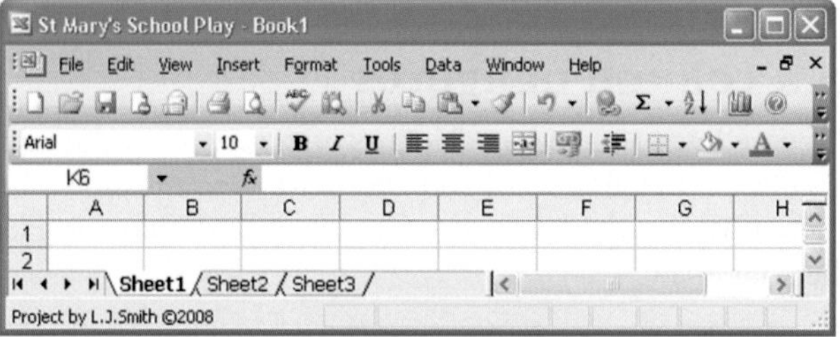

35. Clicking on a cell so it automatically changes 0 to 1 and 1 to 0

(a) You can run a macro so that when you click on a cell containing a 0 its value changes to 1. If the cell contains a 1 it is changed to a 0. (This is useful for booking theatre seats - click on a seat and it is booked. Click again it is unbooked.)
(b) Go into the VB Editor (ALT + F11).
(c) Double click on Sheet1 in the Project Explorer Window (top left of screen). A new module window will open. There are two drop-downs at the top of the window. Choose **Worksheet** and **SelectionChange** as shown.

Figure 7. 33 ▶

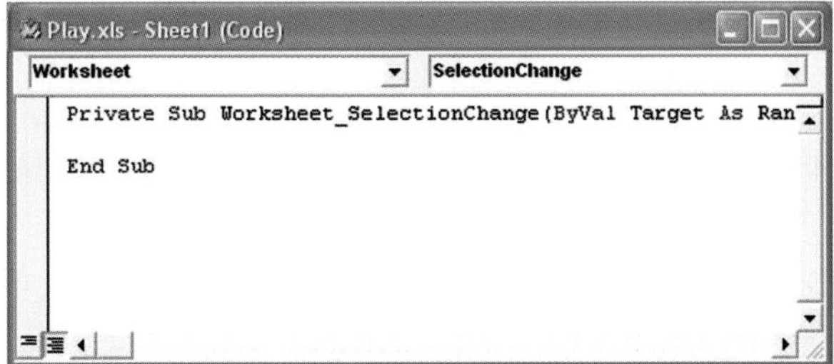

(d) Suppose that we wish to change 0 to 1 when we click on a cell and to change 1 to blank. In the blank middle line of the procedure, enter the coding shown in Figure 7.34.

Figure 7. 34 ▶

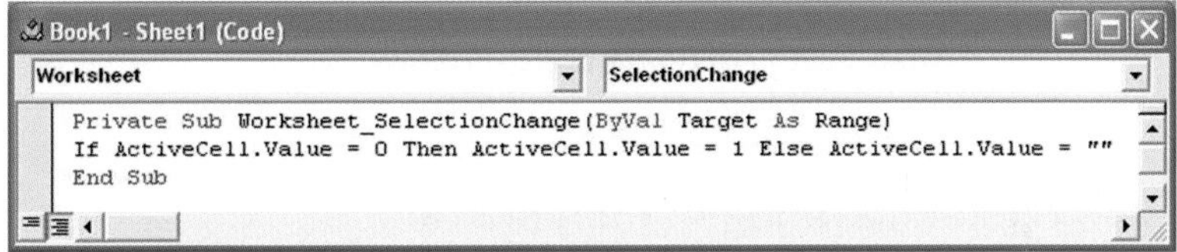

(e) Go back to Excel (ALT + F11 again).
(f) Test it works.

36. MsgBox Carriage Return

Sometimes you may want to put a line of text on a second row of a message box. Try out this example.

(a) Press ALT and F11 to enter the **Visual Basic Editor**
(b) Click on **Insert > Module** and enter this code

```
Sub TwoLines()
MsgBox "Line 1" &  vbCrLf & "Line 2"
End Sub
```

(c) Go back to Excel by pressing ALT and F11 again
(d) Click on **Tools > Macro > Macros > TwoLines**

Figure 7. 35 ▶

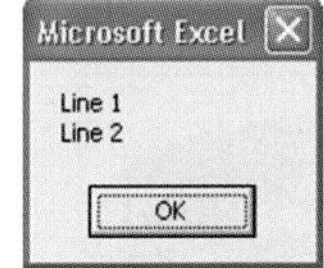

37. Running different macros depending on the value of a cell

Suppose that you want to run different macros depending on the value of a cell. For example, if the value of C4 is 1, you want to run Macro1, if the value of C4 is 2, you want to run Macro2, and if the value of C4 is 3, you want to run Macro3.

(a) Open the Visual Basic Editor
(b) Type in this macro

```
Sub Macrochoice()
If Range("C4").Value = 1 Then Macro1
If Range("C4").Value = 2 Then Macro2
If Range("C4").Value = 3 Then Macro3
End Sub
```

Another way of doing it is as follows:

```
Sub Macrochoice2()
Dim value
value = Range("C4").value
Select Case value
Case 1
Macro1
Case 2
Macro2
Case 3
Macro3
Case Else
Exit Sub
End Select
End Sub
```

38. Selecting an image when you run a macro

In the example below, how can I show a black car if I click on the black option button but a blue car if I click on the blue option button and so on?

Figure 7. 36 ▶

The trick is to have several images, one for each colour choice on your spreadsheet. The images must be the same size.

(a) Create the images and use copy and paste to add them to your Excel spreadsheet.

Figure 7. 37 ▶

(b) Move the images so that they overlap and add the option buttons.

Figure 7. 38 ▶

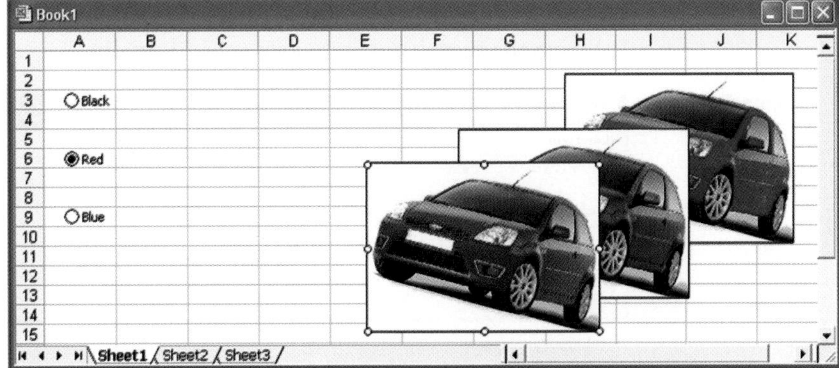

(c) Start recording a macro called **Black**. Right click on the black image and choose **Order > Bring to front**. Stop recording.
(d) Assign the **Black** macro to the option button labelled Black.
(e) Repeat this for all the other colours.
(f) Move the images so that they are on top of each other again and test the macros.
(g) You may want to consider including a plain white image as well. Store this on top of the other images at the start so that if no colour is selected, no car is visible.

39. A splashscreen in Excel

Sometimes it is a good idea to display a splashscreen – a message that appears on the screen for only a few seconds when a file is loaded. How can I do this in Excel?

(a) Press ALT and F11 to enter the **Visual Basic Editor**
(b) Insert a UserForm with **Insert > UserForm**
(c) If the **Control Toolbox** is not visible click on **View** > **Toolbox**
(d) Click on the **Label** icon in the Toolbox
(e) Click on the top left of the UserForm. **Label1** appears.
(f) Delete Label1 and replace it with **Welcome to Morgan's Jam**. (Choose the caption, fonts, font size and colour that you think suitable.)

Figure 7. 39 ▶

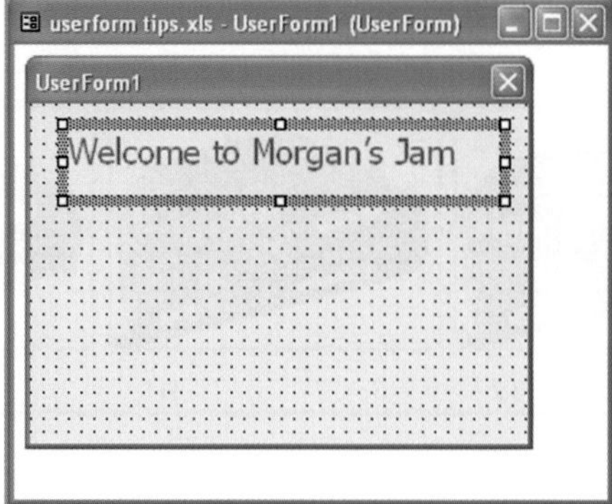

(g) Double click on the **UserForm** (away from the Label)
(h) From the right-hand drop-down select **Initialize**

Figure 7. 40 ▶

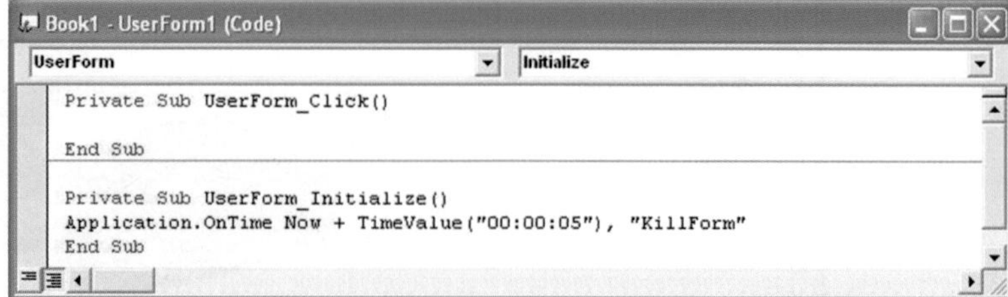

(i) Enter this code:

```
Application.OnTime Now + TimeValue("00:00:05"), "KillForm"
```

Figure 7. 41 ▶

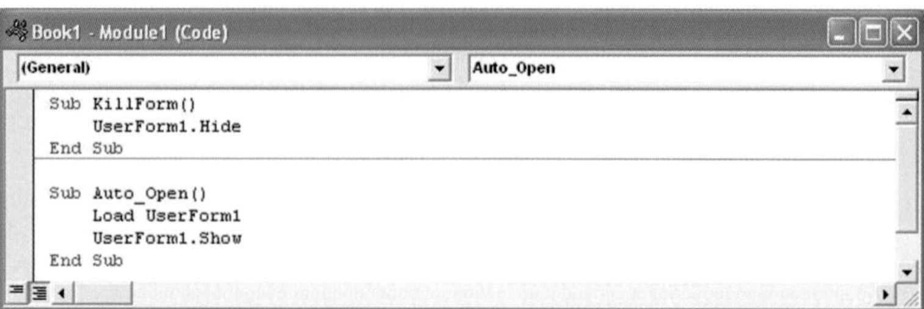

(j) Close this code window
(k) Click on **Insert** > **Module** and enter this code:

```
Sub KillForm()
    UserForm1.Hide
End Sub

Sub Auto_Open()
    Load UserForm1
    UserForm1.Show
End Sub
```

(l) Close the Visual Basic Editor. Save your Excel file and close it
(m) Now re-open it. The UserForm should appear for just five seconds.

40. Synchronising one combo box with another

The data in one combo box is often linked to another combo box. For example, a company may sell two makes of cars, Ford and Honda. The models sold are as shown below:

Figure 7. 42 ▶

Combo exercise

	A	B
1	**Make**	**Model**
2	Ford	Fiesta
3	Ford	Focus
4	Ford	Galaxy
5	Ford	Ka
6	Ford	Mondeo
7	Ford	Puma
8	Honda	Accord
9	Honda	Civic
10	Honda	Prelude
11		

Cars

How can we set up a combo box for the make so that if Ford is chosen, only Ford models appear in a second combo box and so on?

(a) Open a new file in Excel.
(b) Enter the data as shown in the image above. Save your file as combo exercise.
(c) Type Ford into cell D2 and Honda in cell D3.
(d) Using the Forms toolbar, set up a combo box over cells D5 and E5. Right click on the combo box and format it so that the input range is D2:D3 and the linked cell is F5.
(e) Set up a second combo box over cells D8 and E8. Do not format it.
(f) Hold down the ALT key and press F11 to enter the **Visual Basic Editor**. Click on **Insert > Module**. In the window that opens enter this code exactly as shown:

```
Sub Dropdown1_Change()
Dim Make As Integer
Make = Range("F5").Value
Select Case Make
Case 1
ActiveSheet.Shapes("Drop Down 2").Select
With Selection
.ListFillRange = "B2:B7"
.LinkedCell = "F8"
.DropDownLines = 6
.Display3DShading = False
End With
Case 2
ActiveSheet.Shapes("Drop Down 2").Select
With Selection
.ListFillRange = "B8:B10"
.LinkedCell = "F8"
.DropDownLines = 3
.Display3DShading = False
End With
Case Else
End Select
Range("A1").Select
End Sub
```

(g) Go back to Excel by clicking on the View Microsoft Excel icon.
(h) Right click on the first combo box and choose Assign Macro. Choose the macro Dropdown1_Change().

Figure 7. 43 ▶

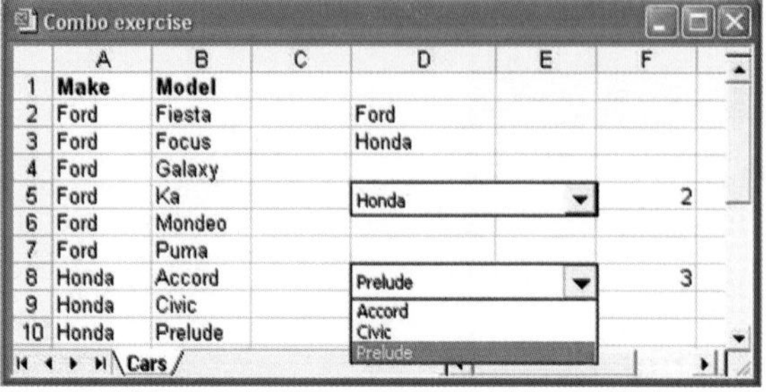

Save the file and test that it works.
(i) If you want to have more makes of car it is easy to edit the macro to include Case 3, Case 4, etc.

41. A real-time clock in Excel

You can set up a real-time clock in an Excel UserForm that ticks by second by second, as follows:

Figure 7. 44 ▶

(a) Open a new Excel workbook or open the workbook in which you wish to put the clock.
(b) Go into the **Visual Basic Editor** by pressing ALT and F11.
(c) Click on **Insert > Module**.
(d) In the new window that opens type in this code:

```
Dim flag As Boolean

Sub auto_open()
flag = False
Load UserForm1
UserForm1.Show
clock
End Sub

Sub clock()
If flag = True Then Exit Sub
Range("a1").Value = Format(Now, "hh:mm:ss")
Application.OnTime (Now + TimeSerial(0, 0, 1)), "clock"
End Sub

Sub stopclock()
UserForm1.Hide
flag = True
End Sub
```

What the code does

The first line sets *flag* as a global variable – a variable that is available in all the macros. Boolean means it can only have two values (True or False).

The first macro loads the UserForm.

The second macro puts the time in cell A1 and updates it every second.

The third macro stops the clock and removes the UserForm.

(e) Still in the Visual Basic Editor set up a UserForm with **Insert > UserForm**.
(f) In the Properties Window set the caption to **The time is...**
(g) Still in the Properties Window, set the **ShowModal** property to **False.** This is absolutely crucial.
(h) Add a **List Box** to your UserForm.
(i) Select the List Box and in the Properties Window set the **RowSource** to **A1**.
(j) Resize the UserForm and the List box as appropriate and choose appropriate colours, borders and fonts.

Figure 7. 45 ▶

(k) Close the Visual Basic Editor.
(l) Set the font colour of cell **A1** to white.
(m) Add a button to run the macro Stopclock. Make the text on the button, Stop the clock.
(n) If you want to, you can add a button to run the Auto_Open macro too.
(o) Save your file.
(p) Test that it works.

Note: You can't exit from this program while the macro is still running but you can do other work on your Excel file.

42. Using Select Case for different responses to different message box buttons

Select Case allows you to set up more options than If Then Else where you are limited to two alternatives. Try this macro:

```
Sub message()
Select Case MsgBox("Are you sure you want to do this?", vbYesNoCancel)
Case vbYes
MsgBox "You chose Yes"
Case vbNo
MsgBox "You chose No"
Case vbCancel
MsgBox "You chose Cancel"
End Select
End Sub
```

43. Importing data from the Internet into Excel

How can you import data from the Internet into a spreadsheet and get it to update?

For this to work you need:

- an always-on connection to the Internet
- a website with regularly updated data such as http://www.x-rates.com/.

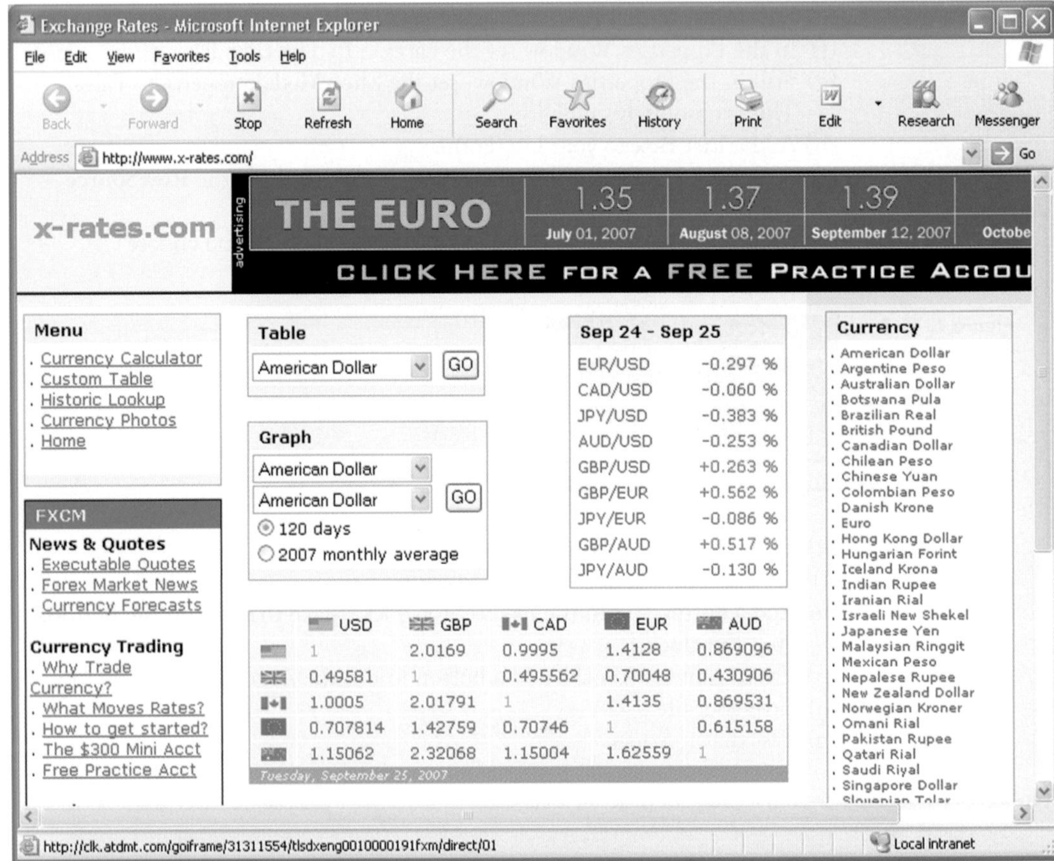

Figure 7. 46 ▲ I want to get updated currency information and will use the table at the bottom of the Web page that gives rates for the US dollar, British pound, Canadian dollar, the euro and the Australian dollar.

(a) Open a new worksheet in Excel.
(b) Click on cell B2.
(c) Click on **Data** > **Import External Data** > **New Web Query**.
(d) Type the address, e.g. http://www.x-rates.com/ in the address box and click on **Go**.

Figure 7. 47 ▶

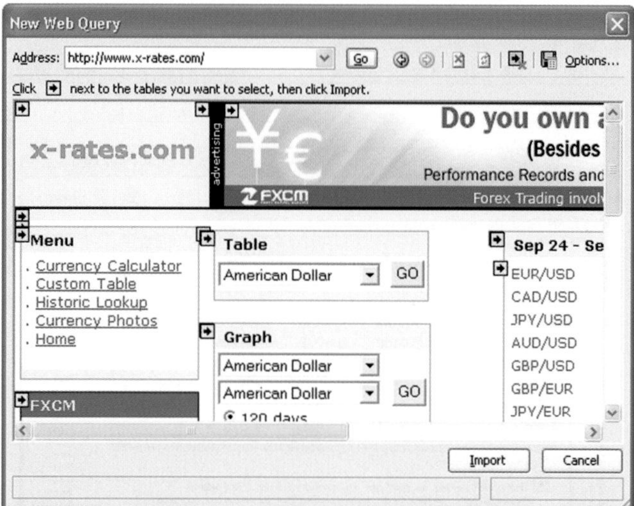

(e) Scroll down and right to the required table.

Figure 7. 48 ▶

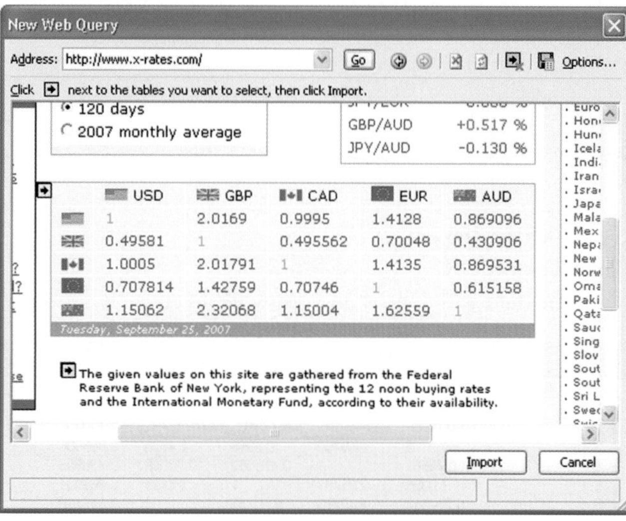

(f) Click on the little black and yellow arrow to the top left of the table.

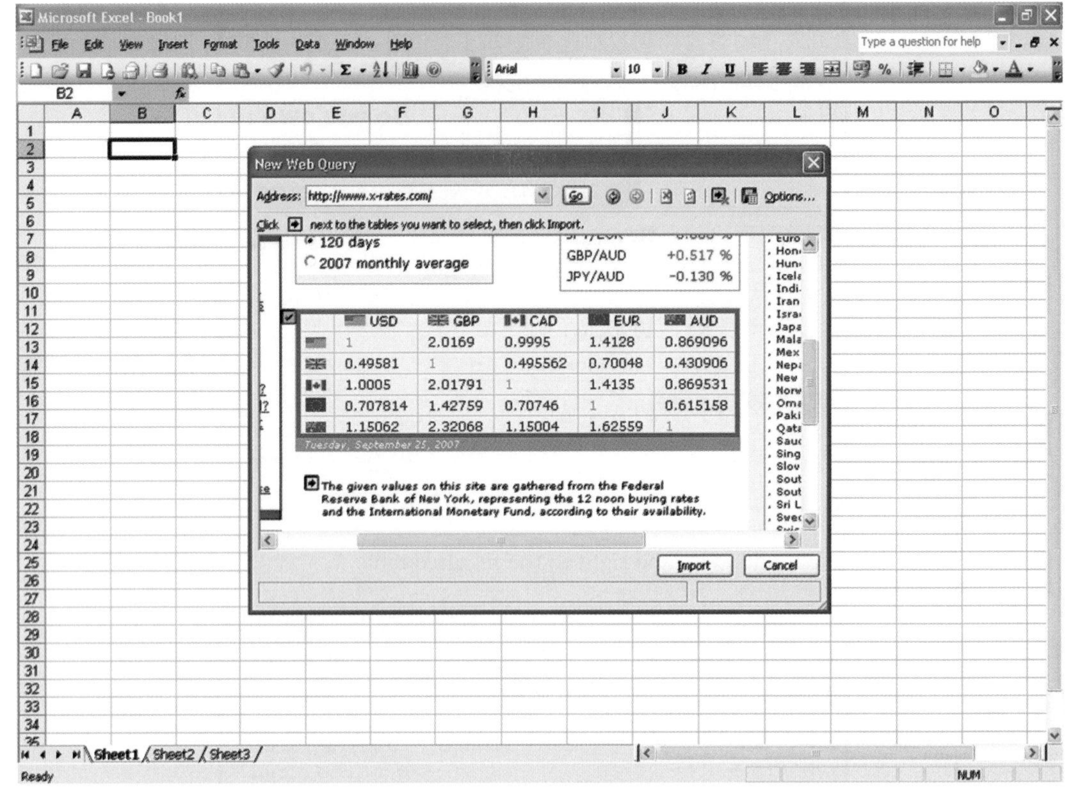

Figure 7. 49 ▲

(g) Click on **Import**.
(h) Click on **OK**.
(i) The data will appear on your worksheet.

Figure 7. 50 ▶

Book1

	A	B	C	D	E	F	G	H
1								
2			USD USD	GBP GBP	CAD CAD	EUR EUR	AUD AUD	
3			1	2.0169	0.9995	1.4128	0.869096	
4			0.49581	1	0.495562	0.70048	0.430906	
5			1.0005	2.01791	1	1.4135	0.869531	
6			0.707814	1.42759	0.70746	1	0.615158	
7			1.15062	2.32068	1.15004	1.62559	1	
8								

Sheet1 / Sheet2 / Sheet3

(j) You can format it as required.

Figure 7. 51 ▶

Book1

	A	B	C	D	E	F	G	H
1								
2			USD USD	GBP GBP	CAD CAD	EUR EUR	AUD AUD	
3			1	2.0169	0.9995	1.4128	0.869096	
4			0.49581	1	0.495562	0.70048	0.430906	
5			1.0005	2.01791	1	1.4135	0.869531	
6			0.707814	1.42759	0.70746	1	0.615158	
7			1.15062	2.32068	1.15004	1.62559	1	
8								

Sheet1 / Sheet2 / Sheet3

(k) Save the file.
(l) To update the data, highlight cells C3 to G7 and click on **Data** > **Refresh Data.**

Figure 7. 52 ▶

	A	B	C	D	E	F	G	H
1								
2			USD USD	GBP GBP	CAD CAD	EUR EUR	AUD AUD	
3			1	2.03889	1.00411	1.4219	0.885496	
4			0.490461	1	0.49248	0.697386	0.434301	
5			0.9959	2.03053	1	1.41607	0.881865	
6			0.703284	1.43392	0.706179	1	0.622755	
7			1.12931	2.30254	1.13395	1.60576	1	
8								

Sheet1 / Sheet2 / Sheet3

(m) You can use macros to transfer data to cells on a different sheet and enter the date. It is possible to create graphs tracking the exchange rates.

44. Sending an email from Excel

How can we send an email from Excel with the Excel file attached?

(a) Press ALT and F11 to enter the **Visual Basic Editor**
(b) Click on **Insert > Module** and enter this code:

```
Sub EmailFile()
    ActiveWorkbook.SendMail _
    Recipients:="put the email address here", _
    Subject:="Here is the file you wanted " & Format(Date, "dd/mmm/yy")
End Sub
```

(c) Save your file.
(d) Go back to Excel by pressing ALT and F11 again.
(e) Click on **Tools** > **Macro** > **Macros** > **EmailFile** to test it.

45. Incrementing an invoice number

Invoices are normally numbered. How can I increase the invoice number by 1 when I clear the data ready for a new customer?

Suppose that you have already recorded a macro called Clear to clear the old data and the invoice number is stored in cell B7.

(a) Press ALT and F11 to enter the **Visual Basic Editor**
(b) Click on **Insert > Module** and enter this code:

```
Sub Newinvoice
Range("B7").Value = Range("B7").Value + 1
Clear
End sub
```

(c) Save your file.
(d) Go back to Excel by pressing ALT and F11 again.
(e) Click on **Tools > Macro > Macros > Newinvoice** to test it.

46. Automatic updating of stock levels (1)

Suppose you have the number of a certain item in stock in cell B5. A number of this item are delivered and this is stored in cell D5. How can you update the stock levels to take account of the delivery?

(a) Press ALT and F11 to enter the **Visual Basic Editor**.
(b) Click on **Insert > Module** and enter this code.

```
Sub Update
Range("B5").Value = Range("B5").Value + Range("D5").Value
Range("D5").Value = 0
End sub
```

(c) Save your file.
(d) Go back to Excel by pressing ALT and F11 again.
(e) Click on **Tools > Macro > Macros > Update** to test it.

47. Automatic updating of stock levels (2)

My spreadsheet stores the stock levels and deliveries of 20 items. The numbers in stock are in column B. The numbers delivered are stored in column D. Can I update all the stock levels at once?

Yes. Suppose that the first item is stored in cell B5.

```
Sub Update2()
Range("B5").Select
For Count = 1 To 20
ActiveCell.Value = ActiveCell.Value + ActiveCell.Offset(0,
2).Range("A1").Value
ActiveCell.Offset(0, 2).Range("A1").Value = 0
ActiveCell.Offset(1, 0).Range("A1").Select 'go down a line
Next Count
End Sub
```

48. Using the Calendar Control to enter dates

(a) Go to the Visual Basic Editor (**ALT** and **F11**).
(b) Insert a UserForm (**Insert** > **UserForm**).
(c) Right click on the Toolbox and choose **Additional Controls.**
(d) Scroll down until you see **Calendar Control 11.0** or something similar. The number may be different for different versions of Excel.

Figure 7. 53 ▶

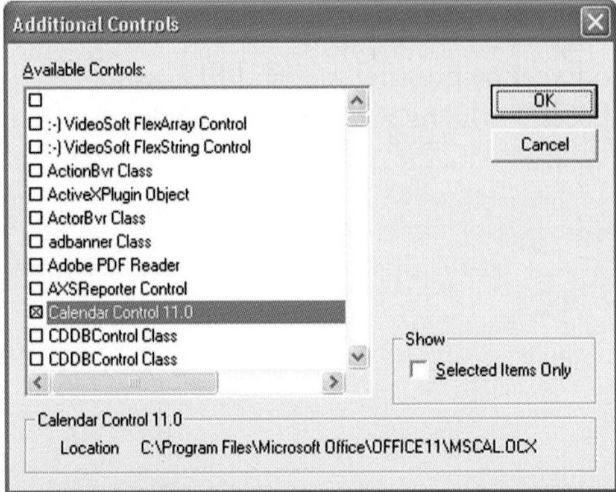

(e) Check the box next to Calendar Control and click on **OK**.

(f) A new icon appears in the toolbox.

Figure 7. 54 ▶

(g) Click on this icon and drag out a rectangle over the whole of the UserForm. A calendar appears.

Figure 7. 55 ▶

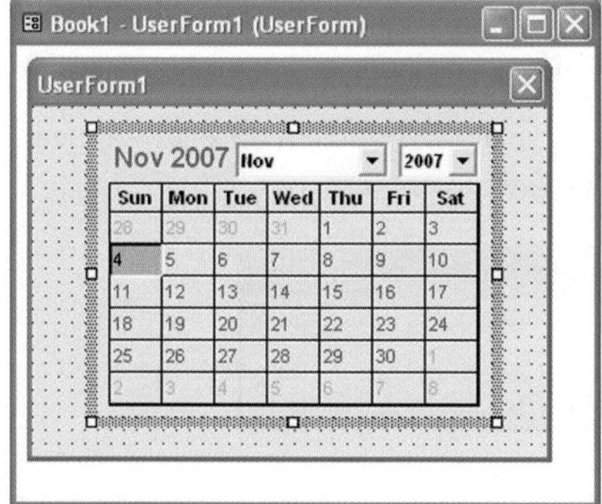

We now need to set up the UserForm so that when you click on a date, that date is entered into a cell, say cell A2.

(h) Double click on the calendar. This VB code appears.

Figure 7. 56 ▶

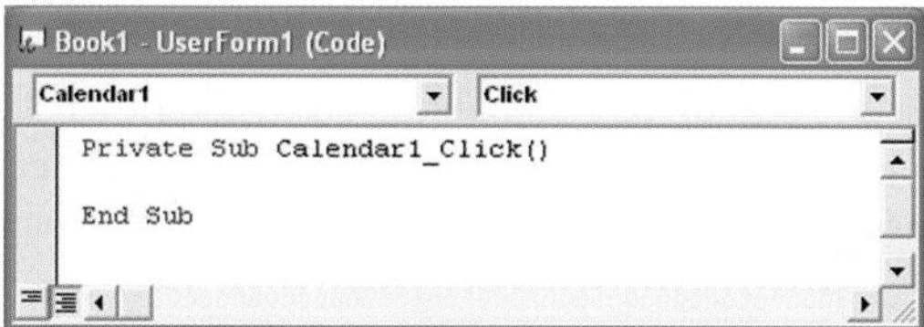

(i) Edit the code so that it reads as follows:

Figure 7. 57 ▶

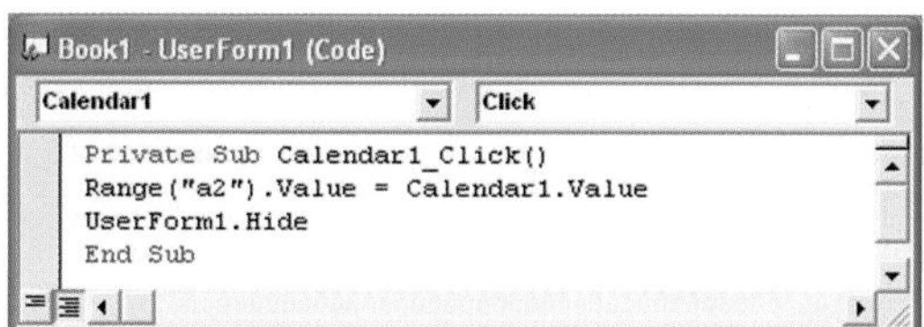

(j) Insert a module (**Insert** > **Module**).
(k) Enter this macro as follows:

Figure 7. 58 ▶

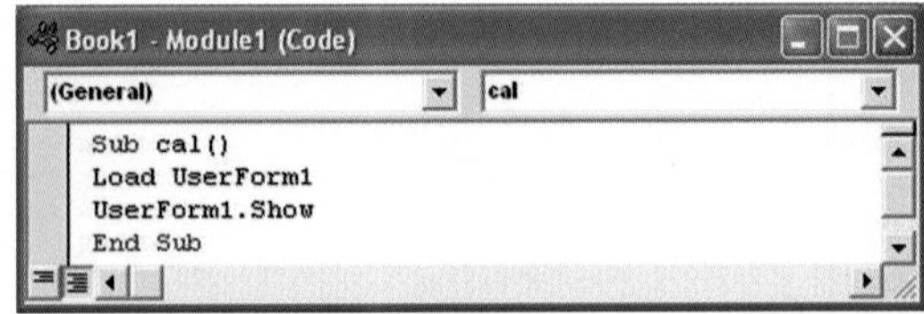

```
Sub cal()
Load UserForm1
UserForm1.Show
End Sub
```

(l) Close the Visual Basic Editor.
(m) Make column A slightly wider.
(n) Run the macro (**Tools** > **Macro** > **Macros**). Select the **Cal** macro. Click on **Run**. The UserForm with the calendar should load with today's date highlighted.
(o) Click on a date in the calendar. You can use the drop-downs to select a different month and year. The chosen date will appear in cell A2. (Make sure that column A is wide enough.)

Figure 7. 59 ▶

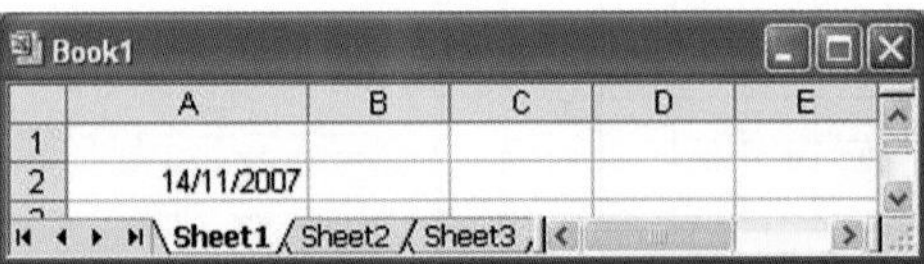

49. Using the Drawing Toolbar

The icons on the Drawing Toolbar enable you to select objects, rotate them, align them with other objects, space them evenly, format the colour of text, background and borders, arrange one in front of another, and group objects together. You can also draw shapes such as lines, arrows, rectangles and circles.

The AutoShapes pop-up menu enables you to add other shapes such as arrows, stars and speech bubbles (called Callouts). These shapes can be made to look three-dimensional using the 3-D icon. To insert a 3-D shape:

(a) Start a new Excel worksheet.
(b) Turn on the **Drawing Toolbar**.
(c) Click on **AutoShapes** and choose **Stars and Banners**.

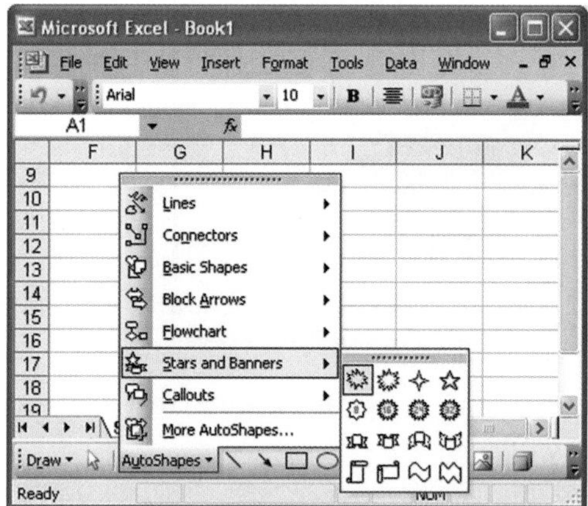

Figure 7. 60 ▶

(d) Choose the first star icon – called **Explosion 1**.
(e) Drag out a rectangle on the screen over cells G3 to H9.

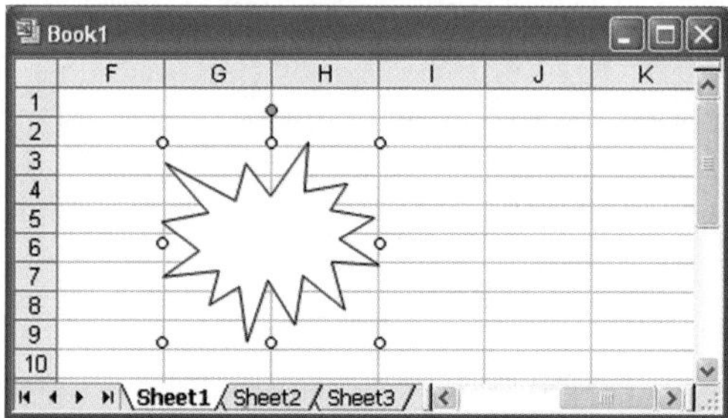

Figure 7. 61 ▶

(f) With the star still selected click on the **3-D Style** icon (the one on the far right of the Drawing Toolbar) and choose the first icon – **3D Style 1**.

You now have a grey three-dimensional shape.

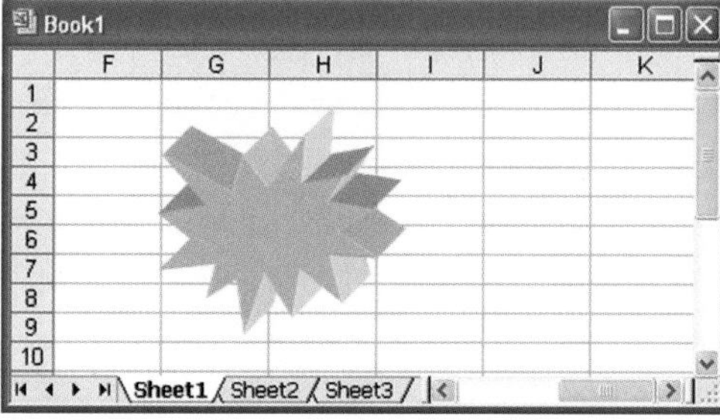

Figure 7. 62 ▶

(g) Right click on the shape and choose **Format AutoShape.** Click on the **Colors and Lines tab** and select the colour **Bright green**. Then click on **OK**.
(h) Right click on the shape and choose **Add Text**. Enter the word **New**!
(i) Set the font to **Century Gothic**, size **18**, colour **yellow, bold** and **centred**.

Figure 7. 63 ▶

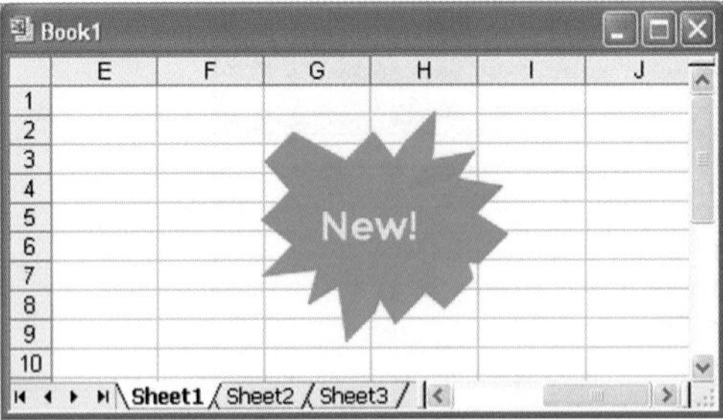

You can assign macros to shapes like these so that when you click on the shape, the macro runs.

50. Shortcut keys

You are probably familiar with some short cut keys such as ALT+ F4 (Close the Program), ALT + F11 (Display the Visual Basic Editor) and ALT + TAB (switch to the next open program).

Here are some others that you may find useful.

Key combination	Action
CTRL + PAGEUP	Move to next worksheet
CTRL + PAGEDOWN	Move to previous worksheet
SHIFT + CLICK	Select the whole area between the active cell and the selected cell
CTRL + SHIFT + DRAG	Replicate selected cells in drop area
CTRL + ' (apostrophe)	Copy a formula from the cell above the active cell into the cell or the formula bar
CTRL + 7	Show or hide the Standard toolbar
F4 or CTRL + Y	Repeat the last action
SHIFT + ARROW KEY	Extend or reduce the selection by one cell
SHIFT + F11	Insert a new worksheet
SHIFT + SPACEBAR	Select the entire row
SHIFT + F3	Paste a function into a formula such as VLOOKUP
SHIFT + F2	Edit a cell comment
CTRL + HOME	Move to the beginning of the worksheet
CTRL + END	Move to the last used cell (lower-right corner)

Index